100 THINGS ILLINOIS FANS
SHOULD KNOW & DO
BEFORE THEY DIE

Kent Brown

TRIUMPH
BOOKS

No part of this publication may be reproduced, stored in a retrieval system, or transmitted in any form by any means, electronic, mechanical, photocopying, or otherwise, without the prior written permission of the publisher, Triumph Books LLC, 814 North Franklin Street, Chicago, Illinois 60610.

Library of Congress Cataloging-in-Publication Data available upon request.

This book is available in quantity at special discounts for your group or organization. For further information, contact:
   Triumph Books LLC
   814 North Franklin Street
   Chicago, Illinois 60610
   (312) 337–0747
   www.triumphbooks.com

Printed in U.S.A.
ISBN: 978-1-63727-619-8
Design by Patricia Frey
Photos courtesy of University of Illinois Athletics

To our grandchildren, current and future,
who will be counted on to carry our
family support of Fighting Illini Athletics.

Contents

Foreword

In my time as the director of athletics at the University of Illinois, I have been fortunate to meet people from across the country and, in some cases, around the globe. Alumni. Donors. Sponsors. Students. Faculty. People who are as diverse as the world itself, with varied backgrounds, upbringings, incomes, religions, nationalities, and political viewpoints. Despite their many differences, however, all of them share one common thread: the University of Illinois.

I am honored to be invited into their homes, to break bread or have an iced tea, and to hear their stories. And as impressed as I am by their individual journeys, I am continually reminded of the power of this place, this university in East Central Illinois with humble land-grant origins that has grown into one of the most dynamic, influential institutions of learning, research, and philosophy in the world.

Central to many of these stories are memories created against the backdrop of Fighting Illini Athletics. We talk often within the Division of Intercollegiate Athletics about the responsibility with which we have been entrusted. Every weekend in the fall, people get engaged at Memorial Stadium. In the parking lots, people host family reunions and run into long-lost roommates. In State Farm Center, the stands are dotted with babies attending their first Illini games. People stand in unison, hold their friends and family, and sway to the singing of "Hail to the Orange." At Demirjian Park, two students meet for the first time and, years later, will be married. In the friendly confines of Eichelberger Field, fathers sit with their daughters and mothers with their sons and enjoy spring weekends that will not soon be forgotten.

Our games serve as markers in our lives. Times shared with children, siblings, parents, grandparents, and friends and neighbors.

Moments etched into our consciousness by not only the people we were with but the extremes of the emotional spectrum stemming from the events themselves. The exhilaration of unexpected victory or the despair of dramatic defeat, all shared with your Fighting Illini famILLy. The people involved in those contests—the coaches, student-athletes, and opponents—gain mythological status, augmented by time and perspective.

Trying to capture the essence of what it means to be a Fighting Illini is an unenviable—and, dare I say, impossible—task. But we can be reminded of the journey that brought us here. And of the history, moments in time, and idiosyncrasies that make the tradition of Fighting Illini Athletics so special—to you, to me, and to all of us.

No one is more qualified to lead us on this exploration than my longtime friend and colleague, Kent Brown. A native of nearby Hammond, Illinois, Kent earned bachelor's and master's degrees from the University of Illinois before embarking on a career in college athletics that spanned four decades before his retirement in 2023. As a childhood fan who became the longest-serving sports information director in Illinois Athletics history, Kent has a unique perspective on what it means to be a Fighting Illini. In the pages that follow, he has made an admirable effort to capture the essence of the Spirit of the Illini: memories, places, and moments that have crystalized in our proud history and shaped the contours of what this program is and the people it represents. Some of these stories will resonate with you on a personal level, others, maybe not. But they are all part of the fabric of this place and, by extension, of each of us who wear the Orange and Blue.

Enjoy this exceptional read, and Go Illini!

—Josh Whitman
University of Illinois Director of Athletics

1 What Is a Fighting Illini?

The Illinois Fighting Illini are the intercollegiate teams that represent the 21 varsity sports sponsored by the University of Illinois Division of Intercollegiate Athletics. The term "Illini" originated when the student newspaper changed names from *The Student* to *The Illini* in January 1874, and the first issue of the *The Illini* implies in an editorial that the term had not formally existed. The term was often used to refer to the students, faculty, staff, and alumni of the University, as well as to the campus as a whole.

The University was one of 37 public land-grant institutions established after the Morrill Land-Grant Colleges Act was signed by Abraham Lincoln on July 2, 1862. Illinois was one of just seven commonwealths that had not formed a state university. The land-grant status made Illinois eligible for a grant of 480,000 acres of public land to support the university, and in 1867 the state established a university for the purpose of fostering access to higher education for working people.

Originally named the Illinois Industrial University, James Newton Matthews became the university's first student, enrolling in March 1868. He was among the founding editors of *The Student* and one of 50 students—all male—who enrolled at the beginning of the first semester. The name was officially changed to University of Illinois more than 20 years after its founding.

The earliest reference to the term "Illini" appears to be in the *Illini Yearbook* summary of the 1907 football season. Illini was more widely used in the 1910s, with the term "Fighting Illini" first appearing in a January 29, 1911, newspaper article describing the basketball team's effort during a game versus Purdue. Within a few months, the athletic teams appeared to have earned the Fighting Illini nickname on a more permanent basis. It was used as an unofficial school nickname for several years before eventually becoming the official name.

Once University of Illinois students and alumni began participating in World War I, which the U.S. entered in 1917, the usage of "Fighting Illini" became mixed, sometimes referring to the soldiers at war and sometimes referring to the University's athletic teams.

In addition to the athletic teams, there are strong links to the term being connected to the soldiers during the war and became a powerful way to honor those Illini who had gone off to fight in Europe. The war-related usage of "Fighting Illini" was central to the fundraising campaign preceding the construction of Memorial Stadium.

So, when did Fighting Illini become the official nickname for UI athletics teams? No one can pinpoint an exact date, but it's clear the term evolved in the 20th century to become one of the nation's most identifiable athletics nicknames.

2 University of Illinois Athletics Hall of Fame

From the time the University of Illinois chartered the Athletics Association in 1883 to oversee its burgeoning athletics teams, thousands of student-athletes, coaches, and staff members have worked tirelessly for excellence and championships.

One of the first major initiatives Josh Whitman established following his announcement as the Illinois director of athletics in the late winter of 2016 was the University of Illinois Athletics Hall of Fame to recognize the incredible efforts and performances over the previous 125-plus years.

In the first eight classes through 2024, 143 all-time greats were inducted and honored forever, with many of those honored being among the most significant people in the world of sports. The names of George Halas, Jerry Colangelo, Mannie Jackson, Red Grange, Dick Butkus, Robert Zuppke, Harry Gill, and Craig Tiley can match up with just about any collegiate department in the nation. Each had careers that have left, and will continue to leave, a proud legacy in sports around the globe.

The first class was honored at a gala held at the Field Museum in Chicago on June 23, 2017, with each living member speaking to the sold-out crowd. Television personality Mike Tirico hosted the event that included interviews with Dick Butkus, Jerry Colangelo, Deron Williams, Tonja Buford-Bailey, Mary Eggers, Perdita Felicien, Mannie Jackson, and many more. Many attendees said afterward that it may have been the greatest U of I athletics event ever held, with certainly the highest number of Fighting Illini athletics royalty ever assembled.

The official induction ceremony was held on campus at State Farm Center on September 30, 2017. Stirring speeches by Butkus and Virginia Halas McCaskey, the daughter of George Halas, highlighted the event. Many of these legends will be detailed in this book, but information on each can be found at FightingIllini. com. Each year since, a new class has been added to help recognize the incredible athletics history that has played out over the decades, while future Hall of Famers are competing on the courts, fields, and courses today. The individuals honored represent every current varsity sport, as well as a few that have been retired.

2017 (28): Nick Anderson (basketball), Lou Boudreau (baseball/basketball), Dee Brown (basketball), Tonja Buford-Bailey (track and field), Dick Butkus (football), Jerry Colangelo (basketball/baseball/contributor to sport), Dike Eddleman (basketball/football/track and field), Mary Eggers Tendler (volleyball), Perdita Felicien (track and field), Harry Gill (track and field coach), Red Grange (football), Abie Grossfeld (gymnastics), George Halas (football/basketball/baseball, contributor to sport), George Huff (football/baseball coach/administration), Mannie Jackson (basketball/contributor to sport), Karol Kahrs (administration), Herb McKenley (track and field), Allie Morrison (wrestling), Harold Osborn (track and field), Andy Phillip (basketball/baseball), Renee Heiken Slone (golf), Steve Stricker (golf), Nancy Thies Marshall (gymnastics), Craig Tiley (tennis coach), Craig Virgin (track and field/cross country), Deron Williams (basketball), Buddy Young (football/track and field), Bob Zuppke (football coach).

2018 (21): Alex Agase (football), Kevin Anderson (tennis), Nancy Brookhart Cherin (volleyball), Chuck Carney (football/basketball), Dave Downey (basketball), Ray Eliot (football coach), Darrin Fletcher (baseball), Maxwell Garret (fencing coach), Kendall Gill (basketball), Jim Grabowski (football), Lou Henson (basketball coach), Dana Howard (football), Tara Hurless (soccer), Red Kerr (basketball), Scott Langley (golf), Celena Mondie-Milner (track and field), Charles Pond (gymnastics coach), Joe Sapora (wrestling), Justin Spring (gymnastics), Tonya Williams (track and field), Willie Williams (track and field).

2019 (16): Ashley Berggren (basketball), Lindsey Nimmo Bristow (tennis), J.C. Caroline (football), Amer Delic (tennis), Don Freeman (basketball), Joseph Giallombardo (gymnastics), Jenna Hall (softball), Joe Hunsaker (swimming and diving), Eddie Johnson (basketball), Bobby Mitchell (football/track and field), Bob Norman (wrestling), Angela Bizzarri Pflugrath (track and field/cross country), Simeon Rice (football), Deon Thomas (basketball), Gary Wieneke (track and field/cross country coach), David Williams (football).

2020 (15): Michelle Bartsch-Hackley (volleyball), Tal Brody (basketball/contributor to sport), Vanessa DiBernardo (soccer), Moe Gardner (football), Kevin Hardy (football), Derek Harper (basketball), Leo Johnson (football/track and field coach), Gia Lewis-Smallwood (track and field), Ray Nitschke (football), Bob Richards (track and field), Art Schankin (fencing/fencing coach), Jenna Smith (basketball), Jake Stahl (baseball/football), Adam Tirapelle (wrestling), Don Tonry (gymnastics).

2021 (28) Pre-1950s: Matt Bullock (athletics trainer), Caton Cobb (gymnastics), John Depler (football), Hoot Evers (baseball/basketball/track and field), Paul Fina (gymnastics), Horatio Fitch (track and field), Charles Flachmann (swimming and diving), Bill Hapac (basketball), Hek Kenney (wrestling coach), Dan Kinsey (track and field), Ed Lindberg (track and field), Justa Lindgren (football/football coach), Carl Lundgren (baseball/football/baseball coach), Bart Macomber (football), Jim McMillen (football/wrestling), Tim O'Connell (tennis), Paul Prehn (wrestling coach), Hartley Price (gymnastics coach/soccer coach), Shorty Ray (contributor to sport), Claude Rothgeb (football/baseball/track and field), Allen Sapora (wrestling), Bernie Shively (football/wrestling/track and field), Ruffy Silverstein (wrestling), Jack Smiley (basketball), Michael Tobin (sports information director), Bill Vosburgh (swimming and diving), Tug Wilson (track and field/basketball), Ray Woods (basketball).

2022 (15): Becky Beach (basketball/golf), Jody Alderson Braskamp (swimming and diving), Bill Burrell (football), Harry Combes (basketball/basketball coach), Dawn Riley Duval (track and field), Charlton Ehizuelen (track and field), Jeff George (football), Ron Guenther (football/administration), Werner Holzer (wrestling), Dr. Nell Jackson (track and field coach), Linda Metheny-Mulvihill (gymnastics), Ken Norman (basketball), Jonelle Polk McCloud (basketball), Emily Zurrer (soccer), Danielle Zymkowitz (softball).

2023 (12): Kenny Battle (basketball), Al Brosky (football), Aja Evans (track and field), Nicole Evans Cazley (softball), Melissa Fernandez (gymnastics), Mike Hebert (volleyball coach), Ken Holtzman (baseball), George Kerr (track and field), Rashard Mendenhall (football), Thomas Pieters (golf), Don Sunderlage (basketball), Jack Trudeau (football).

2024 (8): Darrick Brownlow (football), Laura DeBruler Santos (volleyball), Jannelle Flaws (soccer), Robert Holcombe (football), Pete Velasco (fencing), Nick Weatherspoon (basketball), Frank Williams (basketball), Gary Winckler (track and field coach).

3 From Athletics Association to Division of Intercollegiate Athletics

America's interest in athletics initially formed around the end of the Civil War in 1865, two years prior to the UI's founding in 1867. The student body interest was changing from boating, racing, and cycling to a new team sport called baseball, which history shows originated a couple of decades earlier. It quickly became the nation's most popular sport, including in Champaign-Urbana. The first recorded athletic contest at the University occurred on May 8, 1872, when a group of UI students defeated the Eagle Baseball Club of Champaign by a score of 2–1. It took about seven years before that first game evolved into intercollegiate competition.

On April 20, 1883, UI students combined their original baseball and football organizations to form the Athletic Association, a group that was responsible for caring for the campus gymnasium and for organizing the annual Field Day activities.

In 1891, the AA obtained land on the north end of campus, and on May 15, 1892, Athletic Park was inaugurated. Its name was changed to Illinois Field in 1896, and it remained a part of the athletics facilities as home of the baseball program until Beckman Institute construction began at the corner of Wright Street and University Avenue in the fall of 1986. The UI football and track and field programs also shared space at Illinois Field until the opening of Memorial Stadium in 1923.

In 1896, UI trustees directed by-laws of the Association to be subject to approval of the faculty, and at the turn of the century, an Athletic Advisory Council assisted in the management of the AA. Shortly thereafter, faculty, alumni, and student managers comprised an Athletic Board of Control and Athletic Council to form policy.

On the heels of Title IX legislation, the athletic administration assumed responsibility for overseeing the new Women's Intercollegiate Athletics program in 1974. During the decade of the 1980s, the AA experienced incredible growth and success in many of the sport programs, but several scandals and improprieties were brought to light late in the decade.

Following a thorough investigation by the university, a decision was made to dissolve the AA and a reorganization to the Division of Intercollegiate Athletics was led by Chancellor Morton Weir to bring the division's business within the jurisdiction of the University administration. By July 1989, the DIA and new athletics director John Mackovic reported directly to the chancellor, being treated similarly to deans of the various colleges.

4 The First NCAA Team Champion

The Intercollegiate Athletics Association of the United States was officially constituted as a rules-making body by 62 charter colleges and universities, including the University of Illinois, on March 31, 1906, and in 1910 was renamed the National Collegiate Athletic Association. For several years, the NCAA was mainly a discussion group that made rules to bring fairness to collegiate sports and help protect the safety of athletes.

Conferences had been holding championship events and seasons for years, but a few coaches, including Illinois track and field coach Harry Gill, were looking to expand those events to national competitions. The first NCAA Track and Field Championship, and, thus, the first NCAA championship event, was held June 17–18, 1921, at Chicago's Stagg Field. Gill's Illini squad held off runner-up Notre Dame by 3½ points to bring home the title trophy. Illinois didn't have champions in any of the 15 events but provided enough depth to earn top honors.

1921 NCAA Men's Track and Field National Meet Standings

1. Illinois, 20¼ points
2. Notre Dame, 16¾
3. Iowa, 14
4. Washington, 12¼
5. Wisconsin, 10
6. Nebraska, 8
7. Grinnell, 7
8t. Northwestern, 6
8t. Ohio State, 6
9. Ames College, 5½

Illini athletes collected valuable points from runner-up finishes, including junior Gordon McGinnis in the one-mile run, Russell Wharton in the two-mile run, Dewey Alberts in the high jump, and Harold Osborn in the broad jump (second-place tie).

Illinois has gone on to win national championships in track and field in 1927 under Gill, and with Leo Johnson as head coach in 1944, 1946, and 1947.

The NCAA has gone on to issue thousands of team championships at each of the three levels, but there is only one first.

5 "Papa Bear" George Halas

George Halas, founder, owner, and head coach of the Chicago Bears, was a three-sport athlete at the University of Illinois. He lettered in baseball, basketball, and football from 1916 to 1918, starring in each sport.

With World War I underway, Halas enlisted in the Navy in January of 1918 and was assigned to Naval Station Great Lakes, located in Lake County, north of Chicago. Navy made him a carpenter's mate second class, assigning him to the sports program there. And though he was six hours short of his degree, the U of I issued Halas his degree in civil engineering in June.

At Great Lakes, Halas was joined by football All-Americans Paddy Driscoll of Northwestern, Charlie Bachman of Notre Dame, and Jimmy Conzelman of Washington University. Led by that talented group, the Bluejackets rolled to a 6–0–2 record in 1918, including a 7–0 victory over Halas' alma mater at Illinois Field. Following the season, Great Lakes was invited to play in the fifth edition of the Rose Bowl, known at the time as the Tournament

East-West Football Game, on January 1, 1919. Great Lakes was paired against the undefeated Mare Island Marines and emerged from Pasadena as the champs, winning 17–0. Halas was the star of the game, catching a 32-yard touchdown pass from Driscoll and returning an interception for 77 yards. His performance earned him Most Valuable Player honors and he was inducted into the Rose Bowl Hall of Fame in 2018.

George Halas was a three-sport athlete at Illinois, and was talented enough on the baseball diamond to play right field for the New York Yankees before a hip injury ended his baseball career. The player who followed him in right field was a man named Babe Ruth.

George Halas: By the Numbers

7	Jersey number retired by the Bears in Halas' honor.
8	NFL titles won by Halas-coached teams.
40	Years as a head coach.
63	Years as the Bears owner.
104	Games played in the NFL.
324	Coaching victories (stood as an NFL record nearly three decades).
1963	Year inducted as a charter member of the Pro Football Hall of Fame.
2016	Year inducted into the University of Illinois Engineering Hall of Fame.
2017	Year inducted into the Fighting Illini Athletics Hall of Fame.
2018	Year inducted into the Rose Bowl Hall of Fame.

After his football career ended in Pasadena, Halas turned his attention to baseball and tried out for manager Miller Huggins' New York Yankees. He impressed the club with his speed, arm, and eagerness while earning a position on the 1919 big league roster as a right fielder. His contract called for him to receive $400 a month and a $500 signing bonus. An early hip injury limited Halas' career to just two singles in 12 games. By the time he had fully recovered from his injury, the Yankees had bought the contract for Babe Ruth from the Red Sox prior to the 1920 season and, as they say, the rest is history.

In March of 1920, Halas received a call from the general superintendent of A.E. Staley Company in Decatur, Illinois. He was offered the opportunity to not only "learn the starch business," but also to play on Staley's baseball team and manage and coach the company's football squad. He quickly started recruiting players from colleges around the Midwest.

Next, he needed to assemble a schedule of Midwest competition and coordinated a meeting at Ralph Hay's automobile showroom in Canton, Ohio. Within two hours of the meeting, the American Professional Football Association was created. Olympic gold medalist and football and baseball star Jim Thorpe was elected the APFA's president, and 1920 became the first season of what would be renamed the National Football League in 1922.

When fan turnout was sparse in Decatur during that inaugural season, Staley suggested Halas move the team to Chicago's Cubs Park (now Wrigley Field) to improve attendance. Halas' obligation to the Staley Company ended following the 1921 season

George Halas was a co-founder in 1920 of the present-day NFL and owned the Chicago Bears franchise until his death in 1983, leading the Bears to eight world championships.

and he and co-owner Edward "Dutch" Sternaman established the Chicago Bears Football Club, with the team's nickname a tribute to baseball's Chicago Cubs. The team's official colors of orange and blue were established by Halas and Sternaman as a nod to their University of Illinois roots.

Halas had a hand in just about every aspect of the Bears organization.

"When I joined the Bears, Halas was everything," said Red Grange. "He played right end. He was coach. He was in charge of the tickets. He was in charge of the ground crew. He put out the publicity. I've always said that if anybody ever made a dime out of football, George Halas is the one guy that deserves it more than anybody that ever lived because he put his whole life in it."

Halas died October 31, 1983, at the age of 88, but his oldest daughter, Virginia, continues to serve as the principal owner of the team. She is currently the oldest owner in the NFL and in all major league sports in the United States at the age of 101.

6 A Streak of Fire— Harold "Red" Grange

The first football superstar, Harold "Red" Grange burst on the national scene as a record-setting running back at Illinois from 1923 to '25 before being credited with saving a financially floundering National Football League.

Grange was born in 1903 in Forksville, Pennsylvania, and after his mother died when he was just five years old, Red; his father, Lyle; and his brother, Garland, ended up settling in Wheaton, Illinois, west of Chicago. In four years at Wheaton High School, Grange earned 16 varsity letters in football, baseball, basketball, and track, scoring 75 touchdowns and 532 points for the football team. Grange's high school track and field career was just as legendary. As a sophomore in 1920, he was the state champion in the high jump and placed third and fourth in the 100-yard dash and the 220-yard dash, respectively. In 1921, he won the state title in both the long jump and the 100-yard dash, and as a senior in 1922, he placed third in the 100-yard dash and won the 220-yard dash.

To help the family earn money, he took a part-time job as an ice-toter for $37.50 per week, a job that helped him to build his core strength and where he got the nickname "the Wheaton Ice Man."

Grange enrolled at the University of Illinois in the fall of 1922, where he joined the Zeta Psi fraternity. At first, he had planned to compete only in basketball and track, but his fraternity brothers quickly insisted he also try out for Bob Zuppke's Illini football team. Grange's famous uniform number 77 came about when, according to Grange, "the player in front of me was given 76 and the fella behind me was assigned 78." That number was retired by both the U of I and Chicago Bears.

In seven games as a sophomore in 1923, Grange ran for 723 yards and scored 12 touchdowns, helping the Illini to an undefeated season, a Big Ten title, and the Helms Athletic Foundation national championship.

Grange won the first-ever *Chicago Tribune* Silver Football Award as the Big Ten's Most Valuable Player in 1924, was a three-time consensus All-American from 1923 to 1925, was inducted as a charter member of both the College Football Hall of Fame in 1951 and Pro Football Hall of Fame in 1963, and was named to all-time All-America teams by the Football Writers Association of America in 1969 and Walter Camp All-Century Team in 1989. Grange was named the No. 1 Big Ten Icon by the Big Ten Network in 2010 and one of the top 11 players in the first 150 years of college football in 2019.

Harold "Red" Grange is arguably the most influential football player in the history of the NFL. The barnstorming tour with Grange and the Bears following his Fighting Illini career in 1925 is credited with saving the financially strapped league.

In his 20-game college career at Illinois, Grange rushed for 2,074 yards, completed 40 passes for 575 yards, intercepted 11 passes as a defensive halfback, and scored a total of 31 touchdowns.

The Grange story hardly stops at his final Illini game at Ohio State in 1925, though. With rumors swirling from all directions, Grange announced that he would be leaving U of I immediately after that game to sign a professional contract with the Chicago Bears, who were owned by U of I alumni George Halas and Edward "Dutch" Sternaman. In fact, Grange may have been the first college football player to engage in Name, Image, Likeness opportunities before such a thing existed! Grange is the last player to play both college football and in the NFL in the same season.

Champaign movie theater owner C.C. Pyle, who befriended Grange at a movie showing, quickly negotiated a barnstorming tour for Red to play 19 games in 67 days around the nation with the Bears receiving 50 percent of the ticket gate, while Pyle and Grange got the other half. The contract earned him a salary and share of gate receipts that amounted to $100,000, during an era when typical league salaries were less than $100 per game.

Despite the challenging schedule causing several injuries to players on the Bears roster, the barnstorming tours are generally considered to have saved the NFL and professional football from financial ruin. It has often been said that filling the Polo Grounds with fans who wanted to see Grange and the Bears saved the New York Giants from folding. In his rookie year, Grange made the astounding sum of approximately $125,000, but the value he brought to the NFL was felt for decades in the future.

Grange also starred in several acting roles during the 1920s and '30s before retiring as a player in 1934 and coaching until 1937. He went on to earn a living in a variety of jobs including motivational speaker and sports announcer. Grange was an insurance broker in Chicago during the 1940s and served on the U of I Board of Trustees from 1951 to '55.

Grange and his wife Margaret, nicknamed Muggs, were married in 1941 and remained together until Red's death in 1991 after he developed Parkinson's disease. In honor of his achievements at Illinois, the school erected a 12-foot statue of Grange on the west side of Memorial Stadium that overlooks Grange Grove.

"A streak of fire, a breath of flame
Eluding all who reach and clutch;
A gray ghost thrown into the game
That rival hands may never touch;
A rubber bounding, blasting soul
Whose destination is the goal—Red Grange of Illinois!"
—Grantland Rice

7 Building a Great Stadium

Bob Zuppke and the Illinois football program were firmly established as a national and Big Ten power in the 1910s with national championship squads in 1914 and 1919, and Big Ten titles in 1910, 1914, 1915, 1918, and 1919. Athletics director George Huff was using every trick possible to pack more seats at old Illinois Field, located north of Kenney Gym next to Wright Street. In fact, several times for big games, thousands of fans were turned away, meaning missed revenue opportunities. It was estimated that nearly 20,000 people were unable to obtain seats to the Ohio State game in 1920.

As large stadiums were being constructed in the east, Huff knew there was an opportunity to build a much larger structure in Champaign-Urbana to take advantage of the throngs of fans wanting to attend games.

17

"I haven't the slightest doubt," said Huff, "that we could have sold more than 40,000 tickets, and possibly 50,000 for the Ohio State game if we had had the seating facilities. With the growing interest in our athletics, it is no idle guess to prophesy that every one of the 75,000 seats in the new stadium will be sold for the big games of the next few years."

On April 25, 1921, Huff presented that plan to the U of I student body at the old gym annex. Every seat was filled as bands and horns tooted. The platform was filled with university executives, distinguished Illini athletes, and coaches. President David Kinley first spoke to the masses, then Huff followed.

When the ovation ceased, Huff said, "I want to see a great stadium at the University of Illinois. The stadium will be many

The first game at Memorial Stadium was played on November 3, 1923, just 14 months after groundbreaking ceremonies on September 11, 1922. A spur from the nearby railroad tracks was built to deliver construction supplies directly to the site.

Memorial Stadium was originally dedicated to Illini students, faculty, staff, and alumni who perished during World War I. Since then, the stadium has been rededicated twice to memorialize those who made the ultimate sacrifice in all subsequent wars and military conflicts.

things—a memorial to Illini who have died in the war, a recreational field, and an imposing place for our varsity games. But it will also be an unprecedented expression of Illinois loyalty. What you have started, our alumni will finish!"

Then football coach Bob Zuppke spoke, his hands rigidly clasped behind his back. After a few minutes, Zup ended with his request for voluntary donations of $1,000 for the stadium. Finally, following a few seconds of silence, a Latin-American student named R. L. Cavalcanti shouted out, "I will give, sir!" Within ten minutes, more than $700,000 of the $2.5 million needed to build the great structure had been pledged by the undergraduate student body.

Now, the race was underway to finish funding and start construction. There was some sentiment for building on the site of Illinois Field, but it was too congested to expand the stadium adequately, so a new site was selected in a largely undeveloped area at the south end of campus. English Brothers Company in Champaign, which is still in existence today, was selected as the general contractor.

Work began immediately after the ceremonial ground-breaking on September 11, 1922, ultimately using 12 million pounds of cement, 45,000 tons of sand and gravel, 112,000 cubic feet of cut stone, five million cubic feet of brick, 1,600 tons of reinforcing steel, and 16,000 tons of structural steel.

With much anticipation, the first game was a successful one, defeating the University of Chicago, 7–0, on November 3, 1923, with Red Grange scoring the lone touchdown and rushing for 101 yards on a muddy field. Construction of the stadium began just 14 months prior and was not totally completed, but Huff had pledged that the imposing structure would be ready for the Illini Homecoming Game of 1923.

It rained hard all afternoon, and because the stadium's walkways weren't yet completed, several hundred of the 60,632 fans were forced to abandon their shoes and boots in the mud. Tickets, priced at $2.50 each, yielded record gate-sale receipts of more than $132,000 to the UI Athletic Association.

8 Memorial Stadium Colonnades

Even though the United States didn't formally enter World War I until 1917, almost three years into the conflict, nearly five million Americans served their country, including 9,442 faculty, staff, and students from the University of Illinois.

Memorial Stadium was built as a memorial to Illinois men and women who gave their lives during the Great War. Holabird and

Of the 200 limestone columns that adorn the east and west sides of Memorial Stadium, 184 are dedicated to University of Illinois faculty, staff, students, and alumni who perished during World War I. Their names are forever etched into the stately columns.

Roche (now Holabird and Root), an architecture firm founded in Chicago, designed the stadium with 200 limestone columns that support the east and west sides of the stadium. Of the 200 columns at Memorial Stadium, 184 are dedicated to the men, and one woman, who were Illinois students, alumni, faculty, or staff and made the ultimate sacrifice during WWI. Two additional columns are dedicated to Unknown Illini Dead and Students' Army and Navy Training Corps Dead.

There are two non-Illini honored with columns. Two of Illinois' biggest football rivals sponsored columns for members of their football teams who perished in WWI. University of Chicago's Laurens "Spike" Shull is honored on a column sponsored by George

Carr. Shull played football, baseball, and basketball for UC from 1913–16, winning three varsity letters in each of the three sports and earning First-Team All-Western Conference honors in 1915.

The other column honoring Danville, Illinois, native Curtis Redden was sponsored by Michigan coach Fielding Yost and the men who served with him in the 149th Field Artillery as a bond of union between the two great universities. Redden played for Yost's famous "Point-a-Minute" teams from 1901 to '03 and was selected as an All-Western player in 1903. He was also selected captain of the Wolverine football and baseball teams as a senior. Redden made such an impact on Yost, and since he was from nearby Danville, Yost made a special appeal to include his name on a column. The Curtis G. Redden American Legion Post 210 in Danville bears his name.

The Colonnades are accessible to the general public through the corner ramps on game days on both the east and west sides of the stadium.

9 Memorial Stadium Dedication— October 18, 1924

After Illinois and Michigan tied for the 1923 Big Ten championship without playing each other, the anticipation of the two Midwest powers matching up in 1924 was quite high. Athletics director George Huff and head coach Bob Zuppke each embraced the opportunity to add to the excitement by declaring the Illini-Wolverine tilt on October 18 as the official dedication of the magnificent Memorial Stadium.

Following a ceremony that dedicated the stadium as a memorial to the men and women who gave their lives for their country in World War I, fans from across the region packed into Memorial Stadium for the highly anticipated football game. Officially, 67,886 fans were in attendance for the game, in a time when less than 30,000 people populated Champaign-Urbana!

Michigan entered the game undefeated over the previous 20 games while outscoring their opponents 443–32. Illinois had won 10 straight games since the beginning of the 1923 season.

On that warm October afternoon, Zuppke defied tradition by having his Illini team go sockless, for the first time in Midwest football, and possibly in American gridiron history. According to *The Daily Illini*'s account, "The players wore short socks reaching a few inches above the low shoes and leaving the leg bare to the knee. Whether this style was adopted because of the hot weather or for strategic reason was not officially made known."

As the crowd was still settling into their seats, Michigan kicked off to start the game, and to the joy of everyone wearing orange and blue, Red Grange returned the opening kickoff for a 95-yard touchdown to set the tone for what was about to come.

Rules at the time allowed the defensive team to kick off again to try and pin the opponent deep in their own territory, which Michigan chose to do. The kickoff once again went to Grange, who returned the ball the to the 20-yard line. The Illini didn't move the ball and punted to Michigan, only to regain possession after the Wolverines fumbled a field-goal attempt at the 32-yard line. After Walter McIllwain gained one yard, Grange took the next carry and carved the Michigan defense en route to a 67-yard touchdown run.

After the two teams exchanged possessions, Grange took his next touch 56 yards for his third touchdown. Another exchange of possessions and another Michigan fumble gave Illinois the ball at the Wolverine 44-yard line. On the first carry, Grange circled wide right, then cut back across the field and into the end zone for his fourth score ... all in the first 12 minutes of the game!

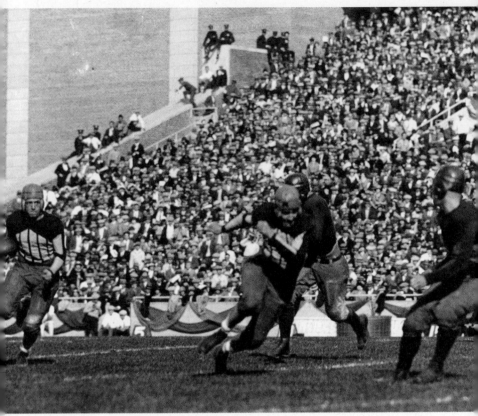

Red Grange shocked the nation with arguably the greatest big-game performance in the history of college football when he scored four touchdowns in the first 12 minutes of a 39–14 victory over Michigan in the Memorial Stadium Dedication Game on October 18, 1924. Grange would later rush for a fifth touchdown and pass for a sixth, while accounting for more than 400 yards.

An exhausted Grange left the field to an eruption of cheers from the sold-out Memorial Stadium crowd. He returned in the third quarter to run for a fifth touchdown and threw an 18-yard touchdown pass in the fourth quarter to finish off the 39–14 rout. Grange's stats for the day: five rushing touchdowns (four in the first 12 minutes) and passing for another; amassed 402 yards rushing and completed six passes for 64 yards. A performance that remains as one of the greatest ever witnessed on a football field.

10 Final Four Minutes to the Final Four

The 2004–05 season was expected to end in St. Louis at the NCAA Final Four following nearly four months as the nation's top-ranked basketball season. Coach Bruce Weber's second Illini squad had won their first 29 games before losing a heartbreaker at Ohio State on the final day of the regular season, then swept through the Big Ten Tournament and first three games of the NCAA Tournament. It just wasn't supposed to end like this.

Trailing by 15 at 75–60 after two made free throws by Arizona's Jawann McClellan with just four minutes to play against third-seeded Arizona in the Chicago Regional Final in Rosemont, things didn't look good for the overall No. 1 seeded Fighting Illini, to say the least.

The highly partisan Illinois crowd of 16,957 at Allstate Arena sat in stunned silence as tournament officials began to plan for a Wildcat celebration when it appeared Lute Olson's squad was going to finish off the Illini and advance to the Final Four.

Tournament officials stashed boxes of the Regional Championship T-shirts and hats behind the Arizona bench so they would be within reach immediately after the game.

"We just kept fighting. We never gave up," Illinois junior guard Deron Williams said. "It looked like the game was over."

But it wasn't.

Williams knocked down a three-pointer before McClellan made two more free throws with 3:26 remaining. Big Ten Player of the Year Dee Brown grabbed an offensive rebound and made a three of his own. Both teams followed with empty possessions before Luther Head made a steal and layup to make it 77–70 with

1:18 remaining. McClellan made one of two free throws before Williams made a layup to make it a six-point deficit.

The final minute was a blur. Arizona's Mustafa Shakur made two free throws with 1:03 to stretch the lead back to eight points. Head knocked down a three-pointer with 54 seconds remaining. Brown knocked the ball away from Shakur and scored a layup on an assist from Williams with 45 seconds remaining to pull within three.

That led to possibly the play of the game. Reserve Jack Ingram, who was in the game because starting center James Augustine had fouled out, knocked away a lobbed inbounds pass that was corralled by Brown, who swung the ball to Williams for his iconic three-pointer that tied the game at 80–80 with 39 seconds still on the clock! The bedlam inside Allstate Arena was heard all the way back in Champaign-Urbana.

Arizona held for a three-pointer by McClellan that missed and was rebounded by Brown, who threw a long pass that was intercepted by Arizona's Salim Stoudamire. It appeared the sharp-shooting Stoudamire would get off an open three to possibly win the game, only to have Head fly in from the side and swat the shot away, sending the game to overtime.

There were many there, including actor Bill Murray, who said it was the loudest crowd they had witnessed. The overtime was as hard fought as the final four minutes of regulation. Williams opened with a three-pointer, only to be countered by a layup and dunk by Wildcat center Channing Frye to take back the lead.

A layup by Illini senior Roger Powell, another three by Williams, and a layup by Head, who was battling a strained hamstring, gave Illinois a 90–84 lead with 1:57 remaining. The Wildcats scored five straight points to pull within one with 52 seconds left on the clock. Frye blocked a jumper by Head to set up another thrilling finish. After calling timeout with 11 seconds remaining, Arizona's Hassan Adams was harassed into missing a long three-pointer at the buzzer. Final Score: Illinois 90, Arizona 89.

The top of Allstate Arena nearly blew off with the reaction of Illinois fans who couldn't believe what they had just seen. The Illini players couldn't believe what had just happened, and an epic celebration started on the floor and continued into the locker

A furious comeback that saw the Fighting Illini overcome a 15-point deficit with four minutes remaining in regulation was capped by this game-tying three pointer by Deron Williams. Illinois would defeat Arizona 90–89 in overtime to propel the Illini to the Final Four.

room. At the NCAA Tournament, the locker room is open to the media following a 10-minute cool-down period, and the exhausted team could only hug and celebrate with each other for those few moments before the media frenzy began.

A few key players are always peeled away from the locker room to appear in a separate media room to be available to all the media in attendance. While waiting in the green room for Arizona coach Lute Olson to finish answering questions on how the game got away from the Wildcats, four Illini players and Weber stood still in shock.

At least until Williams blurted out, "What the hell just happened?"

At that point, Brown, Head, Ingram, and Williams started sharing their recollections of the final minutes.

"I thought I fouled Shakur on the steal, but there's no way I make the layup without the great pass from Deron," said Brown about the spinning lead pass that gave Dee a clear shot to the basket.

"I just did what Coach taught us on defending inbounds passes," added Ingram when talking about his deflection that turned into Williams' game-tying three-pointer.

"My leg was so tight, I didn't think I would make it to the basket," said Head, when describing his steal and dash to score.

Even then, it didn't seem possible.

On the bus trip down I-57 back to Champaign, Illini fans loaded each overpass to cheer their team, including many flashing lights from local fire trucks and other emergency vehicles letting the team know the entire state was behind them. Upon return to the Ubben Basketball Practice Facility parking lot, thousands more had gathered to greet the team and help celebrate the incredible victory.

Certainly, a night that everyone involved will never forget.

11 Interception King—Brosky Holds Tight to Record for More than 70 Years

The one record held by a Fighting Illini football player that may never be broken is the career interceptions mark achieved by defensive back Al Brosky from 1950 to '52. But just as impressive, and possibly an even longer shot to be broken, is his streak of an interception in 16 consecutive games.

The youngest of 12 children to immigrant Czechoslovakian parents, Brosky attended Harrison Tech High School in Chicago. Upon his graduation, he enlisted in the Army and served for more than 15 months. He was discharged in 1948 and enrolled at St. Louis University, but he left after a semester and came to the University of Illinois.

During the next three seasons, Brosky was simply amazing, developing into the most productive Illini pass defender ever … during an era in which teams generally didn't attempt many pass attempts each game. In 28 career games at Illinois, he picked off a national-record 30 interceptions.

In 1950, he finished with 11 interceptions and followed that up with 11 interceptions again in 1951, when the Illini won the Big Ten championship and defeated Stanford in the 1952 Rose Bowl. Brosky finished his Illini career with eight interceptions as a senior in 1952. At the time, the NCAA didn't count bowl game statistics in career numbers, so his numbers in the record book stand at 29 career interceptions, career interceptions per game at 1.1 (29 interceptions in 27 games), and most consecutive games with an interception at 15. Since he had a pick in the 1952 Rose Bowl, his Fighting Illini interceptions records are 30 for his career and a streak of 16 straight games.

In addition to being a captain and Most Valuable Player of the 1952 squad, Brosky also was an All-Big Ten and All-America selection.

A severe back disorder as well as other complications prevented him from pursuing a career in professional football other than one season with the Chicago Cardinals, so he went into business for himself.

Brosky was inducted into the College Football Hall of Fame in 1998 and the University of Illinois Athletics Hall of Fame in 2023. He died at the age of 82 in 2010.

12 Bret Bielema Makes Immediate Jolt as Head Coach

When the University of Illinois made a football head coaching change at the end of the 2020 season, one person was an immediate candidate: Illinois native son Bret Bielema.

His background included growing up and playing high school ball in Illinois, playing in the Big Ten, coaching and serving as a coordinator in the Big Ten, leading a Big Ten program as a head coach, and winning three Big Ten titles.

Bielema grew up on an 80-acre hog farm near Prophetstown, Illinois, not far from the Quad Cities. Bielema starred as a tight end and linebacker for the Prophetstown High School Panthers while also competing in track and wrestling.

He walked on as a defensive lineman at the University of Iowa under coach Hayden Fry, playing from 1989 to 1992. Bielema lettered four years, earned a scholarship, and served as team captain as a senior while playing on the 1990 Iowa squad that won a share of the Big Ten title.

Bielema made a meteoric rise in the coaching profession after starting under Fry as a graduate assistant in 1994. In 1996, he was promoted to linebackers coach. In 1998, Fry retired and was replaced by Kirk Ferentz, who retained Bielema on his staff for three seasons before Bielema left for Kansas State as co-defensive coordinator under the legendary Bill Snyder. He coached the K-State defense for two seasons, helping the Wildcats win the 2003 Big XII championship.

The next break in Bielema's career came when Wisconsin head coach Barry Alvarez lured him to Madison as the Badgers' defensive coordinator. He served in that role for two seasons, and in July 2005, when Alverez announced he would retire after that season, the longtime leader of the Badgers named Bielema as the head coach in waiting.

As head coach, Bielema led the Badgers to Big Ten championships in 2010, 2011, and 2012 before leaving to become head coach at Arkansas from 2013 to '17. Prior to the 2018 NFL season, he was hired by the New England Patriots as a defensive consultant to head coach Bill Belichick before being promoted to defensive line coach for the 2019 season. Bielema helped the Patriots to a Super Bowl title when they defeated the Los Angeles Rams in Super Bowl LIII.

After his second season in New England, Bielema was hired by the New York Giants as their outside linebacker coach. However, during his three years in the NFL, Bielema was learning and planning for his return as a collegiate head coach when the opportunity came along.

As a native of Illinois, and with his Big Ten background, he kept an eye on the Fighting Illini head coaching position, and when UI athletics director Josh Whitman made the decision to make a change from Lovie Smith, Bielema immediately knew this was a golden opportunity.

Following a national search, a small group of Illinois administrators boarded a plane on December 18, 2020, and flew to New

Jersey to finalize the deal with Bielema. The next morning, on December 19, Fighting Illini fans woke up to the news that a new football era was underway with Bielema making national television appearances before heading to State College, Pennsylvania, where the Illini were scheduled to play Penn State in the final game of the regular season.

At the end of a bizarre football season when games were played in empty, or near empty, stadiums because of the COVID-19 pandemic, Bielema watched his future team from the press box before flying to Champaign the next day, where he would meet with his players and media.

Bielema immediately connected with his squad by giving everyone on the team the opportunity to return, which set a tone of coming together as a family (later changed to FamILLy). This would be a bedrock of the program.

The initial 2021 season included two road wins over Top 20 opponents with victories at No. 7 Penn State and No. 20 Minnesota. The Illini victory at State College earned national attention, not just because it was a win over a Top 10 opponent, but because it took an NCAA-record nine overtimes before quarterback Brandon Peters connected with Casey Washington to stun the Penn State crowd with a score of 20–18.

Bielema and his team made a huge jump in 2022, beginning the season with seven wins in the first eight games and earning an invitation to the 2023 ReliaQuest Bowl in Tampa on January 2. The Illini dropped a hard-fought game against Mississippi State, 19–10, but finished the season with eight wins and their first winning season since 2011.

13 Pregame Traditions— Grange Grove and Illini Walk

The area on the west side of Memorial Stadium has been many things over the decades including practice fields, tennis courts, parking lots, and intramural fields. Envisioning a tailgating space that compares to any in the nation, starting in 2015, Grange Grove became the premier tailgating spot for fans attending Fighting Illini football games.

Stretching nearly the length of Memorial Stadium from Kirby Avenue to Erwin Drive and from the stadium sidewalk to First Street, fans have a great place to set up and enjoy the tailgating experience. Concerts, food trucks, autograph signings, performances by the Marching Illini, and merchandise opportunities are just some of the activities offered in the well-kept grassy space.

Fans can also welcome their favorite team's arrival to the stadium during the traditional Illini Walk that begins approximately two and a half hours prior to kickoff when the team busses unload at the First Street entrance.

Reservations for tailgating spaces can be made in advance, are inexpensive, and the spaces can be set up the night before games. Grange Grove opens at 7 a.m. on game days and is open until 10 p.m. after games. The north end of the space is normally used by students and student groups for tailgating.

The imposing Red Grange statue overlooks the space that is also used as one of the primary entrances to the stadium and includes brick columns that recognize each of the Fighting Illini consensus All-Americans.

14 Claude "Buddy" Young— The Bronze Bullet

In a college career split by the armed services, 5'4" halfback Claude "Buddy" Young earned All-America football honors in 1944. Young scored 13 touchdowns that season to tie Red Grange's Illini record while rushing for 842 yards with an amazing 8.9 yards-per-carry average.

In his Illini debut on September 16, 1944, Young, dressed in football jersey No. 66, quickly established himself as a star. The nation's fastest halfback played just nine and one-half minutes for Illinois against Illinois State, averaging more than 28 yards every time he touched the ball. Young lost four yards on his first carry, then scored touchdowns of 22 and 82 yards on his next two attempts. He also ran 51 yards for a TD, only to have it called back by a clipping penalty as Illinois handily defeated ISU 79–0.

Following that All-American season, he was drafted by the Navy and played for a service team. After his stint in the Navy, Young returned to Illinois and helped the Illini win the 1946 Big Ten football title before rushing for 103 yards in Illinois' 45–14 upset of unbeaten UCLA in the 1947 Rose Bowl, where he was selected as the game's co-MVP.

But his athleticism wasn't limited to the football field. Also known as the "Bronze Bullet," Young won 1944 NCAA outdoor track and field titles in the 100- and 220-yard dashes, tied the world record for the 45- and 60-yard dashes (6.1 in the latter), and was the Amateur Athletics Union 100-meter champion.

Young was a trailblazer as the first nationally famous Black athlete at Illinois and as one of the first Black players in the NFL. He played 10 years of pro football and was the first Baltimore Colts player to have his number retired (22).

But it may have been his skills off the field where Young left his greatest legacy. In 1964, Young became the first Black executive hired by a major sports league when NFL Commissioner Pete Rozelle snatched him from the Colts to be his confidante and insider as it related to the rapidly growing number of Black NFL players.

In one of his first major projects, a memorandum dated August 3, 1966, Young meticulously produced a revealing five-page synopsis that was titled "Some Observations on the NFL and Negro Players."

It's a document that renowned sociologist Harry Edwards says, "should be in Canton, enshrined in a case like the Declaration of Independence."

Young was inducted into the College Football Hall of Fame in 1968, Rose Bowl Hall of Fame, and the inaugural Illinois Athletics Hall of Fame in 2017. Young was the first Illini player to show up in Heisman Trophy voting, finishing fifth in 1944.

At his death in 1983 in a tragic car wreck on a highway in Texas, Young was 57 years old and Director of Player Relations for the NFL. Legendary *New York Post* sportswriter Jerry Izenberg praised him in a stirring tribute.

"Buddy was just 57 years," Izenberg wrote. "Few men are loved in so short a span of time the way he was. It is generally said of such a man that he walked among giants. In this case, it's not quite so. Buddy was larger by far than most men. He was 5–4 and the world looked up to him."

15 Homecoming—An Illinois Tradition Since 1910

For decades following an idea hatched by Clarence Williams and Elmer Ekblaw back in 1910, the University of Illinois claimed to be the original college to celebrate the Homecoming tradition … but so did several other schools, including Missouri, Indiana, Michigan, and Northern Illinois.

What is known, though, is that Williams, better known as "Dab," and Ekblaw, the editor of *The Daily Illini*, conceived of the very first Homecoming on the UI campus while sitting on the old YMCA steps during the fall of 1909 discussing a way to contribute to their alma mater. They presented the idea to Shield and Trident, a senior honorary society, then called upon UI President Edmund James and Dean Thomas Arkle Clark. A year later, during that first Homecoming weekend (October 14–16, 1910) more than 1,500 UI graduates returned to campus, nearly one-third of the school's alumni. The culmination of the inaugural Homecoming weekend was a 3–0 victory by the Illini football team over the University of Chicago when Illinois' Otto Seiler kicked a field goal to provide the winning margin.

The Daily Illini declared that first Homecoming to be an unqualified success and touted the University as the originator of the affair:

"The echoes of the events of this great 'Home-coming' will be heard as long as the University endures, for it is now almost a certainty that it will be adopted as a permanent annual institution the like of which no other University can boast. Illinois may well pride itself on being the originator of the plan for drawing home the alumni, a plan which will undoubtedly be adopted general."

Unfortunately for *The Daily Illini*'s assertion, on November 24–25 of the previous year—1909—Baylor University had sponsored an alumni event called a "Home-coming" featuring a concert, pep rally, parade, bonfire, and football game. However, Baylor's next Homecoming apparently wasn't held until 1915. Several other schools claim to have hosted alumni events around a football game since early in the century, but, other than Baylor, none had called their celebration a Homecoming. No matter the circumstances, Illinois can always claim to have hosted one of the very first continuous Homecoming celebrations for alumni.

Illinois has hosted Homecoming festivities each year since. The exception is 1918, when, as World War I was winding down, no preparations for the annual tradition had been made by early autumn, early Big Ten football games were canceled, and Homecoming never took place. The Spanish Flu Pandemic was

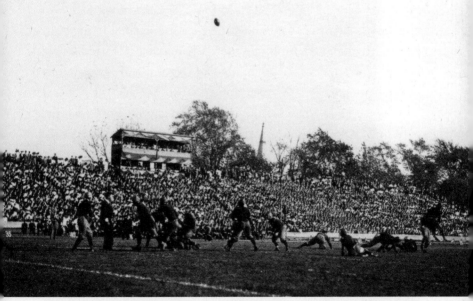

Dab Williams and Elmer Ekblaw are credited with originating the Homecoming tradition on the University of Illinois campus in 1910. It is the longest-running continuous Homecoming celebration in the nation.

also raging across the nation and most of the games played that season were behind locked gates with no fans.

The COVID-19 pandemic caused another hiccup in the Homecoming tradition in 2020. Football games that season were played with either no fans or very limited fans allowed inside stadiums. The Homecoming game was played against Iowa in front of 875 fans and a virtual Homecoming celebration was held with a week-long schedule of events that alumni, fans, and friends could participate in via their home computers.

16 Walking Among Illini Royalty at Roselawn and Mt. Hope Cemeteries

For those who are interested in history and enjoy poking around cemeteries, the Rose Lawn and Mt. Hope Cemeteries, located just east of Memorial Stadium, are spots where one can find the final resting places for several Fighting Illini royalty and many locally prominent names.

George Huff, the longtime athletics director for the University of Illinois who was the driving force behind the construction of Memorial Stadium, is buried in the first row next to Fourth Street at the 50-yard line extended from inside the stadium. Huff was best known for having devoted his life to the honor and glory of the University with honesty and fair play. On October 1, 1936, uremic poisoning claimed the life of "The Father of Fighting Illini Athletics" at age 64.

Just to the north of Huff's grave, you'll find the stone of legendary football coach Robert Zuppke. He coached the Fighting Illini from 1913 to 1941, capturing national titles in 1914, 1919, 1923, and 1927, along with seven Big Ten crowns. Zuppke was football's most innovative coach in the early decades of his career and was honored in 1951 by being selected a charter member of college football's Hall of Fame. Zup died in 1957 at the age of 78.

Several yards to the south of Huff is the gravesite of Dwight "Dike" Eddleman, considered to be the greatest all-around athlete in Fighting Illini history. Not only was Eddleman a member of Illinois' first Rose Bowl championship team in 1947 and the leading scorer on the UI's first Final Four basketball team in 1949, but he also finished in a three-way tie for second place in the high jump at the 1948 London Olympic Games. Dike's 11 varsity letters at Illinois also stand as a record.

A short distance to the north of Zuppke is the grave of Michael Tobin, the first full-time collegiate athletics publicist in the country, a position more commonly known as sports information director. It was his job to spread the word on the athletic exploits of Fighting Illini stars, including Red Grange. Tobin died in 1944 at the age of 64.

A few rows in from Zuppke is Ray Eliot, who played for Zup then followed him as head coach from 1942 to 1959. Known as "Mr. Illini," Eliot passed away on February 24, 1980.

Just inside the main driveway to Rose Lawn is the gravesite of legendary basketball coach Lou Henson, who led the Fighting Illini from 1975 to 1996 and is Illinois' all-time leader in victories with 423 and a member of the National Collegiate Basketball Hall of Fame. Henson died July 25, 2020.

Other prominent Fighting Illini buried in Rose Lawn include baseball All-American and longtime coach Lee Eilbracht; major donor Clint Atkins; longtime sports information director Chuck Flynn; basketball stars Rod Fletcher and Fred Green, who served the area as a judge; Olympic medalists Don Laz and Frank Murphy; wrestling coach Paul Prehn; and football players Justa Lindgren, Jim Reeder, and Stan Wallace.

One important name in the history of Illinois athletics who is buried at Rose Lawn may not be as well-known as many but is no less important. Hiram Hannibal Wheeler was one of two men who broke the color barrier for Illinois athletics in 1904. Wheeler participated in both football and track as a student-athlete, lettering as a sprinter in track and becoming the first Black athlete to win a track event by winning the 100-yard dash in a dual meet with Purdue in 1904. He died as a victim of the Spanish influenza pandemic in 1918.

Two prominent former Illini athletes in Mt. Hope Cemetery are College Football Hall of Famer J.C. Caroline and former Whiz Kid and athletics director Gene Vance.

17 Dick Butkus— Monster of the Midway

There is probably no football name in the history of the game that personifies defensive toughness like that of Illini Hall of Famer Dick Butkus.

A native of the South Side of Chicago who attended Vocational High School, Butkus chose Illinois as his collegiate home in 1961 and became the dominant defensive player of his era, and maybe of all time.

He was exceptionally large for a linebacker playing in the 1960s at 6'3" and weighing 245 pounds, with terrific foot speed that allowed for relentless pursuit and ferocious tackling.

Butkus played both center and middle linebacker, with many observers saying that he might have been the greatest offensive center they had ever seen. Because of his value on the defensive side of the ball, however, he was normally brought in at center in short yardage situations.

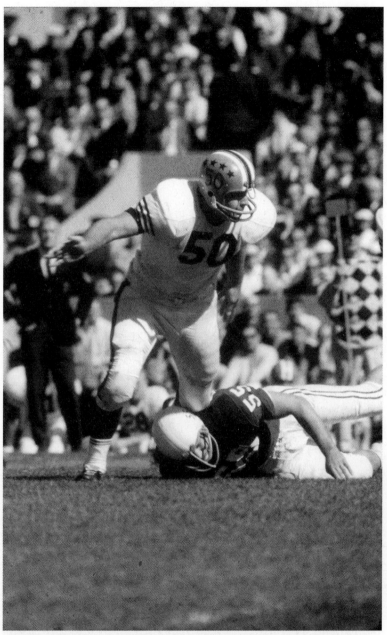

Dick Butkus became the most feared football player on the planet during his career at Illinois from 1962 to '64. His physicality set the standard for all linebackers who followed in his shadow.

After he earned Second-Team All-Big Ten honors in 1962, Butkus was a consensus All-American in both 1963 and 1964 and won the Big Ten Silver Football Award as the conference's Most Valuable Player and finished third in voting for the Heisman Trophy as a senior in 1964.

Butkus helped lead the Fighting Illini to the 1963 Big Ten championship and a 1964 Rose Bowl victory over Washington. He was named the 1964 Collegiate Player of the Year by the American Football Coaches Association.

Butkus was drafted in the first round of the 1965 NFL Draft by his hometown Chicago Bears and in the second round of the 1965 AFL Draft by the Denver Broncos of the American Football League. After several days of recruiting by both the teams and leagues, his decision to sign with the Bears was considered a major victory for the NFL.

He went on to be named NFL Defensive Player of the Year in both 1969 and 1970, earn All-Pro honors eight times (five times First-Team), and was placed on NFL All-Decade teams for both the 1960s and 1970s as well as earning spots on the NFL 75th and 100th Anniversary All-Time Teams.

Butkus was named to the Big Ten Diamond Anniversary Team in 1970, The *Sporting News* College Coaches All-Time Team, the Walter Camp All-Century Team, the University of Illinois All-Century Team, and as one of the 11 greatest collegiate players of all time by ESPN when celebrating 150 years of the game, joining fellow Illinois alum Red Grange on the esteemed list. An award in his honor, given annually since 1985 to the most outstanding linebacker at the high school, college, and professional levels, is named the Butkus Award and is sponsored by the Butkus Foundation.

Following his incredible playing career, Butkus moved to Florida and then to the West Coast to start an extensive acting career that included appearances in many movies including *Mother, Jugs & Speed* (1976), *Johnny Dangerously* (1984), *Necessary*

Roughness (1991), and *Any Given Sunday* (1999). He was a regular character on TV shows such as *Blue Thunder*, *My Two Dads*, *Vega$*, *MacGyver*, and *Hang Time*. Throughout the late 1970s and early 1980s, Butkus appeared alongside former NFL star Bubba Smith in a series of ads for Miller Lite, which were released to high acclaim.

Butkus was named to the Pro Football Hall of Fame in 1979, the College Football Hall of Fame in 1983, and the University of Illinois Athletics Hall of Fame as an initial class member in 2017. Illinois retired his uniform number 50 in 1986 and the Bears followed suit by retiring his number 51 in 1994. The numbers 50 (Butkus) and 77 (Grange) adorn the front of the Memorial Stadium Press Box.

The Dick Butkus Center for Cardiovascular Wellness is a non-profit organization in Orange County, California, with a cardiac screening program that uses specialized testing to help identify those at risk of heart disease. He underwent quintuple bypass surgery in 2001 to remove blockages in his arteries, which led to him starting the organization.

Butkus passed away at his home in Malibu in his sleep on October 5, 2023, at the age of 80.

18 Illini in National and International Leadership Roles

As charter members of both the NCAA and Big Ten Conference, it should be no surprise that that Illini athletes, coaches, and administrators have played major leadership roles in several national and international sports organizations.

In 1895, it had become apparent that with the growth of state universities had come a burgeoning interest in intercollegiate athletics. The new interest meant new loyalties, hot competition, and an insatiable desire to win. It was also apparent that rules and regulations were sorely needed to keep things square on the field of competition. Baseball, track, and football were considered the "varsity" sports at the time, with football soon passing baseball as the leading attraction.

On January 11, 1895, Purdue president James Smart issued invitations to the presidents of six other universities to attend a meeting at the Palmer House Hotel in Chicago to discuss ideas on how to gain control of intercollegiate athletics.

The initial group of presidents represented Purdue, Minnesota, Wisconsin, Illinois, Northwestern, Michigan, and Chicago. Initially named the "Intercollegiate Conference of Faculty Representatives," the group of schools would go on to become the Big Ten Conference.

Since that time, several people closely connected to the University of Illinois, either as alumni or staff members, have gone on to major leadership roles.

Major John L. Griffith, the first Big Ten commissioner, was head of the physical education program and coaching school at Illinois following his service in World War I. While at Illinois in 1921, he collaborated with famed Chicago football coach Amos Alonzo Stagg and Wisconsin track coach Tom Jones to help start the first NCAA outdoor track and field championships. The meet was a success and formed the cornerstone for other NCAA championship events. He was named the first Big Ten commissioner in 1922 and served in that position until his sudden death in 1944. Griffith also served the NCAA as secretary-treasurer.

Kenneth "Tug" Wilson, a native of rural Atwood, Illinois, about 30 miles south of the Illinois campus, was a track and field Olympian and basketball team captain during his years as an Illini. After beginning his athletics administrative career as an assistant to George Huff at Illinois, he went on to become the athletics director at Drake, then Northwestern before following Griffith in the role as the Big Ten's second commissioner from 1945 until 1961. He followed Griffith as the NCAA secretary-treasurer, served as chairman for the 1948 Olympic Games in London, and was president of the U.S. Olympic Committee from 1953 until 1965.

Avery Brundage, a great all-around track star for Illinois before World War 1, went on to international eminence, and controversy, as president of the U.S. Olympic Association and later president of the International Olympic Committee from 1952 to 1972 and probably did more to set the tone of the modern Olympic Games than any other individual. He also played basketball at Illinois while earning his degree in civil engineering.

Brundage competed in the pentathlon and decathlon at the 1912 Olympics in Stockholm and was the U.S. champion in the all-around in 1914, 1916, and 1918. He served seven years (1928–33, 1935) as president of the Amateur Athletic Union and was president of the U.S. Olympic Association and Committee from 1929 to 1953. In 1936 he was elected to the IOC and served as vice president from 1945 to 1952 until his time as president.

Illinois alum Jim Phillips, who served the Illinois basketball program as a team manager and student assistant to Lou Henson, left the coaching profession in 1997 for administrative positions at Tennessee and Notre Dame before being named athletics director at Northern Illinois and Northwestern. He was named the fifth commissioner in Atlantic Coast Conference history in 2021.

19 Illini Who Went on to Own the Team

Over the decades, several University of Illinois alumni worked their way to the top of the organizational chart by becoming the team owner.

Possibly the most important NFL meeting in league history occurred on September 17, 1920, when a group of men representing professional football teams gathered in Canton, Ohio, at the Hupmobile showroom of Ralph Hays, owner of the Canton Bulldogs. One attendee who would go on to play a major role in the NFL for more than 60 years was former Fighting Illini George Halas, who was representing the Decatur Staleys. The result of that meeting was the birth of the NFL.

Two years later, another meeting in Canton included a strenuous afternoon of meetings that included the contested ownership of the Decatur/Chicago Staleys franchise between Halas and his partner, Edward "Dutch" Sternaman, who were teammates at Illinois in the late 1910s, and the Harley brothers (Bill and Charles). Apparently, Halas had pursued Ohio State All-American Chic Harley and other Buckeyes, and agreed to share his profits with Bill Harley, Chic's brother who was doing the negotiating. At this meeting in 1922, Bill Harley showed up in Canton and claimed he was an equal owner with Halas and Sternaman.

The owners eventually voted 8–2 to award the Chicago franchise to the Illini graduates, who immediately changed the name to the Bears. Halas eventually bought out Sternaman in 1933, but not without peril. The two men agreed to an installment plan that included a clause stipulating that if Halas defaulted on any of the payments, ownership of the team reverted to Sternaman.

"When the final payment came due in '33, I was exactly $15,000 short," Halas wrote in a published series of stories about Bears history. "It was a case of finding $15,000 in a hurry—or losing everything I'd worked for since moving the Staleys from Decatur to Chicago in 1921.

"From this desperate situation, I was rescued by the joint efforts of my mother and my friend Charley Bidwill," Halas wrote. "Mother bought $5,000 worth of stock from her savings, Bidwill purchased $5,000 in stock and arranged a bank loan for the remaining $5,000 needed to pay off Sternaman. But it was a mighty close call. As I remember, I finally got all the money together at 11:10 a.m. on the day the final note came due. Forfeit time was 12 o'clock noon."

Another Illinois alum from Chicago was also earning the reputation as a sports pioneer and entrepreneur in the 1920s. Abe Saperstein was only five feet tall, but competed in baseball, basketball, and track as a high school student, and wasn't given a tryout for the University of Illinois basketball team as an undergraduate student. Following graduation, Saperstein moved back to Chicago, where he founded and coached what would evolve into the world-famous Harlem Globetrotters.

In 1926, Saperstein took over a team composed entirely of Black players named the "Savoy Big Five," named after team sponsor the Savoy Ballroom. The next year, he formed the Saperstein's Harlem, New York, Globetrotters, which later became simply the Harlem Globetrotters.

Saperstein traveled around the world as owner and coach of the Harlem Globetrotters until his death in 1966. He was inducted into the Basketball Hall of Fame in 1971.

Along with some of the famous Globetrotter names over the decades like Curly Neal, Wilt Chamberlain, Meadowlark Lemon, Marques Haynes, Goose Tatum, Geese Ausbie, and Connie Hawkins, were two former Fighting Illini in Mannie Jackson and Govoner Vaughn.

Jackson and Vaughn were pioneers of their own merit as the first Black Illinois basketball starters and letter winners from 1958 to 1960. Both players went on to standout stints with the Globetrotters in the 1960s. After a long and successful career as a business executive, Jackson became the first Black person to own a major international sports/entertainment organization when he purchased the Globetrotters in 1993.

He achieved a dramatic corporate turnaround, reviving the near-bankrupt organization and restoring its status as one of the most admired and publicized teams in the world while rebuilding the fan base to near record levels.

Jackson sold 80 percent of the team to Shamrock Capital Growth Fund in 2005 and stepped away from his day-to-day operations of the team. He remains the Globetrotters' chairman of the board and still owns 20 percent of the team.

One of Mannie Jackson's teammates at Illinois went on to an incredible sports story of his own. A native of Chicago Heights, Illinois, Jerry Colangelo started his collegiate basketball career at the University of Kansas, where he spent his freshman year as a teammate of Wilt Chamberlain. Following that season, when Chamberlain left college to play a season with the Globetrotters prior to his Hall of Fame NBA career, Colangelo transferred closer to home and became an Illini.

During his time at Illinois, Colangelo played both basketball and baseball from 1960 to '62 before embarking on a long and influential career in professional sports as a coach, general manager, and even team owner.

At the age of 28, he became the youngest general manager in professional sports, hired to direct the newly franchised Phoenix Suns. And, as GM with the Suns, he was involved with one of the most famous coin flips in sports history. The Milwaukee Bucks and Suns paired off with the winner of the flip claiming the first pick of the 1969 NBA Draft, where Lew Alcindor (later known as Kareem

Abdul-Jabbar) of UCLA was the obvious prize. Unfortunately for Colangelo, the Suns' call of heads ended up on the wrong side of the flip.

After working with the Suns for nearly 20 years, Colangelo stepped up and coordinated a group of investors who purchased the club in 1987. He would be directly connected with the Suns for 40 years. In 1994, he put together another group of investors and purchased the Arizona Diamondbacks franchise, a Major League Baseball expansion team. He delivered the first major sports championship to the Phoenix area when the Diamondbacks defeated the New York Yankees in the 2001 World Series, becoming the fastest expansion team to win a World Series title.

Colangelo was also instrumental in the start-up of other teams such as the Women's National Basketball Association's Phoenix Mercury and the Arena Football League's Arizona Rattlers. He was paramount in bringing the NHL to Arizona in the form of the Winnipeg Jets in 1997, playing as the Phoenix Coyotes before relocating to Utah.

But he wasn't done excelling on the big stage. After the United States Men's Basketball Team struggled at the Olympics, Colangelo took the reins as chairman and managing director of the team, where he recruited and served as architect of an all-star powerhouse team that restored the U.S. reputation on the international basketball landscape. He was the driving force behind the Senior Men's National Team winning the Gold Medal at the 2008, 2012, 2016, and 2020 Olympic Games.

Sheila Crump Johnson graduated from Illinois in 1970 with her bachelor's degree in music while also serving on the Fighting Illini cheer squad. It was here that she also married Robert Johnson in 1969. In 1980, the Johnsons co-founded Black Entertainment Television (BET), a cable network geared toward Black audiences.

In 1999, Johnson left BET to pursue her own interests and moved to the Washington, D.C., area. She became involved in the Washington Mystics WNBA franchise, and in 2005 purchased the team. This, and similar moves in relation to the Washington Capitals (NHL) and the Washington Wizards (NBA), earned her the distinction of being the first woman to be a stakeholder in three professional franchises.

Shahid (Shad) Khan is a 1971 graduate of the University of Illinois Grainger College of Engineering with a degree in industrial engineering. An immigrant from Pakistan, Khan bought Flex-N-Gate from his former employer in 1980.

An engineer, his design for a one-piece truck bumper was the basis for his business success as the company now has more than 75 plants worldwide and more than 27,000 employees.

Kahn bought the NFL's Jacksonville Jaguars in 2012 and the UK's Fulham Football Club in 2013. He and his son, Tony, launched All Elite Wrestling, a professional wrestling entertainment company and a competitor to WWE, in 2019. In 2024, Forbes ranked him as the 12th richest U.S. Sports Team Owner and among the top 70 richest people in the nation.

Halas was a charter member of the Pro Football Hall of Fame while Jackson and Colangelo are both members of the Naismith Memorial Basketball Hall of Fame.

20 Ayo and Kofi Lead Illini Golden Era in Hoops

When Brad Underwood was named head basketball coach at Illinois in March 2017, the Fighting Illini were coming off just three NCAA Tournament appearances in the previous 10 seasons, and none since John Groce's initial season in 2013.

It was evident an injection of top talent was in order, and Underwood identified the Illinois high school star and five-star recruit Ayo Dosunmu as the key prospect to start the turnaround. At a highly covered press conference at Niketown in downtown Chicago, the two-time state champion and all-stater thrilled Illini fans everywhere by committing to his home-state school.

The 2018–19 season record didn't exactly show the wanted success on paper with a 12–21 record, setting the mark for most losses in school history. However, the promise of future success was evident with Dosunmu being named to the Big Ten All-Freshman Team after leading the Illini in scoring at nearly 14 points per game, classmate Giorgi Bezhanishvili scoring 12.5 points per game, and sophomore Trent Frazier dropping more than 13 points each night.

Dosunmu, Frazier, Bezhanishvili, Da'Monte Williams, and junior college transfer Andres Feliz all had proven themselves as legitimate Big Ten players. Missing from the lineup was a big man in the middle.

That changed immediately with the introduction of Jamaican Kofi Cockburn to the college basketball world. Illinois had never seen a player of Cockburn's physical stature of seven feet tall and nearly 300 pounds. His addition to Underwood's lineup was just the ingredient to push Illinois back on the national radar.

The 2019–20 season started with a mixed bag of results before dominating fifth-ranked Michigan State at home in early December. A seven-game conference winning streak to end January firmly placed Illinois in the Top 25 before stumbling with four straight losses to open February. A road win at ninth-ranked Penn State on February 18 stemmed the tide that led to five wins in the last six games of the regular season to finish with a 21–10 overall record.

The Illini were finishing the season with a high level of confidence heading into the Big Ten Tournament when a double bye pushed their first game to Friday, March 13. A return to the NCAA

Ayo Dosunmu and Kofi Cockburn can be credited with leading the return of Fighting Illini basketball to the list of the nation's top programs. Both players earned Consensus All-America honors and helped the Illini to Big Ten tournament and regular-season titles.

Tournament was all but assured. That is, until a new virus labeled COVID-19 thrust itself into the sporting world on Wednesday, March 11, and nearly every athletics team in the nation was shut down by the end of the day on Thursday, March 12.

The 2020–21 season came with sky-high expectations for the Fighting Illini, but also with a bizarre set of rules and policies as the world continued to struggle with COVID-19. Games would be played, but only after extensive testing of everyone on the teams and on the basketball courts. Fans would be prohibited from arenas for much of the country, and only limited attendance allowed in some venues.

Illinois would be ranked inside the Top 25 for the entire season. The schedule was changed so that every game, beginning December 15, would be Big Ten Conference contests only. The

Illini began conference play with five wins in the first six games before tough back-to-back home losses to Maryland and Ohio State.

Looking up at Big Ten leaders Michigan and Ohio State, the Fighting Illini reeled off 11 wins in the last 12 regular season games to finish with a Big Ten–best 16 victories against only four losses.

Three games of that streak stand out, including a 75–60 win over 19th-ranked Wisconsin when Dosunmu posted the third triple-double in school history with 21 points, 12 rebounds, and 12 assists, while Cockburn damaged rims with eight slam dunks on his way to 23 points and 14 boards against the overmatched Badgers.

A few weeks later, following a physical loss at Michigan State when Dosunmu was injured on a hard foul late in the game where he suffered a broken nose, the Illini found themselves having to play down the stretch without their national player of the year candidate. A road swing at No. 2 Michigan and seventh-ranked Ohio State seemed daunting.

The performance at Ann Arbor on March 2, 2021, was one for the record books as the Illini dominated the Wolverines 76–53. It was the NCAA's largest victory margin over a top–2 team on the road since 1995.

Four days later in Columbus, Dosunmu would return having to wear a mask to protect his face and scored a game-high 19 points. The victory improved Illinois to 16–4 in the Big Ten, its winningest conference season in school history. Iowa was within two victories of Illinois at 14–6, but Michigan was named Big Ten regular season champion with a 14–3 mark and better winning percentage after having to cancel three games with COVID-19 issues within the program.

The next week at the Big Ten Tournament in Indianapolis, games were scheduled at Lucas Oil Stadium and would allow a limited number of fans inside to watch. Four Top 10 teams promised to provide a high level of basketball, and the tournament didn't disappoint.

Illinois opened with a 90–68 win over Rutgers with Dosunmu scoring a game-high 23 points. Then, the third-ranked Illini took down No. 5 Iowa, 82–71, with Cockburn leading all scorers with 26 points and Dosunmu following with 18 points, nine assists, and seven rebounds.

The championship contest with Ohio State would be the tie-breaker after the teams split games in the regular season. Six Illini scored in double figures to lead a balanced attack in a heavyweight bout that ended with an Illini 91–88 overtime victory. While the team celebrated on the floor and was receiving the tournament championship trophy, the NCAA Selection Show was underway and announced that Illinois would be a No. 1 seed for the tournament, creating another loud roar from the Illini fans who stuck around.

To try and ensure the NCAA Tournament would be played in 2021, all 68 teams were brought to Indianapolis and kept in "bubbles" to minimize the chance of COVID-19 spreading among the student-athletes, staff, and officials. Games were scheduled at sites in and around Indianapolis, including two different courts inside Lucas Oil Stadium, the Indiana Farmers Coliseum, Bankers Life Fieldhouse, Hinkle Fieldhouse, Mackey Arena, and Assembly Hall in Bloomington.

The Fighting Illini opened with a 78–49 victory over Drexel at the Indiana Farmers Coliseum on the Indiana State Fairgrounds. Dosunmu led the way with 17 points, 11 rebounds, and six assists, while Cockburn added 18 points.

The following matchup against Chicago Loyola at Bankers Life Fieldhouse proved to be the end of the road for the outstanding season when the Ramblers pulled off a 71–58 upset over the top-seeded Illini and left them with a 24–7 record.

All eyes immediately turned to the future to see if the two Fighting Illini consensus All-Americans, Dosunmu and Cockburn, would return for another run in the Orange and Blue.

21 Kofi Returns, Ayo Declares for NBA, and Illini Win Big Ten Title

Junior Ayo Dosunmu earned a National Player of the Year Award from *USA Today* and was a consensus All-American after his incredible 2020–21 season. This all meant decisions about his future had to be made. Where did he fall in the minds of the NBA? Could he help his draft status by returning for another season?

Head coach Brad Underwood helped him make the decision when he told Dosunmu that he needed to go to the next level. There was very little that could be added to his game at the collegiate level. In early April, Dosunmu submitted his name, which led to being selected in the second round by his hometown Chicago Bulls.

On deck was center Kofi Cockburn, who was a consensus Second-Team All-American. In a different era, he surely would have been a lottery pick, but style of play in the NBA has changed considerably and three-point shooting became a critical part of the grading process.

Cockburn was coming off one of the most dominant seasons by a post player in Big Ten history and was clearly ranked as one of the best big men in Fighting Illini history. After competing in workouts with several NBA teams, he decided to return to Illinois and work on his game to better prepare for a professional career.

Sophomore Adam Miller, who started all 31 games in 2020–21, made the decision to leave the program and transferred to LSU during the offseason.

Underwood knew he had a great nucleus, including the massive Cockburn, returning for a veteran ballclub that promised to compete for the Big Ten title. High expectations were quickly tempered when Cockburn was served a three-game suspension to start the season after selling some team gear before announcing his return to Illinois, just a couple of weeks before that would have become legal under changing NCAA rules.

In addition, sophomore point guard Andre Curbelo, who expected to take over much of Dosunmu's role as a floor leader, suffered a concussion and was sidelined for several weeks in December, never regaining his stellar play that earned him Big Ten Sixth Man of the Year honors in 2021.

After starting Big Ten play with a home win over Rutgers and road victory at Iowa in December, Illinois won its first four games in January before running into fourth-ranked Purdue for a rare Monday matinee appearance on Martin Luther King Day. In two overtimes, Purdue pulled out a 96–88 win at State Farm Center, handing the Illini their first Big Ten loss of the season.

The two top teams in the conference met again in West Lafayette three weeks later when the 13th-ranked Illini made the short trip to Purdue against the third-ranked Boilermakers. Purdue broke open a two-point game at halftime to hand Illinois their third loss in conference play and drop them into a first-place tie with the Boilermakers and surging Wisconsin.

Just one week earlier, Illinois dominated the Badgers, 80–67, with Cockburn playing one of the best games of his career with 37 points and 12 rebounds.

As the season wound down, a critical home loss to Ohio State dropped Illinois to 12–5 in the conference, which would require help to claim a piece of the title. Wisconsin had played itself into the driver's seat with a win over Purdue in Madison on March 1.

Illinois hung around the top with a critical win at Ann Arbor over Michigan followed by a home victory over Penn State on March 3.

Wisconsin entered the final day of the Big Ten regular season only needing a victory over last-place Nebraska to win the outright conference title. But things don't always go as expected. The Huskers rallied from 10 down in the second half to upset the 10th-ranked Badgers in Madison, 74–73. And, with that, an Illinois victory over No. 24 Iowa on the final game of the day would mean the Illini could claim a share of the Big Ten championship.

The electric atmosphere inside State Farm Center on March 6 was apparent from the moment doors opened. Everyone in the building knew what was at stake, with the hated Hawkeyes standing between Illinois and a Big Ten championship.

In a memorable senior night, it was only fitting that fifth-year seniors Trent Frazier and Da'Monte Williams would play a major role in determining the outcome. Williams made a free throw with just seconds remaining to give Illinois a two-point lead, then Frazier grabbed the final defensive rebound to secure the 74–72 victory and the Fighting Illini's first regular-season title since 2005.

What followed the final buzzer was the greatest court-storming in the nearly 60-year history of State Farm Center. Thousands of jubilant fans rushed Lou Henson Court and celebrated with the Illini team, which was presented a Big Ten championship trophy at midcourt.

The 44 wins in Big Ten play over the last three seasons (2020–22) is the winningest three-year stretch in school history, including at least 13 conference wins in each of the three years for the first time. Seniors Frazier, Williams, and Jacob Granderson, along with Cockburn, were mainstays for all three seasons. Cockburn would go on to earn consensus All-America honors for the second consecutive season while establishing himself as Illinois' most dominant big man. He would forego his senior season while making himself available for professional basketball, where he played internationally the next season.

22 Howard Griffith Scores Again, and Again, and Again ...

The Illinois football team entered its September 22, 1990, football game against in-state rival Southern Illinois with a 1–1 record after losing the opener at Arizona and bouncing back with an impressive 23–22 victory over ninth-ranked Colorado.

That victory moved Illinois to No. 15 in the national poll and established the Illini as prohibitive favorites over the Salukis. However, no one told that to the SIU team.

Griffith put the Illini on the scoreboard first, but the Salukis used two turnovers, including one when SIU linebacker Kevin Kilgallon ripped the ball from Griffith's hands and ran 27 yards into the end zone, to take a 21–7 lead in the first quarter.

The turnover by Griffith, and following touchdown, seemed to light a spark that inspired one of the all-time great performances.

"We're losing the game," Griffith said. "And we had a really good team that year, but it just goes to show when you don't respect your opponent, you can find yourselves in those types of games. We were able to turn it around, but before we got it turned around, I was taking a draw play running to my left, and I take the handoff—the ball, obviously, should be in my left hand since I'm going left, but I was one of those people that just wanted to hold it in my right all the time. The linebacker comes up, rips the ball out of my hand, and goes the other way and scores a touchdown.

Fighting Illini running back Howard Griffith broke a 39-year-old NCAA record by rushing for eight touchdowns against Southern Illinois on September 22, 1990. His incredible performance that day has only been equaled once in more than three decades since.

Howard Griffith's Eight Touchdowns

1. 5-yard burst off right tackle, 10:06 left in 1st quarter
2. 51-yards up the middle, 8:50 left in 2nd quarter
3. 7-yard up-the-middle run, 4:53 left in 2nd quarter
4. 41-yard dash, left side, 3:10 left in 2nd quarter
5. 5-yard run off right tackle, 12:34 left in 3rd quarter
6. 18-yard, tackle breaker, 10:10 left in 3rd quarter
7. 5-yard run off right tackle, 6:07 left in 3rd quarter
8. 3-yard drive off right tackle, 1:25 left in 3rd quarter

It was the most humiliating situation I had been in, and then we went off on a run after that."

Did they!

Beginning in the second quarter, Griffith scored three touchdowns to regain the lead. In the third quarter, he added four more scores as the Illini defense shut out the Salukis for the remaining 46 minutes of the game. He scored on runs of five, 51, seven, 41, five, 18, five, and three yards.

As each touchdown was scored, the sports information crew in the Memorial Stadium press box was busily tracking school, Big Ten, and NCAA records. Griffith's fifth and sixth touchdowns tied and then broke legendary Red Grange's Illinois and Big Ten records set in 1924 during the dedication game of the stadium, and his eighth TD broke Mississippi State legend Arnold "Showboat" Boykin's record of seven set back in 1951.

Griffith finished the day with 21 carries for 208 yards in front of a crowd of 64,469 and was carried off the field by his teammates after his eighth touchdown.

Griffith's 48 points also broke Syracuse legend Jim Brown's record of 43 points scored in a game set against Colgate in 1956.

Trailing 21–7 made the decision to keep Griffith in the game easier to understand, but head coach John Mackovic also knew a moment like this would likely never come again and gave him an opportunity to score one last time to break the 39-year-old record. It took until November 28, 2020, before Buffalo's Jaret Patterson tied the record with his eight-touchdown performance in a 70–41 victory over Kent State.

"It was really, just really, a crazy game," Griffith said. "I should have played the lottery that day."

In his final season at Illinois, Griffith rushed for 1,115 yards and 15 touchdowns. For his career, he rushed for 2,477 yards and 31 scores. Griffith went on to win two Super Bowl rings with the Denver Broncos during his eight-year NFL career.

Illinois would go on to claim a share of the Big Ten championship with an 8–4 overall record, including 6–2 in conference play, earning a spot in the Hall of Fame Bowl on New Year's Day.

23 Marching Illini

Just like the Fighting Illini football team gathers in the weeks before classes start, the Marching Illini begins its own preseason practice schedule in preparation for a year full of performances.

Since 1868, the Marching Illini have entertained millions of fans with traditional and innovative performances that have made them "The Nation's Premier College Marching Band." The Marching Illini continues its pursuit of the highest level of musical, visual, and thoroughly entertaining performances at Memorial Stadium.

In the 1920s, John Philip Sousa called the Illinois Band the "World's Greatest College Band." Superlatives like this have come to be expected during the long and illustrious history of the University of Illinois Bands.

Shortly after the Illinois Industrial Technology opened in 1868, a military band was organized. The military band became the Concert Band and gave its formal concert in 1890. The University of Illinois Bands of today are the top of a pyramid of university band organizations, both concert and marching, that regularly enroll more than 800 students each year.

The unique style of the Marching Illini represents a combination of time-honored traditions and exciting innovations. The MI is a select organization that annually includes many of the University's finest and most dedicated students, while representing virtually every college and major on the UI campus. Each year, the Marching Illini numbers around 375 members, which includes musicians, guard, the Illinettes Dance Team, drum majors, and the undergraduate and graduate staff members.

The "3-in-1" is a tradition forged in the early years of the band's history from three distinct pieces of the University's heritage. The Marching "ILLINI" formation was created by A.A. Harding and his assistants in the early 1920s, making it the oldest part of the "3-in-1." The present-day version of the Marching ILLINI is like the original but is highlighted by an intricate countermarch that allows the band to form the ILLINI letter by letter as it marches back down the field.

The musical portion of the "3-in-1" consists of three distinct Illinois pieces: "Pride of the Illini," "March of the Illini," and "Hail to the Orange."

In addition to its performances, the University of Illinois Bands could claim the honor of holding the largest collection of original works and papers by John Philip Sousa, until 1994 when these items were transferred from the possession of the band to the University of Illinois Archives.

One of the band's favorite traditions each year is when the Alumni Band, including Alumni Illinettes and Featured Twirlers, returns for Homecoming and performs with the current version.

The alums, who range in age from people in their twenties to some in their nineties, can be found at many of their old haunts around campus.

Other Marching Illini firsts:

- Birthplace of the college concert band—first formal concert given in 1890
- First school song—"Illinois Loyalty" was first performed March 3, 1906
- First Football Halftime Show—in 1907 for the game vs. University of Chicago
- First band to former school letters (Block I in parade)
- First Band with a website—first advertised in April 1994
- First college marching band to release a compact disc (*The Marching Illini* in 1986)
- Performed at the first nationally televised football game and the first football game televised in color.

24 Black Pioneers Wearing Orange and Blue

Hiram Hannibal Wheeler and Roy Mercer Young were instrumental in changing the course of intercollegiate athletics at the University of Illinois. In 1904, Wheeler and Young broke the color barrier at the Illinois campus, integrating varsity rosters that had previously only included White men. They came on the scene in Champaign-Urbana about 14 years after the first known Black collegiate football players—W.T.S. Jackson and W.H. Lewis—arrived at Amherst College in Massachusetts.

Wheeler participated in both football and track and field as a student-athlete at Illinois, lettering for first-year track coach

Harry Gill in 1904. In a dual meet with Purdue on May 13, 1904, Wheeler became the first Black player to win a track event by winning the 100-yard dash.

Young, from Springfield, lettered twice as a tackle for the Illini football team. He later attended Northwestern University's Dental School and served as a dental surgeon during World War I in the U.S. Army.

A third Black Illini, George Kyle, competed as a non-letter-winning sprinter in track and field on the 1924 and 1925 teams. Kyle was the first Black athlete to acquire his bachelor's degree (Liberal Arts and Sciences in 1926), then a master's degree (psychology in 1930).

During the late 1920s, a man named Douglas Turner became the first Black student to play tennis at Illinois. He took second place in the 1930 Western Conference (Big Ten) singles competition, then a few weeks later won the national championship among Black men at the American Tennis Association Tournament.

A swimmer named Ralph Hines competed for Coach Ed Manley in 1947 but did not letter. He also briefly ran track as a junior in 1948, the same year he served as president of UI's junior class.

While Mannie Jackson and Govoner Vaughn are most widely recognized as Illini men's basketball Black pioneers in the late 1950s, it was Walt Moore who initially integrated Illinois hoops in 1951. Moore's Illini career lasted only one semester as a freshman in 1951–52 before transferring to Western Illinois, where he earned NAIA All-American honors in 1957 and was head coach of the Leathernecks from 1973 to '77.

The color barrier in fencing at Illinois was initially broken by Richard Younge in 1948, though he did not letter. John Cameron came along a few years later to compete in sabre for Coach Maxwell Garret and letter for Illinois' undefeated teams and Big Ten champions in 1952 and 1953. Cameron captured the conference title in sabre in 1953 and became UI varsity athletics' first Black captain.

The first Black man in Illinois' wrestling room was in the mid-1960s when Al McCullum joined Coach Buell "Pat" Patterson's squad. Wrestling at 130 pounds, McCullum lettered from 1964 through '66.

It wasn't until 1965 that a Black man played baseball at Illinois. Trenton Jackson had already made an impact with the Illini football team, lettering in 1962 and 1965, and the Illini track and field squad (1963, 1964 and 1965). He was part of UI's NCAA-winning 440-yard relay team and won Big Ten titles in the 100 and 220. Jackson hit .235 in the only season he played for Coach Lee Eilbracht's baseball squad.

In the sport of gymnastics, former Illini star Charles Lakes accomplished firsts more than once. Not only was he Coach Yoshi Hayasaki's first Black athlete, lettering from 1983 to '85, but Lakes departed the UI in 1986 to become one of the first Black American gymnasts to compete in the Olympics. He won six Big Ten titles at Illinois and won the 1984 NCAA high bar championship.

Will Clopton, who played in the mid-to-late 1980s, is believed to be the first Black student-athlete to be a member of Illinois' golf team.

When women's varsity athletics debuted at the University of Illinois in 1974–75, Black female athletes were present, though sparse in numbers. Some of the most prominent in the early days of Illini women's athletics were track and field's Bev Washington and basketball's Kendra Gantt. Terry Hite, who directed Illinois' volleyball program from 1975 to '77, was the university's first Black head coach.

25 Astrolllini

There are kids who stare at the stars and dream of being astronauts, and then there are a few who figure out what it takes to make their dreams come true.

That is the story of Fighting Illini football captain Mike Hopkins, who would reach for the stars and complete an incredible 14-year career with NASA that included 334 days in space and five spacewalks during two assignments on the International Space Station.

After growing up in Lebanon, Missouri, Hopkins arrived at the University of Illinois as a walk-on defensive back in 1987 after not being recruited out of School of the Osage in Lake of the Ozarks. It was the reputation of the U of I College of Engineering that drew his attention and he completed a bachelor of science degree in aerospace engineering in 1991. He attended Stanford to study for a master's degree in aerospace engineering in 1992 prior to being commissioned as a second lieutenant in the U.S. Air Force.

On the football field, Hopkins redshirted during Mike White's last season in 1987 and began competing for playing time after John Mackovic arrived in 1988. From that unassuming start, Hopkins became one of the great Fighting Illini success stories, earning First-Team Academic All-America honors and being named a three-time Academic All-Big Ten selection. He was a four-year letter winner and team captain as a senior in 1991. Hopkins helped lead the Fighting Illini to the 1990 Big Ten co-championship and four consecutive bowl appearances from 1988 to 1991.

"Illinois gave me a chance. I was a walk-on here and they didn't even have to give me a shot," Hopkins said. "When I came out of high school, I wasn't recruited anywhere. Zero. Zero recruiting visits. Zero offers anywhere. When they said, 'Yeah, we'd welcome to have you come and try out with us,' that was a start. When I came to the team, I didn't even think I was ever going to see the field other than practice. To have it go from there and actually get to play, get to be a full-time starter, get to have the privilege of being a captain, blows your mind away that it happened for me.

"Quite frankly, that has been a driving force for me throughout my career in the Air Force, the Space Force, and with NASA as well. I tell people all the time, believe it or not, I've been able to go out the door and do five spacewalks and what I learned here at the University of Illinois helped me through those spacewalks."

Col. Hopkins retired from NASA in the summer of 2023. His last spaceflight was as commander of NASA's SpaceX Crew-1

Former Fighting Illini defensive back Michael Hopkins graduated from both Illinois and Stanford with degrees in aerospace engineering. He completed two different assignments on the International Space Station during his NASA career as an astronaut.

mission to the International Space Station in 2020. Crew-1 was the first flight of a NASA-certified commercial human spacecraft system as part of the agency's Commercial Crew Program, and the first flight of the SpaceX Dragon crew spacecraft *Resilience*.

During his Air Force career, Hopkins became special assistant to the vice-chairman of the Joint Chiefs of Staff in 2008. In 2009, he was selected as part of NASA's 20th astronaut class and graduated from astronaut candidate training in 2011. Hopkins' first assignment in space was in 2013. Along with two Russian cosmonauts, he traveled to the ISS aboard the Soyuz TMA–10M spacecraft as a flight engineer of Expedition 37/38, where he spent 166 days in space and orbited the Earth 2,656 times.

Hopkins has returned to campus several times to meet with students in the College of Engineering and the Fighting Illini football team. He delivered the commencement address during the University of Illinois graduation ceremonies in 2014.

26 Dana Howard Locks Down Butkus Award

Following an All-America season as a junior in 1993, Fighting Illini linebacker Dana Howard was on every list for postseason awards in 1994. One of the most consistent star players in Illinois football history, Howard recorded at least 147 tackles in each of his four seasons and was on his way to a Big Ten record 595 tackles for his career.

Howard was a captain for head coach Lou Tepper and was one of the team's emotional leaders and toughest players. He was also one of the most-requested players by media who covered Big Ten football. To help accommodate the media and to try and make it as easy as possible for Howard, a media teleconference was scheduled each Monday where members of the media could call and ask him questions. This was also a valuable tool being used to help publicize Howard for national awards, including the Butkus Award, named after all-time Illini great Dick Butkus and given to the nation's most outstanding linebacker.

Illinois had started the 1994 season with two wins against Missouri and Northern Illinois and two losses to Washington State and Purdue. The 22–16 loss to Purdue was especially difficult after a potential game-winning touchdown pass from Johnny Johnson to Martin Jones was called back because of a penalty. Then future NFL tight end Ken Dilger was stopped just inches from the end zone as time expired.

Illinois' next game was at 17th-ranked Ohio State, and the Illinois season seemed to be in a spot where it could go either way. Howard appeared on his weekly media teleconference to provide his comments to the media and one of the first questions from a Ohio reporter asked him how he thought the team would respond after such a tough loss to Purdue.

Howard barely hesitated in answering that his team would respond by going to Ohio State and winning the game. His direct answer broke many of the unwritten sport rules of predicting victory, especially over the powerful Ohio State Buckeyes at Ohio Stadium.

To the reporter's credit, he offered Howard a chance to clarify his answer since it sounded like a guarantee that Illinois would win the coming Saturday. But Howard didn't back off and repeated that he expected his team to bounce back, go to Ohio State, and win the game. The reporter gave him one more chance to soften the statement, but Howard didn't shy away. He believed in his team and was confident they would take care of business on Saturday.

Thus, the storyline that week was that Dana Howard was guaranteeing an Illini victory over the Buckeyes. At practice later that day, when the team was called together at the end of the workout, Howard stepped up in front of his teammates and said he had told the media earlier that this team was going to win over Ohio State and that he wanted his teammates to know that he believed in them.

To say the least, Coach Tepper was not happy that Howard had stepped out and made such a strong public statement. But there was no turning back at this point.

The game in Columbus was televised nationally by ABC with the legendary Brent Musburger serving as the play-by-play announcer. All eyes were on Howard and how he would respond to all the attention given his statements earlier in the week.

What does he do? Howard totaled 14 tackles, including two quarterback sacks, recovered a fumble, and stepped in front of a Buckeye pass on first and goal for an interception to lead Illinois to the guaranteed 24–10 victory. He delivered in a big way! Musburger couldn't stop mentioning the Butkus Award each time Howard's name was spoken.

Howard would go on to win the 1994 Butkus Award and was a consensus All-American. He would be inducted into the College Football Hall of Fame in 2018.

27 Jim Grabowski

Success for the Fighting Illini football teams from 1962 to '65, and especially the Big Ten championship season of 1963, centered around the stubborn defense led by Dick Butkus and a physical running game behind fullback Jim Grabowski.

Grabowski was a two-time Associated Press selection at fullback in 1964 and 1965. He was inducted into the College Football

Hall of Fame in 1995, the GTE Academic All-American Hall of Fame in 1993, and the Rose Bowl Hall of Fame in 1997.

In his first season as an Illini in 1963, Grabowski led the Illini with 616 yards and, after helping Illinois to the Big Ten title that season, earned MVP honors in the 1964 Rose Bowl while gaining 125 yards in the win over Washington.

After rushing for 1,004 yards and earning All-America and First-Team All-Big Ten honors as a junior in 1964, Heisman Trophy chatter followed Grabowski into the 1965 season. After leading the Big Ten in rushing with 1,258 yards and setting the Big Ten record for career rushing yards with 2,878 yards, Grabo finished third in Heisman Trophy voting. Other honors include *The Sporting News* co-Player of the Year, Back of the Year by the Washington Touchdown Club, and the *Chicago Tribune* Silver Football as the Big Ten Most Valuable Player.

His sterling college career made him a hot choice in the following professional football drafts in a time when the NFL and AFL battled in bidding wars against each other to sign selections.

Grabowski was selected ninth overall by the Green Bay Packers in the 1966 NFL Draft and was also selected No. 1 overall by the Miami Dolphins in the AFL Draft that same year.

He found himself in the Packers boardroom, sitting directly across from Vince Lombardi, a man he considered "next to God as far as the NFL goes."

"I had the ability to try and play off one against the other," said Grabowski. "It was a very interesting time for a kid who was 21 years old, grew up in Chicago, and didn't know too much about anything."

Eventually, he decided to play in Green Bay where he shared the nickname "Gold Dust Twins" with teammate Donny Anderson.

During five seasons as a Packer, Grabowski won two Super Bowl titles in Super Bowls I and II in 1967 and 1968 as a teammate of former Illini linebacker great Ray Nitschke. His final season as a pro was spent with his hometown team, the Chicago Bears, in 1971. With knee problems limiting his effectiveness, Grabo ended his pro career with 1,731 rushing yards and 11 touchdowns.

Following his football career, Grabowski became a color radio analyst for Fighting Illini football, broadcasting games for 26 seasons.

28 Flyin' Illini of 1989

The 1987–88 Illinois basketball season ended in disappointment after the third-seeded Fighting Illini were upset by Villanova in the second round of the NCAA Tournament. But, after losing just three of ten players who played the majority of minutes, expectations were extremely high entering the 1988–89 season.

Returning were Nick Anderson, Kenny Battle, Kendall Gill, Lowell Hamilton, Stephen Bardo, Larry Smith, and Ervin Small, with the addition of High School National Player of the Year Marcus Liberty.

The Big Ten was loaded that year, with Iowa, Michigan, Indiana, and Illinois all spending large portions of the season ranked in the Top 10.

Coach Lou Henson was losing big man Jens Kujawa, who returned to his native Germany to play professionally, so he was concerned about lack of size. What he found out with his squad of super-athletic players, which had eight of his top nine players listed between 6'3" and 6'8", was that quickness, speed, and athleticism could overcome the lack of a true big man.

The depth of the team also played to its strength as Henson had several interchangeable parts to his squad. Basically, the Illini could

The Flyin' Illini of 1989 was the first Illinois basketball team to advance to the NCAA Final Four since 1952. Junior Nick Anderson (left) and senior co-captains Lowell Hamilton (center) and Kenny Battle (right) were three of the team leaders for Lou Henson's historic squad.

switch defensively just about anywhere on the court and not be at a disadvantage. Henson installed a full-court press with the aptly named Battle at the point, causing many opponents nightmares in advancing the ball against intense pressure.

The season started with 17 straight victories that moved the Illini from No. 9 in the preseason polls to No. 1. Victories along the way included a 97–67 blowout over 19th-ranked Florida, who featured a 7'1" force in Dwayne Schintizius, to prove that the lack of size wouldn't be an issue.

One of the iconic wins that season came in the annual Braggin' Rights game in St. Louis when the sixth-ranked Illini took on 10th-ranked Missouri. The Tigers raced out to a 39–21 lead before Battle and his teammates roared back for an 87–84 win.

"We had two ways to go when we were down 18," said Battle. "We could get beat by 40 points or we could man up and show all the Illinois fans that this team was going to be special—so don't ever give up on us."

The regular season peaked on Super Bowl Sunday, January 22, when the Illini hosted Georgia Tech in a fired-up Assembly Hall. When Duke lost to North Carolina four days prior and to Wake Forest a day earlier, everyone was aware that an Illinois victory would move them to the top of the polls. Maybe it was that pressure that allowed the Illini to play tight and fall behind by 16 points. But the Illini wouldn't give up this historic opportunity and came out flying around the court in the second half to tie the game at 74–74 and force overtime.

A play near the end of regulation, when Gill landed on someone's foot during a rebound attempt, nearly completely derailed the season. The rising junior star was helped off the floor and was later diagnosed with a broken fifth metatarsal.

The Illini forced a second overtime, and when foul trouble shortened the Georgia Tech lineup, the Illini pulled away for a 103–92 victory with the game ending to the crowd chanting, "We're Number One!"

Vitale can take credit for nicknaming this squad the Flyin' Illini, which matched perfectly with the high flying and dunking of Battle, Anderson, Gill, Hamilton, Bardo, and Liberty.

Gill's broken foot would keep him out of the lineup for 12 games, in which the Illini went 8–4, likely keeping them from winning the Big Ten title they lost by just one game.

Illinois would win its last six games of the regular season, including an instant classic over eventual Big Ten champs and third-ranked Indiana at Bloomington when Anderson drilled a 30-foot jump shot to beat the buzzer and quiet a huge Hoosier crowd.

Gill returned the next game when the Illini defeated 15th-ranked Iowa 118–94 during Senior Day at Assembly Hall. The final regular season game was another Top 10 matchup against No.

8 Michigan at Ann Arbor. The Illini made their statement for a No. 1 seed in the upcoming NCAA Tournament with an impressive 89–73 victory over the Wolverines.

Illinois entered the postseason ranked No. 3 in the nation and with a No. 1 seed in its regional that also included powerhouse Louisville, Syracuse, and Missouri squads in the Sweet Sixteen round at Minneapolis. The four competing teams sported no less than 13 future first-round NBA draft picks.

During the open practice period prior to the first game, Battle slipped on water that had leaked through the Hubert H. Humphrey Metrodome ceiling and banged his knee on the floor. Then, during the victory over Louisville, Hamilton sprained his ankle. Trainer Rod Cardinal became the unsung Illini hero of the weekend when he nursed Battle's knee and Hamilton's ankle through each night in Minneapolis using all the tools at his disposal.

With a trip to Seattle and the Final Four on the line, Illinois took on No. 7 Syracuse in the round of eight with the floor loaded with future pros. Battle (28 points) and Anderson (24 points) teamed up for an astounding 89–86 defeat of the Orangemen in two of the most courageous games in Fighting Illini history and sent Illinois to the Final Four for the first time in 37 years.

The Final Four at the Kingdome in Seattle was played in front of 39,187 fans and the Illini were paired against 10th-ranked Michigan, whom the Illini had defeated twice already, including the embarrassing 16-point win at Ann Arbor on their Senior Day. This time around, the Wolverines were coached by assistant coach Steve Fisher, who had replaced Bill Frieder after Frieder was fired by athletic director Bo Schembechler for announcing that he had accepted the Arizona State job.

What followed was an epic battle with 33 lead changes, not counting ties. Battle outscored Michigan's Glen Rice 29–28 but Michigan prevailed 83–81 as Sean Higgins knocked in Terry Mills' miss with two seconds remaining.

That magical season ended a game earlier than Illini fans wanted, but the memories from that 31–5 Flyin' Illini season will never be forgotten by all those who witnessed it.

29 Buzzer Beaters—1960s and '70s

Basketball buzzer beaters create some of the most memorable moments in sports, especially during championship seasons when one shot can snatch victory from defeat or overtime. Over the decades, there have been several significant buzzer beaters that will forever remain a part of Illini lore. Here are a few:

Bob Starnes Throws in a Miracle

Illinois 78, Northwestern 76, January 14, 1963: After scoring 106 points in a 24-point win over Purdue just a few days earlier, the fifth-ranked Fighting Illini struggled making baskets nearly the entire next game at Evanston against Northwestern. The Illini battled back to tie the game at 76–76 near the end of regulation, but Northwestern had the ball and stalled for the final 65 seconds. But Wildcat guard Marty Riessen, later of professional tennis fame, threw an errant pass into the hands of Bill Small, who called timeout with two seconds remaining. After a timeout, and everyone in the gym expecting overtime, Tal Brody passed the ball into Illini guard Bob Starnes, who took two dribbles to the far free throw line before launching into the air what Ed O'Neill of *The News-Gazette* called a "push-hook-throw" or, as Starnes recalled, a combination of a baseball pass and a hook shot. The impossible happened. Starnes' miracle chuck from 60 feet away cleanly dropped in the middle of the basket, touching nothing but the bottom of the net. The victory helped give Illinois a share of the Big Ten title with an 11–3 record and advance to the Elite Eight of the NCAA Tournament.

Rich Adams Gives Lou Henson First Illini Victory

Illinois 60, Nebraska 58, November 28, 1975: There would be hundreds to follow, but Lou Henson's first Illini victory was certainly special. The Illini were heavy road underdogs in Lincoln. Slender left hander Rich Adams scored 19 points in the second half to give Illinois a chance against the Cornhuskers. With just over a minute remaining, Nebraska had the ball with the game deadlocked at 58. The Huskers stalled for over a minute before finding forward Bob Siegel open in the left corner.

Siegel missed off the side of the rim and the ball landed out of bounds to the Illini. Larry Lubin took the inbounds pass and raced up the floor, penetrating to the lane where the Husker center had to cover, which allowed Lubin to pass to an open Adams, who was wide open on the right baseline from six feet away.

Adams' short jumper hit nothing but net to give him a game-high 25 points and win number one of the Henson era.

Eddie Johnson Jumper Sinks Magic and Top-Ranked Spartans

Illinois 57, Michigan State 55, January 11, 1979: It was one of the most anticipated home games in Illinois basketball history, and it didn't disappoint. The 15–0 Fighting Illini were ranked No. 4 in the nation, while the Spartans were the No. 1 team in the nation and featured the most recognizable player in college basketball in Magic Johnson.

"I loved playing every game in the Hall, but that night was something special," recalled the game's hero, Eddie Johnson. "It was so loud in there and every time we scored the fans acted like it was the last shot of the game. It was just unbelievable."

The second half of the game was especially tense with solid defense at both ends. With the game tied at 55 and under a minute to play, Illinois forward Levi Cobb lost the ball off his foot and the ensuing struggle for the loose ball resulted in a jump ball. The rules at the time meant the two players would be a part of a jump ball at the free throw line closest to the play.

Cobb won the tip and Illinois had the ball with 37 seconds remaining before calling timeout. After running some clock, point guard Steve Lanter penetrated the lane when MSU forward Greg Kelser took a step in to help, leaving Eddie Johnson open for a 15-footer from the right wing and with four seconds remaining. Johnson's shot splashed cleanly through the net to give Illinois the lead. After taking the in-bounds pass, Magic Johnson could only throw up an air ball from beyond the midcourt line to seal the Illini victory and lead to pandemonium in Assembly Hall.

Illinois was poised to move into the nation's top spot in the rankings if they could win two days later at home against Ohio State. Lanter suffered a knee injury in that game and the Illini couldn't overcome the Buckeyes in a three-point overtime loss.

30 Buzzer Beaters—1980s and '90s

Harper's Buzzer-Beater in Second Overtime Sends Illinois to the Tourney

Illinois 70, Minnesota 67, March 13, 1983: The final regular-season game of 1983 at Assembly Hall was for all the marbles. Win and the Illini would receive a spot in the NCAA Tournament field. Lose and the season-long goal was dashed, and the team would hope for an NIT bid.

The Big Ten portion of the schedule started with an embarrassing 26-point loss to those same Gophers in Minneapolis. After building a double-digit lead in the first half, the Gophers rode the shoulders of 7'3" center Randy Breuer, who finished with 24 points and 12 rebounds, to tie the game as regulation was ending. With the game tied at 56, junior guard Derek Harper had a shot to win it, but missed from 24 feet.

"I remember thinking after I missed that shot that I was the goat," Harper said. "Walking back to the huddle, I just couldn't believe I had the chance to end the game and didn't do it. I told everyone who was around me that I wanted the ball in the overtime."

The teams remained deadlocked after the first timeout. Illinois tied the game in the second OT when Efrem Winters slammed home an alley-oop with a minute left to play. Minnesota attempted to hold for the last shot, but a missed shot under 10 seconds led to an Illini rebound and advancement to the front court with four seconds remaining.

There was little doubt who was going to get the final shot for Illinois.

"Coach Henson is drawing up a play with all these Xs and Os in the huddle and I am listening intently as he told us to do this and do that," said freshman guard Bruce Douglas, who was the inbounds man on the play. "We come out of the huddle, Derek looks at me, and says with this serious look, 'Throw me the ball,' and that's exactly what I did."

Douglas threw the ball into Harper about 35 feet from the basket and the rest is history.

After receiving the pass, there was time for a couple of dribbles and a quick shake-and-bake before Harper pulled up from 27 feet straight in front of the basket and drew nothing but the bottom of the net to secure the victory. The moment started a string of eight straight NCAA Tournament appearances.

The play would be Harper's final shot in Assembly Hall when, after the NCAA Tournament appearance, he announced his eligibility for the NBA Draft, where he was the 11th overall pick in the first round by the Dallas Mavericks.

"Personally, that shot meant everything to me," Harper said. "Growing up as a kid I spent countless days on the basketball courts in the projects counting down the clock and dreaming of hitting a game-winning shot like that. For my mother to be there to see it in front of a sold-out Assembly Hall was just amazing. It is one of the greatest moments of my basketball career, one that I will take with me for the rest of my life, and I get goose bumps even thinking about it."

In the Nick of Time

Illinois 70, Indiana 67, March 3, 1989: This matchup was of two teams fighting for a No. 1 seed in the upcoming NCAA Tournament. The injury of Kendall Gill that helped lead to four Illini losses in the middle of the conference schedule basically took the Illini out of contention for the Big Ten title, but he was close to returning. Indiana had taken full advantage of the Illini losses and taken a stranglehold on first place and entered this game with a three-game lead over Illinois with only three games remaining. A Hoosier victory would clinch the Big Ten title.

It was a classic back-and-forth battle between the two Top 10 teams in front of a highly partisan Hoosier fan base and national television audience on ABC with Keith Jackson and Dick Vitale calling the action.

The Illini were clinging to a two-point lead with 17 seconds remaining and there was no doubt that the Hoosiers would go to Jay Edwards for their shot at tying or taking the lead. He had already hit incredibly clutch shots in several Indiana wins during the season to put them in the position to win the title.

The Assembly Hall broke out into a frenzy when Andy Kaufmann sank a buzzer-beating three pointer at the end of the 78–77 victory over Iowa on February 4, 1993. The emotion of the rivalry against Iowa and the climatic shot led to one of the greatest court stormings in Fighting Illini basketball history.

KENT BROWN

As the clock ticked under 10 seconds, Edwards, being guarded by Nick Anderson, got the ball and drove hard left to the baseline, where Lowell Hamilton jumped over to help. With his foot inches from being out of bounds, he faded back and threw a high-arching shot over the outstretched hands of Hamilton that seemed to cleanly clear the backboard and drop straight through the basket to tie the score at 67. Illini guard Stephen Bardo quickly called time out, and even though the final buzzer had sounded, official Ed Hightower correctly ruled that two seconds would be returned to the clock.

The play called by Lou Henson was for Kenny Battle to set a screen for the Indiana player guarding Bardo on the throw in while Anderson would come off a screen in front of the Illinois bench. Indiana coach Bob Knight chose not to guard the pass and Battle dropped back toward the far end of the court, where the Hoosiers were double teaming guard Larry Smith.

The final message Henson gave Anderson at the end of the timeout was to take a dribble after catching the pass before going up for his shot.

"We told Nick that when he got the ball off the catch to make sure to take a bounce before he shot it," Henson said. "He was a much better shooter off the dribble than from a stationary position."

After taking the ball from the official, Bardo fired a perfect strike to Anderson, who was coming off a double screen by Hamilton and Battle.

"When Kenny and Lowell set the screen on Jay Edwards, I came off it wide open," recalled Anderson, who caught the ball, took a hard dribble with the left hand, and then rose up for a 35-foot jumper. "When I released it, you could see the rotation of the ball. It felt so good and the whole arena was dead quiet."

The ball seemed to take minutes hanging in the air, but the clock struck all zeros as the ball quietly nestled into the net to give the Illini a 70–67 victory that led to an immediate dog pile and celebration by the Fighting Illini bench. Assembly Hall was completely silent except for the few dozen Illinois fans lucky to be in attendance.

Illinois finished the season one game behind Indiana in the Big Ten standings but earned a No. 1 seed for the NCAA Tournament and opened play in Indianapolis, likely taking the spot that the Hoosiers expected to be. The Flyin' Illini finished the regular season with convincing wins over Iowa and Michigan before advancing to the 1989 Final Four in Seattle.

Kaufmann Buries Hawkeyes at Buzzer

Illinois 78, Iowa 77, February 4, 1993: There were so many storylines to this matchup between the Illini and the ninth-ranked Hawkeyes. Iowa assistant coach Bruce Pearl was a primary character in an NCAA investigation into the recruitment of Illinois star Deon Thomas, which led to an icy relationship between coaching staffs as penalties stifled Illini recruiting. Iowa was still struggling with the sudden death of star forward Chris Street in a car crash just over two weeks earlier. The Hawkeyes were coming off extremely emotional victories at Michigan State and over fifth-ranked Michigan in Iowa City.

The Assembly Hall crowd was in a frenzy after Richard Keene tied the game at 75 on a three-pointer and it's hard to describe exactly what happened when the Hawkeyes played for the final shot, which was a 15-foot baseline jumper by center Acie Earl.

"I remember the shot bounced hard off the side of the rim," said Thomas, who was battling for rebounding position. "I reached for the ball. It hit my arm, flew back up there, and kissed off the backboard and went into the basket. I mean, what are the chances of something like that happening? I remember thinking, *Did it have to happen in the Iowa game?*"

With the entire Assembly Hall crowd in shock and the Iowa bench in jubilation, only Illini guard Rennie Clemons was aware enough to call timeout. The referees added 1.5 seconds back to the clock to give Illinois one last unlikely chance.

Illini guard T.J. Wheeler, who had played quarterback in high school, took the ball at the north end of the court as Andy Kaufmann came off a double screen set by Robert Bennett and Thomas. Wheeler fired a strike to Kaufmann, who caught the ball, took a hard dribble, and let go of a three-point attempt from right in front of the Illinois bench.

When the shot dropped cleanly through the south basket, Assembly Hall erupted into bedlam on the court as the Illini team, coaches, and Orange Krush swarmed to celebrate the incredible finish.

In 1.5 seconds, the Illini turned a demoralizing loss into an exhilarating victory that will forever have a place in Illinois basketball lore.

31 Buzzer Beaters—2000s

Griffin's Shot Extends Illini Home Winning Streak

Illinois 68, Wisconsin 67, February 13, 2001: The fourth-ranked Fighting Illini entered this game with a 16-game home winning streak and were fighting for a Big Ten title in Bill Self's first season as coach. The Badgers had different ideas, however, and dominated the first half by shooting 61 percent from the field, making six of nine three-pointers in building a 35–22 lead.

It took nearly the entire second half for Illinois to scratch and claw their way back against the stubborn Badgers as eventual Big Ten Player of the Year Frank Williams scored 18 of his 22 points, including a three-pointer with four minutes remaining to pull

Coach John Groce drew up one of the greatest end-of-game plays in Fighting Illini history, which allowed Tyler Griffey to break open and receive a pass from Brandon Paul for the buzzer-beating layup in a 74–72 Illinois victory over top-ranked Indiana on February 7, 2013.

within one point. The teams seesawed through the final minutes with Marcus Griffin scoring on a put-back in the final seconds to give the Illini a 66–65 lead.

However, Wisconsin's Kirk Penney was fouled with 10 seconds remaining and knocked down both free throws to give the Badgers a one-point lead. The result looked dismal when Williams missed a shot on the final possession, but the ball tipped off a Badger player and went out of bounds with 2.5 seconds remaining.

"We called out of bounds play number four," remembered Self. "Usually, Frank always took it out, but we decided to let Sean Harrington be the passer on that one. We thought if Frank set the screen, there wasn't any way they weren't going to help on him because they would be nervous about him getting the ball."

Harrington had two choices with his pass. "If Marcus was open off the screen, I was going to lob it to him and, if not, Frank was going to post up on the block."

Griffin was being guarded by 6'11" freshman Dave Mader, and when Marcus made the move, Williams was able to screen the Badger big man, allowing Griffin to step into the lane where Harrington placed a perfect lob.

"It seemed like the ball was in the air forever," said Griffin. "I just went up, caught it, and guided it back the other way."

The "other way" was right into the hoop with 0.8 seconds remaining. A long Badger pass was intercepted by Williams and Assembly Hall erupted into celebration.

Illinois would go on to share a piece of the Big Ten title and earn a top seed in the NCAA Tournament.

Williams Buzzer Beater Wins Big Ten Title

Illinois 67, Minnesota 66, March 3, 2002: The Fighting Illini had won seven games in a row entering the regular season finale at Minnesota and needed a victory to gain a share of their second straight Big Ten title. The Gophers had different plans on their senior day and after Minnesota guard Kerwin Fleming made a three-pointer with 3:12 remaining to give them a nine-point lead, it appeared Illini chances were slim.

But the Illini didn't totally fold. A three-pointer by Cory Bradford and two free throws by Robert Archibald cut the lead to four while taking just a minute off the clock. With 31 seconds remaining, Frank Williams ripped the ball from Fleming, where it trickled into the hands of Bradford, who rose up and nailed another three-pointer to make it a one-point game.

Using full-court pressure, the Illini trapped after the in-bounds pass and Gopher Kevin Burleson tried a desperate cross-court pass that sailed out of bounds with 6.9 seconds remaining to give Illinois one more chance.

In the Illini huddle, there was no doubt who was going to get the ball.

"I remember Frank saying, 'Give me the ball,' and you could see in his eyes that there wasn't another person on that team that was going to take that shot," said Lucas Johnson. "Everybody in the building knew it, everyone watching on television knew it, and Frank knew it."

The play set by Self had one of the bigs set a pick on the wing and let Frank penetrate, telling him that once he turned the corner and could go all the way, just go.

Williams caught the ball on the wing guarded by 6'7" Big Ten Defensive Player of the Year Travarus Bennett. He got a brush screen, dribbled right, and turned the corner. As the lane opened, he rose up, glided through the air, and put up a soft bank shot from just outside the lane.

"For Frank to be able to elevate over Bennett was amazing," Johnson said. "He didn't shoot when everybody expected him to shoot. He hung in the air, let Bennett fly by him, and then shot it off the glass with ease."

The bucket set off a wild celebration in Minneapolis as the Illini had won back-to-back Big Ten titles for the first time since 1951 and 1952.

Heady Play Gives Illinois Big Ten Title

Illinois 81, Purdue 79, March 3, 2004: In the right spot at the right time, junior guard Luther Head made a play for the ages to give the Fighting Illini a Big Ten title in a game played at Mackey Arena.

Purdue's Kenneth Lowe hit a three-pointer with 11 seconds left in overtime to tie the game at 79, and Head was given the inbounds pass. From near half-court, he tossed a long pass to Roger Powell, whose layup was blocked by Purdue's Brett Buscher.

That's where Head's hustle paid off. Following the pass to Powell, Head grabbed the rebound and banked in a game-winning shot with a second remaining as he was crushed by a Boilermaker defender, ending the play flat on his back.

"I don't know how he made the thing," Coach Bruce Weber said.

Head intercepted Purdue's inbounds pass to seal the win and a share of the title they would clinch outright the next game after beating Ohio State. The game was especially emotional for Weber as it was his first game at Mackey Arena as coach of the Illini after spending 18 seasons as an assistant to Gene Keady.

Griffey Layup Knocks Off Top-Ranked Hoosiers

Illinois 74, Indiana 72, February 7, 2013: The top-ranked Indiana Hoosiers came to Champaign-Urbana having spent a total of 10 weeks as No. 1, including the season-opening poll. The Hoosiers were in charge until the final 3½ minutes, when the Fighting Illini finally put together a run to take the lead and then retake the lead.

Indiana had taken a 69–59 lead with just under five minutes remaining and things were looking glum for the Illini. D.J. Richardson then went on a one-man run, first burying back-to-back three-pointers and then hitting a midrange jumper on the run to tie it at 70 with 1:17 to play.

With the clock under 30 seconds and the game tied at 72, Indiana had the ball for what would have been a last shot, but Victor Oladipo coughed up the ball. Richardson picked it up and tried a breakaway layup that Oladipo just swatted out of bounds to set up a final play for Illinois.

The out-of-bounds play Illinois coach John Groce drew up was meant to create confusion with the four Illini on the court convening at the elbow before breaking off on individual runs.

With 0.9 seconds to go, Tyler Griffey left defenders Cody Zeller and Christian Watford behind on an inbounds play from the baseline, took the pass from Brandon Paul, and delivered the uncontested buzzer-beater.

"I just made a simple curl cut and left two guys behind me, and Brandon got off a heck of a pass," Griffey said. "Zeller and Watford were both right in front of me and just kind of stayed there.

"Zero-point-nine seconds is not a lot of time. I know the notion of 0.4 whether you can tip or hold it. I had enough time to get it up there and guide it in. Brandon made a great pass, so all I had to do was catch it and guide it up there."

What followed was one of the great court rushes in State Farm Center history as he was carried off the court by the Orange Krush.

Rayvonte Rice Adds Wrinkle to Braggin' Rights Legacy

Illinois 62, Missouri 59, December 20, 2014: The annual Braggin' Rights basketball series in St. Louis always brings out the best from the Illinois and Missouri basketball teams and their fans. There have been matchups when both teams were in the Top 10 and games when neither team was ranked. It doesn't matter, the emotion inside the arena that night is always red-hot.

The 2014 version had neither team ranked, but the rivalry game turned into an instant classic thanks to Illini guard Rayvonte Rice.

"At first, I didn't understand how big a rivalry it was," Rice said. "Fans can't wait to go all year."

Mizzou's Wesley Clark hit a jumper from the key to tie the game with 17.8 seconds remaining. Illinois then held for the final shot with the ball staying in Rice's hands for most of the way. He dribbled for several seconds before stepping to the top of the key and drilling a fade-away three-pointer over two Tiger defenders, watching the shot fall from his back before getting mobbed by teammates.

Ayo Sinks Dagger at Michigan

Illinois 64, Michigan 62, January 25, 2020: As with many of their Big Ten opponents, Illinois has had many classic matchups with Michigan, with incredible finishes going both ways. The 2019–20 season was a year Illinois basketball was returning as a contender for championships and the matchup in Ann Arbor was always seen as a tough road game.

As the final seconds ticked away in a tie game, Ayo Dosunmu was guarded by Zavier Simpson, one of the top defenders in the Big Ten. Ayo's length at 6'5" gave him a five-inch height advantage over Simpson, and he used it to sink a contested jumper from the free-throw line with 0.5 seconds remaining to give Illinois a two-point victory.

The Illini tied the game at 62 on a pair of free throws by Trent Frazier with 52.3 seconds remaining. Michigan's Jon Teske missed an inside shot and after garnering the rebound, Illinois had the ball back for a final shot.

"Coach just said, 'No ball screen,'" Dosunmu said. "He told me just make sure I got the last shot. He believed I was going to make the right play. Simpson, he played great defense. He couldn't have guarded that any better. But I just got into my pull-up, got into my moves, and then just knocked the shot down."

Illinois finished the 2020 Big Ten basketball season one game out of first place and earned a double bye at the Big Ten Tournament before the collegiate athletics world shut down because of the COVID-19 pandemic.

Dosunmu finished with 27 points in the huge road win and added this to the list of many game-ending shots during his Fighting Illini career. Many longtime Illini basketball observers named Dosunmu as the best clutch player in Illinois basketball history.

32 The Harris Mansion Heist of 1929

The Illinois football team rolled into the much-anticipated Army game of 1929 with a 3–1–1 record and as a favorite to win their third straight Big Ten Conference title to close off a highly successful decade of football.

In just their fifth season at Memorial Stadium, the Illini, under head coach Bob Zuppke, had become one of the best teams in the nation. During the Roaring '20s, when college football far surpassed the interest in pro football, Illinois piled up 55 wins against just 19 losses. The Illini won three conference titles (1923, 1927, 1928) and two national championships in 1923 and 1927.

The game against powerful Army on November 9, 1929, was one of the most anticipated games of the year when Zuppke's Fighting Illini faced off with the Cadets, led by head coach Ralph Sasse, at Memorial Stadium in front of a season-high 69,509 fans.

The large crowd was notable for the number of dignitaries in attendance. Among them was Secretary of War James Good, who joined Illinois Governor Louis Emmerson, U.S. Senator Charles Deneen, Illinois Constitutional officers, and Illinois Supreme Court justices, among many other politicians. Army had brought several high-ranking officers from West Point for the trip west.

Following Illinois' 17–7 victory over the Cadets, the Harris family hosted an opulent party at the magnificent mansion located at the corner of Church Street and Prospect Avenue. That night there were approximately 60 guests in attendance at the party with the list including many well-known locals of Champaign-Urbana as well as notable guests from Chicago and across the Midwest as the game earlier in the day drew many out-of-towners into Champaign.

The site of the party, and eventual crime scene, was built by First National Bank President Benjamin Harris in 1904 to the tune of $200,000. The estate, called Elmshade, was completed in 1907 and was considered the largest and finest home in Champaign for many years.

As the party celebrating the Illini victory moved late into the evening, an interruption occurred around 11 p.m. with the arrival of four assailants who were there to take advantage of the wealth in the mansion. At gunpoint, they forced Mr. Harris to surrender a diamond ring and roll of currency. Two of the robbers marched him up the stairs to the ballroom, which held most of the guests, beating him with the butt of a revolver on the way.

The guests were moved into the ballroom and two bedrooms, where they were forced to abandon their valuables and furs. One of the guests had called the Champaign police, and upon arrival, shots were exchanged, with Officer Clyde Davis getting wounded in the wrist. One of the holdup men, C.W. Katzschman (from Mattoon), was shot through the abdomen by Officer Gilbert Brown. He was admitted to Burnham Hospital in critical condition and later died.

The second man captured, Harold Smith (AKA "Tuscoly Smitty") of Charleston, escaped injury in the gun fight but was arrested. Hearing the gunshots upstairs, the other two assailants, who were doing their business on the lower level, ran from the home and escaped. Getaway driver Carl Wilson, who sported a wooden leg, was arrested in Decatur, but provided information that the two remaining at-large suspects were heading to California.

The culprits stole cash, furs, and jewelry worth more than $30,000 from the guests, which would equal nearly $500,000 today.

Verne Katz (AKA "Jerry O'Malley") and Clifford Henderson (AKA "Cappy Henderson"), both of Chicago and railroad workers, were arrested in Los Angeles after the nationwide hunt and returned to Champaign County on December 7, 1929.

When Benjamin Harris died suddenly at age 52 in 1920, the home was passed to his wife, and later to his son H.H. Harris. In 1931, two years after the robbery and as the Great Depression was in full force, the Harris family moved and left the home to decline nearly to ruin. It was abandoned until 1947, when the home found new life as Cole Hospital. The mansion served in this capacity for many years until ownership was transferred to The Pavilion mental health clinic and the Harris Mansion was demolished in 2012 to make way for expansion.

33 The Dave Wilson Game at Ohio State

When Mike White took the reins as head football coach in 1980, he promised to bring the wide-open West Coast passing offense he learned from the legendary Bill Walsh that would excite the Fighting Illini fan base.

White delivered.

He immediately dove into the California junior college ranks to revamp the Illini football roster and came up with two strong-armed quarterbacks from Northern California who would change the total storyline for Illinois football.

Dave Wilson and Tony Eason battled through that first camp with Wilson earning the starting position, which would allow Eason to redshirt and keep two years of eligibility.

After several years of subpar play that relied primarily on running plays, White and his squad opened the season against Northwestern. To prove that there was a new game plan, White had Wilson unleash a bomb on the very first play from scrimmage, and even when it fell incomplete, the Illini crowd roared with approval and gave the play a standing ovation.

As the season went along, the Illinois passing game continued to improve, including a shootout at Memorial Stadium on October 18 against Purdue when Boilermaker quarterback Mark Herrmann eclipsed the Big Ten record with four touchdown passes and 371 yards. After falling behind, Wilson began a passing streak like no one in the conference had ever seen. Shortly after stadium PA announcer Tom Trent announced Herrmann's Big Ten record, Wilson blew past that mark with 58 attempts, 35 completions, and 425 passing yards, and Trent would have to update his record-setting announcements for all three statistics.

The Wilson passing trend continued for the remainder of the season but peaked on November 8 when the Illini traveled to Columbus to take on the seventh-ranked Buckeyes.

"Ohio State was rated about seventh in the nation and, deep down, we really didn't figure to win," Wilson later recalled. "Coach White told us to just go out there and have some fun, not to worry about it. We studied Ohio State film and put together a game plan. And I'll never forget as I came up to the line that day, it was like watching that film over again. The coaches had me prepared and I recognized each defense as it came up."

Illinois ran 76 offensive plays after that, 69 of them Wilson passes and 43 of those completions. Six of Wilson's passes turned into touchdowns. The final passing yardage number … 621 yards. All, except the six touchdown passes, bettered or equaled NCAA records and came against perhaps the best secondary in the conference. The Buckeyes were allowing just over 100 passing yards per game.

The Illini trailed 35–7 at one point in the third quarter, but the wild second half brought Illinois roaring back before losing 49–42.

Illinois had made it a one-possession game despite seven turnovers during the day.

"The passing numbers were announced to the crowd, and we left the field to a standing ovation," Wilson said after the game. "An old man, who said he'd been attending Ohio State games for more than 40 years, took a Buckeye cap off his head and handed it to me in appreciation."

"It's a good thing Wilson didn't have a good first half or he would've had a thousand yards," said stunned Ohio State coach Earle Bruce after the game.

The 1980 season was extremely hard on Wilson as the Big Ten had ruled him ineligible based on a single snap he had taken in a previous season before being injured and missing the remainder of the year. The Conference declared that he had played three years of college football and had not acquired the appropriate number of academic hours to be eligible. In August 1980, shortly before the season began, Wilson sued in an Illinois state court alleging that the Conference's refusal to waive its rules denied him equal protection of the laws and due process of law. Each week, he filed an injunction in a local court against the Big Ten ruling and needed a judge to approve it by Friday before being able to play.

Wilson played each game during the 1980 season, but during the following spring, the court dismissed the complaint. Possibly facing more legal challenges from the Big Ten in 1981, Wilson made himself available for the NFL Supplemental Draft that summer where the New Orleans Saints made him the number one overall choice.

The incredible performance that afternoon in The Shoe in Columbus remains one of the legendary games in Fighting Illini and Big Ten history.

34 The Incredible Whiz Kids

Illinois basketball had already been established as one of the top programs in the nation, but head coach Doug Mills took the Illini to a different level when a group of the state's top players arrived on the UI campus together in the early 1940s.

Art Mathisen was already on campus and established as a varsity starter in 1941 when the quartet of Andy Phillip, Jack Smiley, Gene Vance, and Ken Menke became eligible for the 1941–42 season. That group of athletes, who all stood around 6'3", allowed Mills to mix and match his team on the floor in a position-less system.

Their fast-paced style of play earned the nickname "Whiz Kids," as the team took the Big Ten and nation by storm, rolling to a cumulative Big Ten record of 25–2 in 1942 and 1943 and winning two Big Ten titles.

Huff Gym was packed nearly every night as they rolled through the schedule with an 18–5 overall record in 1942 and 17–1 in 1943.

The young team traveled to New Orleans for the 1942 NCAA Eastern Playoffs and dropped tough games to Kentucky (46–44) and Penn State (41–34) in their first postseason experience.

Expectations from both the team and Illinois fans were sky high entering the 1942–43 season with the entire team returning. The only Whiz Kids hiccup came at Camp Grant in a game at Rockford when Mills started the reserves and allowed his stars to rest much of the game.

The 1943 version was undefeated in conference play with a 12–0 mark but didn't play in the NCAA Tournament because of service in World War II.

The Fighting Illini Whiz Kids of 1942 and 1943 were widely considered the nation's best team at the end of the '43 season when the team finished with a 17–1 record, including a perfect 12–0 mark in the Big Ten. When three members of the starting lineup were drafted into the Army before the NCAA Tournament, the team decided to pass on playing shorthanded in the postseason.

Before the NCAA Tournament began, the Army drafted Mathisen, Menke, and Smiley. That left only Vance and Phillip, both of whom would be named to Illinois' All-Century team in 2005. But Coach Mills made a decision in February 1943 that all five supported.

At the end of the season, the Illini were blowing past all opponents, including a 50–26 win over Wisconsin, an 86–44 victory over a Northwestern team that featured Otto Graham, and finally a 92–25 crushing of Chicago when Phillip scored a conference-record 40 points.

The scoring numbers were astounding when you consider the team outscored opponents by an average of 57.7 points to 37.1 points per game that year. Dominance was verified when the All-Big Ten First Team was made up of Phillip, Vance, Smiley, and Mathisen. Phillip was the Big Ten and National Player of the Year.

"If all five guys could not get a chance to play in the tournament, then two of us shouldn't have either," Vance said in a 2005 interview. "So, we didn't play. It was the right choice.

"I think not being able to go to the NCAAs was the biggest disappointment I've ever had. We just had five guys who played off each other well, didn't have specific roles, and nobody cared who scored all the points as long as we were winning," he said.

Despite being the overwhelming favorite to win a national title, Illinois did not participate without three of its top players. In June, Vance (ROTC) and Phillip (Marine Corps) signed up for military service as well.

Without Illinois in the eight-team field, Wyoming went on to defeat Georgetown in the 1943 title game.

All the Whiz Kids except for the older Mathisen reunited for the 1946–47 season and stepped back into their starting positions, but it wasn't quite the same.

"They had gone through terrible war experiences, and they had changed," recalled Mills. That 1947 team finished with a 14–6 overall record, including 8–4 in the Big Ten, which placed them in a tie for second place. Phillip, who led Granite City High School to the 1940 state title, served as a first lieutenant in the Marine Corps, participating in the battle at Iwo Jima.

Smiley, from Waterman (Illinois) High School, served with the Army's 106th division as an artillery corporal and was engaged in one of the war's deadliest skirmishes, the Battle of the Bulge. It was written that Smiley fired his Howitzer for 96 continuous hours during that battle when his division reported a 90 percent casualty rate. Smiley was named the UI basketball MVP in 1947.

Menke, who played for Dundee High School's 1938 state champs, served with the Army's 193rd Field Artillery Battalion in the European theater of operations from 1943 to '46.

Vance, a native of Clinton, Illinois, wore a U.S. Army uniform during WWII duty in Europe, then also later during the Korean conflict. He earned two Bronze Stars, awarded for heroic achievement and service.

The 1946–47 season would be Mills' last as basketball coach before moving into the athletic director's chair until 1966. Vance stepped into the permanent AD role from 1967 to 1972 and was the last living Whiz Kid until his death in 2012.

35 Illini on Stages, Sets, and Big Screens

Ever since Red Grange starred in his first film, not surprisingly the silent football drama *One Minute to Play* (1926), several Fighting Illini athletes dabbled in acting careers once their playing days were over.

Grange was associated with FBO (Film Booking Offices of America), the studio that Joseph Kennedy later merged into RKO Studios. Grange followed up with *A Racing Romeo* (1927), which had an auto racing theme and was once again directed by Sam Wood.

To take advantage of his national fame, Grange toured big-time vaudeville in 1927 and 1928 with an act called *C'mon Red*. He returned to films in 1931, this time in a low-budget mascot adventure serial called *The Galloping Ghost*.

Another early entertainer was former Illini track and field athlete George Chandler, who graduated in 1922. After time on the vaudeville circuit, he began in films starting in 1928 and appeared in more than 450 movies and television shows through the 1970s. His highest-profile projects included *The High and the Mighty* (1954), *Roxie Hart* (1942), *Every Which Way But Loose* (1978), and almost 60 appearances in *Lassie* in the late 1950s.

Several years later, Illini tackle Peter Palmer, who lettered in 1952 and 1953, began a long acting career highlighted when he starred in the title role of *Li'l Abner*, both on Broadway and in the 1959 movie adaptation. A music major, Palmer sang the national anthem in his full uniform before some of the games he played. Illinois won a Rose Bowl and two Big Ten titles during his collegiate playing career.

Later roles included Broadway performances in *Brigadoon* and *Lorelei* as well as recurring roles on TV's *The Legend of Custer* and *The Kallikaks*. Palmer made guest appearances on TV shows such as *Emergency!, Three's Company, Dallas,* and *Charlie's Angels*. His other movies include *Edward Scissorhands* (1990).

Hall of Fame linebacker Dick Butkus compiled a long list of television and movie appearances following his playing career. After appearing with fellow football star Bubba Smith in some classic Miller Lite Beer commercials during the 1970s and '80s, Butkus' list of appearances in film and television is impressive. Some of his films include *Mother, Jugs & Speed* (1976), *Gus* (1976), *Johnny Dangerously* (1984), *Hamburger: The Motion Picture* (1986), *Necessary Roughness* (1991), and *Any Given Sunday* (1999). He was a regular character on TV shows such as *Blue Thunder, My Two Dads, MacGyver,* and *Hang Time*. He also portrayed himself in the critically acclaimed TV movie *Brian's Song* (1971).

NFL Hall of Fame linebacker Ray Nitschke also starred in the Miller Lite commercials but may be best known for his role of Bogdanski in *The Longest Yard* (1974) as one of the players on the prison guard team. In that role, he found the wrong end of three straight passes thrown by Burt Reynolds' character Paul Crewe.

Former Illini women's basketball star Cindy Dallas also made a move to Hollywood after a series of knee surgeries ended her brief pro basketball career. Dallas has worked in commercials, theater, television, and film, while also going on to write, direct, and produce her own short films. She has appeared in several TV series including *The Bold and the Beautiful, Shameless, The Mick, Days of Our Lives, 2 Broke Girls,* and *Westworld.*

Former Illini walk-on tight end Ryan McPartlin is an established television actor with the shows *Chuck, L.A.'s Finest,* and *Hunter Killer* among the many shows on his résumé.

McKinley Freeman, who was on the Illini basketball team in the early '90s as David Freeman, has appeared in many television series and movies following his time on campus. The Champaign native is known for his work in *End of Watch* (2012), *Greencard Warriors* (2013), and *Delta Farce* (2007).

All-American running back Rashard Mendenhall was a writer and executive story editor for the award-winning HBO series *Ballers* from 2015 to '19 following his NFL career. Another All-American and Illini Athletics Hall of Famer, Simeon Rice, has acted in and produced multiple films, including *Unsullied* (2014).

Jim Blondell, who was a defensive lineman for the Illini in the late 1980s, is a writer and director who has written and directed numerous commercials and shorts. His directorial debut was the feature film *Angel* (2019). He also created and wrote the award-winning graphic novel *Black Jesus.*

The legendary Bob Richards, known as the "Vaulting Vicar," portrayed himself in a few television appearances over the decades. Levi Cobb, who was an Illini basketball player in the late 1970s, has a few acting credits to his name.

Mark Kelly, former Illini defensive back from the 1980s, was cast in a few episodes of *Proven Innocent, Chicago P.D.,* and *Chicago Fire.* Jon Lee Brody was on the Illini football roster until suffering an injury that ended his playing career during his sophomore season before earning his degree in 2007. Brody is best known for appearances in *Furious 7* (2015) and *Malignant* (2021) and directing *DC Universe All Star Games.* Troy Prior also had a football career cut short by injuries, but has gone on to be an actor, producer, director, and writer.

Illini football player Godfrey Danchimah and tennis star Michael Kosta have established careers as comedians. Danchimah, professionally known as Godfrey, was a member of the football team in the early '90s and has appeared on BET, VH1, and Comedy Central, along with feature films such as *Soul Plane* (2004), *Original Gangstas* (1996), *Zoolander* (2001), *Americanish* (2021), and *Johnson Family Vacation* (2004). He continues to tour around the nation with his stand-up comedy act.

Michael Kosta starred on the Illini tennis team from 1998 to 2002, helping the Illini to three Big Ten titles in his four seasons before playing professionally for two years. After giving collegiate coaching a try, Kosta explored his opportunities as a stand-up comedian and hasn't slowed down since. He has made several television appearances, including many on *The Daily Show*. He also continues to tour around the nation with his stand-up comedy act.

Many former Illini players have also gone on to careers as sports announcers in football and basketball. Former members of the Flyin' Illini of the late 1980s, Stephen Bardo and Kendall Gill have both found a home on TV talking about basketball. Bardo has worked as an analyst for ESPN, FOX, and Big Ten Network along with several NBA games. Gill continues to provide pre- and postgame analysis on the Chicago Bulls TV network. Johnny "Red" Kerr called games as an analyst for the Bulls for more than three decades, while former Illini stars Derek Harper and Eddie Johnson have worked as announcers for the Dallas Mavericks and Phoenix Suns, respectively, for several seasons.

Sean Harrington has called games on the ESPN family of channels and Big Ten Network for several years. He is joined by Deon Thomas and Doug Altenberger as former Illini who have been color analysts for Illini and Big Ten basketball games. Thomas, Altenberger, Bardo, Jerry Hester, Rick Schmidt, and Dave Downey have all worked multiple seasons calling Illini basketball games on the radio.

Baseball Hall of Famer Lou Boudreau was a longtime radio announcer for the Chicago Cubs and played himself in the movie *The Kid From Cleveland* (1949), along with a few other appearances in the 1970s.

All-time Illini football great Doug Dieken played in every game (203 consecutive regular season games) of his 14-year NFL career with the Cleveland Browns before transitioning to the radio booth from 1985 through the 2021 season. David Diehl, who played on the 2001 Big Ten championship squad and won two Super Bowls with the New York Giants, tried his hand as a network football television analyst.

Another former Illini who was a longtime NFL offensive lineman and also made the move to the announcer booth is Larry McCarren. He played 162 consecutive games as the center for the Green Bay Packers. He served as an analyst on the Packers' radio broadcasts starting in 1995 while also working for a local television station as a sports reporter.

In the Fighting Illini football radio booth, All-American running back and two-time Super Bowl champion Jim Grabowski provided analysis for many years. He handed over his spot in the booth to former quarterback Kurt Kittner, who led the Illini to the 2001 Big Ten championship. Kittner was followed by former All-American offensive lineman Martin O'Donnell in the booth.

36 The History of Huff Gym

Located at the corner of Fourth Street and Gregory Drive on the UI campus, Huff Hall was originally called the "New Gymnasium" when it was completed in 1925. Designed in the Georgian-Revival style by Charles Platt and University Architect James White, the building's architecture matches that of the Armory, Main Library, the Student Union, and other campus buildings.

At the conclusion of its $772,000 construction in 1925, Huff Hall replaced Old Men's Gym (now known as Kenney Gym Annex) as the home for Fighting Illini basketball. The "New Gymnasium" was renamed Huff Gym in 1937 following the long-time athletic director's passing.

Illinois athletics has enjoyed a proud tradition in the gymnasium, serving as home of Illinois basketball from 1925 to 1963, when the Fighting Illini hoopsters won 339 out of 418 games (.811), eight Big Ten championships, and earned three NCAA Final Four appearances.

Even though it was more than twice the size of the old Drill Hall at Kenney Gym, where the Illini had previously played, it was realized soon after construction that the building was still too small to accommodate all the fans who wanted to attend games.

Many years, students were issued split season tickets to allow more the opportunity to experience the magic of Huff Gym.

The name was changed from Huff Gym to Huff Hall in the 1980s as several sports moved into the building for home competitions, including volleyball, women's basketball, men's gymnastics, women's gymnastics, wrestling, and fencing.

The gym has hosted its fair share of championships at the collegiate and high school levels over the years. In 1940 and 1947, the Fighting Illini hosted the NCAA Wrestling Championships at Huff. In 1930, 1933, 1946, 1948, and 1958, the Big Ten Wrestling Championships were held there.

Huff served as host for the 1991, 1995, and 2003 Big Ten Women's Gymnastics Championships; the 1992, 1995, and 2004 Big Ten Men's Gymnastics Championships; and the 1993 and 1999 NCAA Men's Gymnastics East Regional.

The Fighting Illini volleyball team moved from cramped Kenney Gym to Huff in 1990 and immediately saw attendance jump from a sold-out number of around 1,800 to more than 4,000 in the venerable facility. For the first match at Huff on September 4, 1990, the Whiz Kids basketball team from the 1940s returned to campus to help celebrate the excitement generated in the building.

Huff Gym was the home of the original March Madness when it served as the site for Illinois' annual high school basketball championships from 1926 to 1962, when the tournament moved down the street to Assembly Hall (now State Farm Center). One of the great traditions of the high school tournament was the large state of Illinois map with light bulbs placed where the 16 teams that advanced to Champaign were located. As teams would lose, the bulbs would be turned off until the champion was determined.

The building housed training rooms, a weight room, equipment rooms, and locker rooms in the basement used by several different teams until space has opened in other athletics facilities on campus. There is also an underground tunnel that connects Huff to the indoor track inside the Armory on the other side of Gregory Drive.

The legendary Dike Eddleman once won the high jump competition in a meet at the Armory, slipped through the tunnel to Huff to change into his basketball uniform, and helped the Illini to a victory on the hardcourt.

37 From Illinois to Super Bowl Champ, Ray Nitschke

As a member of the Green Bay Packers, Ray Nitschke was one of the most menacing NFL middle linebackers of the 1960s. He helped build the Packers' historic dynasty that decade when they won three NFL championships and two Super Bowl titles.

Nitschke earned one Pro Bowl, two First-Team All-Pro, and five Second-Team All-Pro selections from 1962 to '69 and was a starting linebacker on the 50th Anniversary Team of the NFL. Eventually, Nitschke earned his rightful place in the Pro Football Hall of Fame in 1978.

Nitschke grew up around tragedy and held a grudge against life for many years. His father, Robert Sr., died when Ray was three years old in 1939 after a wayward trolley smashed into his car when Robert was on his way home from work.

Ray's older brother, Robert Jr. (Bob) acted as his surrogate father and actually worked for the local railway company when he was just 14 years old to help with the family's income.

Anna Nitschke started working as a waitress after her husband passed away, but she, too, died at a young age when she succumbed to a blood clot in 1949 when Ray was just 13 years old.

According to his biography, *Nitschke: The Ray Nitschke Story*, he chugged whiskey and got into fistfights with reckless abandon in his youth. As a teenager, Ray became a golf caddie at an upscale River Forest neighborhood golf course where he developed a love for golf that remained for the rest of his life.

Ironically, Nitschke grew up a Bears fan and idolized Sid Luckman and Bronko Nagurski. Later during his professional career, that turned into a heated rival as a member of the Packers. At Proviso East High School, Nitschke played quarterback for the football team while also excelling in baseball and basketball for the Pirates. There is legend that he once launched a 560-foot home run in a high school state tournament game.

Nitschke chose to play football for Ray Eliot and the Fighting Illini from 1954 to '57, teaming up with future NFL Hall of Fame running back Bobby Mitchell and five-time Pro-Bowl selection Abe Woodson in the Illini backfield. Prior to his sophomore season, Eliot gave Ray the news that he was moving from quarterback to fullback and linebacker, news that Nitschke didn't take well.

In a day when facemasks were not required, Nitschke took an Ohio State lineman's helmet flush in the mouth and lost four teeth, which eventually became his trademark as a snarling middle linebacker.

He was a very effective fullback for the Illini, gaining 998 yards in his career, including 170 yards against Northwestern as a senior in 1957.

Chosen as the 36th overall pick by the Green Bay Packers in the NFL Draft, Nitschke needed a map to find out where Green Bay was, but the relationship became a lifelong love affair between the Hall of Famer and the Packer faithful.

After Lombardi took over as the head coach, it became evident he was the perfect coach for Nitschke. Lombardi was a stickler for discipline, while Ray was anything but. Eventually, Nitschke fell into line with Lombardi and drove the team to victories in Super Bowls I and II on his way to Canton, Ohio, and the Pro Football Hall of Fame.

The other great middle linebacker from the 1960s was fellow Illinois alum Dick Butkus, and both men had a mutual respect for other even though they played in a fierce rivalry. After 15 years in the league, Nitschke retired during the preseason camp in 1973. He finished his career with 25 interceptions, two defensive touchdowns, two forced fumbles, and 23 fumble recoveries. Oh, and five world championship rings as captain and leader of the Packer defense.

A member of the Illinois All-Century Team in 1990, Nitschke made several visits back to Champaign following his career to catch a football game and meet with the Illini team. One such visit can be found on YouTube. During his returns, Nitschke's first stop was always at Uncle John's Pancake House (later called Aunt Sonya's Pancake House) at the corner of State and Kirby in Champaign.

Tragically, Nitschke died in 1998 at the age of 61 after suffering a massive heart attack while living in Florida.

38 "Frosty Peters Out"

One of the more interesting names of Fighting Illini football history has mostly gotten lost over the decades. Forest "Frosty" Peters was a star quarterback and kicker in 1926, 1928, and 1929, helping the Illini to the 1928 Big Ten championship.

Before Peters set foot on the UI campus, he had already set a world record as a member of Montana State's freshman team, the Bobkittens, in 1924 when he drop-kicked 17 field goals against Billings Polytechnic (now Rocky Mountain College). MSU freshman coach Schubert Dyche admitted the event was planned in advance, with full participation of all team members.

At a time when drop-kicking was becoming obsolete because of the effectiveness of place-kicking, Peters was widely referred to decades after his playing career ended as the last of the great drop-kickers.

During that November 1 game in Billings, Montana, Peters attempted a total of 25 drop-kicked field goals, making 17, including a streak of ten consecutive makes spanning halftime. The previous record was seven in a game set by E.C. Robertson of Purdue in 1900. The entire MSU freshman squad helped with the record by running the ball to within 10 or 15 yards of the goal post, only to go down and give their captain another chance at the record. The game ended with a 64–0 Bobkittens win with both touchdowns coming in the fourth quarter.

Peters also starred with the MSU track team, and in the spring of 1925 competed at the Drake Relays in Des Moines, Iowa. The *Big Timber Pioneer* newspaper mentioned that a Billings resident who had attended the University of Illinois urged Peters to consider playing football there. Illinois newspaper reports indicate that football coach Bob Zuppke recruited Peters after his freshman season. Illinois also competed at the Drake Relays and former Illini star athlete Tug Wilson was the Drake athletics director at the time, to raise even more speculation on how contact was made. Whatever factors were involved, he transferred to Illinois in the fall of 1925.

While practicing with the Illini in the fall of 1925, Peters and J.A. Timm were noted as good material to replace the legendary Red Grange and Earl Britton in Zuppke's backfield. In fact, by the start of his varsity career in 1926, Peters was already labeled "Second Red Grange," which had to be quite daunting considering Grange's accomplishments.

The Illini finished 6–2 in 1926, losing only to Michigan and Ohio State, with Peters handling kicking chores and playing quarterback. In the season opener against Coe College, Peters scored a touchdown and converted three of his four drop-kick PATs in the 27–0 victory.

Peters suffered a knee injury prior to the 1927 season, when Illinois would win Big Ten and national titles with a 7–0–1 record. Out for the season, Peters moved back to Helena, Montana, and attended classes at Mt. St. Charles (now Carroll) College, creating a bit of a stir and a memorable *Daily Illini* headline, "Frosty Peters Out," that likely caused some snickers on campus.

Frosty returned to Illinois in 1928 and helped lead the Illini to a 7–1 mark and another Big Ten title, scoring the only touchdown in the UI's 8–0 win over Ohio State to clinch the title in the final game of the season. As a senior, Peters again played quarterback and helped lead the Illini to a 6–1–1 mark, including a 27–0 win at Ohio State when he completed 10 of 13 passes.

Peters was also a track and field standout and helped the Illini win the NCAA Outdoor Track and Field Championships in 1927.

During his three seasons wearing the Orange and Blue, the Illini were an impressive 19–4–1. Peters would go on to play 25 games in the NFL with the Providence Steam Roller and

Portsmouth Spartans in 1930, for the Brooklyn Dodgers in 1931, and the Chicago Cardinals in 1932. He is credited with two field goals and nine extra points made. From 1933 to '35 he starred in pro football's minor league, serving Memphis as player-coach in 1933–34 and in the same capacity with the St. Louis Gunners in 1935.

Living in Montana in the offseason and after retiring from football, Peters' name began showing up frequently in baseball box scores as an umpire. He would go on to toil as an umpire in the minor leagues for three years before serving as a sergeant in the Army Air Forces as director of the physical training program while stationed at the University of Michigan.

After World War II ended Peters resumed his umpiring career until was assaulted by an American Association manager in 1946. Peters then moved to Decatur, Illinois, and helped design bridges for an engineering firm. After retiring he wintered in Texas and worked at the Scovill Golf Course in Decatur managing the driving range before dying in his Decatur apartment in 1980, thus ending the long and fascinating life of Forrest Ingram "Frosty" Peters.

39 Bruce Weber Leads Illini Basketball to the Final Four

Big Ten Player of the Year and All-American Brian Cook took his game to the NBA following his graduation in 2003. Also leaving the program was head coach Bill Self, who took the offer from Kansas after agonizing for several days over the decision to leave or not.

And it was agonizing.

Self thought Illinois could and would win at an extremely high level in the years to come, but he had begun his coaching career at KU and knew the tradition at Kansas would help keep the Jayhawks among the nation's blue bloods.

To the chagrin of Illini basketball fans, Self boarded a private jet on Sunday, April 20, and flew to Lawrence, Kansas, where he took over the head coaching position for the Jayhawks. Billy Gillispie and Norm Roberts would follow.

The coaching change certainly caused a major disruption within the walls of the Ubben Basketball Practice Facility as team members wondered what would happen next.

Players were thinking about transferring. Director of athletics Ron Guenther could only ask them to be patient through the search process.

There were several top coaches on Guenther's short list, but one coach who had caught his eye when the Illini played his team in Las Vegas and had his squad put on an impressive NCAA Tournament appearance was Southern Illinois head coach Bruce Weber.

Weber had been a longtime assistant coach under Gene Keady for 18 seasons at Purdue prior to making the move to SIU, where he built the Saluki program into a Missouri Valley Conference power from 1998 to 2003.

There was no doubt about Weber's basketball knowledge and experience, and knowing the team that was returning in Champaign-Urbana, it didn't take much for Guenther to convince Weber to make the move up I–57 on April 30, 2003.

The transition was in no way easy. The Illini players knew the system that was heading to Lawrence had worked very well with this group and were skeptical of major changes.

An unsung hero during the entire transition was point guard Jerrance Howard, who had walked through Senior Day festivities at the end of the 2003 season. But he had one year of eligibility remaining if both parties were open to his return.

The importance of Howard's personality and leadership within the tight-knit group was quickly apparent to Weber. He asked Howard to return for his final year, and Jerrance quickly agreed.

Weber preferred a motion offensive system that primarily uses the fundamental elements of passing, cutting, screening, or dribbling, while incorporating player and ball movement to create scoring opportunities. Self used a high-low style of play on offense, with many more set plays.

It was clear that this system was a perfect fit for the three primary ball handlers of Dee Brown, Deron Williams, and Luther Head, along with athletic front-line players like James Augustine and Roger Powell, Jr.

It wasn't a simple transition by any means. Early in the 2003–04 season, the Illini lost by 19 points to Providence at Madison Square Garden and Weber saw very clearly that the team needed to trust the motion offense and buy into the new system.

His tactic was to hold a mock funeral of the Self Era, wearing a black suit and declaring the former coach's time as head of the program dead. It was time to move on.

"He had a good point behind it," Howard told the *Chicago Tribune*. "He wanted to make sure we were doing things his way … the way he had been successful."

Following a 20-point loss at Wisconsin in late January, team togetherness was in doubt. It was Howard who called a team meeting to clear the air, getting everyone back on the same page and pointing the way forward.

The Illini won their final 10 games of the regular season to win an outright Big Ten title. They earned a five-seed at the NCAA Tournament and advanced to the Sweet Sixteen before losing to Duke in Atlanta.

The second-round victory over fourth-seeded Cincinnati was as impressive as any win that season. After Bearcat players confronted the Illinois squad as they left the court during the open practice session the day before, Williams and his teammates were determined not to just beat Cincinnati, but to bury them. The final score of 92–68 was proof enough.

Weber now firmly had everyone believing in the system with all eyes looking at the 2004–05 season.

40 How One Week in 2004 Set Expectations

Following the finish to the 2004 basketball season, expectations within the Illini program and with its fan base were sky high. Deron Williams had made a huge jump in his game and earned First-Team All-Big Ten honors as a sophomore. His running mate, Dee Brown, was on the Second-Team All-Conference squad. The Illini were ranked sixth in the preseason national polls.

Weber didn't back away from high-level opponents, scheduling a matchup against Gonzaga at the Wooden Tradition doubleheader in Indianapolis, followed by top-ranked Wake Forest in Champaign four days later as part of the Big Ten/ACC Challenge. He also scheduled games against Arkansas in Little Rock; at Georgetown in Washington, D.C.; Oregon at the United Center in Chicago; the annual Braggin' Rights game against Missouri in St. Louis; and a rematch against Cincinnati at the Las Vegas Holiday Classic.

Thousands of Fighting Illini fans followed the team to each stop.

The week from Saturday, November 27, through Saturday, December 4, may go down as one of the best in Illini basketball history.

With the legendary John Wooden watching from courtside, the Illini annihilated the Zags, who featured All-American Adam

The backcourt of Dee Brown (left) and Deron Williams (right) proved two point guards could thrive together in the right system. As classmates, the two helped the Fighting Illini to consecutive Big Ten titles in 2004 and 2005, and a run to the National Championship Game in 2005.

Morrison, building a 58–27 lead at halftime, increasing the lead to 38 points in the second half, and coasting to an 89–72 victory.

The nation's basketball world turned all eyes to Champaign a few days later when Chris Paul and his top-ranked Demon Deacons entered a delirious Assembly Hall.

It wasn't close. The Illini won every phase of the game, leading by as much as 32 points in the second half.

"They played infinitely better than we did. I don't know how much more clearly I can say it," Wake Forest coach Skip Prosser said afterwards. "They made shots that were open, they made shots that were contested. Their offense was exponentially better than our defense, hence the score of the game."

The Orange Krush chanted, "We're Number One! We're Number One!" but no one watching had to be told who was moving to the top of the rankings if the Illini could defeat Arkansas the following Saturday.

In fact, the next week the Fighting Illini moved to the top spot in the national rankings, where they would stay for 14 straight weeks through the end of the regular season.

Illinois had already clinched another outright Big Ten title when the Illini traveled to Columbus for the regular season finale against Ohio State. Buckeye sharpshooter Matt Sylvester would plant himself in Ohio State lore with a 25-point performance that included a three-pointer with 5.1 seconds remaining to hand the Illini their first loss of the season after 29 straight wins by the score of 65–64.

Illinois swept through the Big Ten Tournament at the United Center in Chicago with James Augustine earning tournament MVP honors. The biggest storyline, though, was the tragic death of Bruce Weber's mother, Dawn, from a ruptured aorta suffered prior to Illinois' victory over Northwestern.

An emotional Weber returned to the Illini sidelines the next day in the victory over Minnesota and again in the championship game victory over Wisconsin.

Earning the overall No. 1 seed in the NCAA Tournament allowed the Fighting Illini a path to the Final Four without getting on a plane. The first two rounds were played in Indianapolis and featured wins over Farleigh Dickinson and Nevada.

The Chicago Regional was next at Allstate Arena in Rosemont. First up was Wisconsin-Milwaukee and their head coach Bruce Pearl, who is at or near the top of Illini fans' most-hated list. The Illini flexed to a 77–63 victory.

The regional final against Arizona would go down as one of the greatest moments in Fighting Illini basketball history. The final four minutes are documented in another chapter, but every Illinois fan worth their salt knows exactly what they were doing that Saturday afternoon.

Bill Murray sitting in the stands, the steal by Jack Ingram, the shot by Deron Williams, the steal and layup by Dee Brown, and the toughness shown by Luther Head will always be remembered on that amazing day.

The victory allowed the Illini another bus trip to St. Louis for the 2005 Final Four. Following the team was the largest media contingent in NCAA history, an NCAA Final Four–record crowd of 31,500 fans in attendance at the open practice on Friday, and incredible hopes for a team that had caught the nation's fancy.

During the weeklong Orange and Blue party in St. Louis, it was announced that three Illini players had earned consensus All-America honors with Brown making the First Team and Head and Williams chosen for the Second Team. It was the first time three guards from the same team received consensus All-America honors in the same season. Weber also collected a total of eight National Coach of the Year Awards that week.

In front of more than 47,000 in attendance on April 2, the Illini took down Louisville in the National Semifinal by the score of 72–57. The win gave Illinois its 37th victory, tying the most wins in a single season in NCAA history (since broken).

The championship game on the final Monday of the season featured the No. 1 Fighting Illini against No. 2 North Carolina. The Illini battled through an off-shooting night and foul trouble to fight back from a 15-point deficit and tie the game at 70-all with two minutes remaining. Illinois had a number of open shots to take the lead or tie it in the final minutes that just would not fall, and the Tarheels went on to win the title by the score of 75–70.

Despite not winning the national championship, this team left Fighting Illini fans with a lifetime of memories. A final tribute came the next day when the team was welcomed back to Champaign-Urbana by a crowd of 25,000 at Memorial Stadium as the players, coaches, and fans gathered to celebrate the most successful year in the history of Fighting Illini basketball.

41 Football Rivalry Trophies—The Cannon, Lincoln's Hat, and IlliBuck

The Fighting Illini football team has been involved with three different rivalry trophies in series against three Big Ten foes.

The Cannon
Illinois-Purdue since 1943

The "Cannon Trophy," also known as the "Purdue Cannon" by Illini fans, began when Purdue students took a cannon to Illinois for the 1905 game, planning to fire it after a Boilermakers win. Purdue won 29–0, but when the students went to find the hidden cannon, it was missing! Quincy Hall, an Illinois student, had stumbled across it near old Illinois Field and moved it. Hall moved it to his farmhouse near Milford, Illinois, where it survived a fire and gathered dust for nearly 40 years. Hall donated it back to the schools in 1943 to symbolize the rivalry.

The actual small cannon was last fired in 2001 after a Fighting Illini victory during a Big Ten championship season. A replica Cannon Trophy now goes to the winner each year.

Since Purdue is Illinois' closest Big Ten rival, with only about 90 miles between stadiums, fans from both schools often make the short trip across state lines to attend the games.

IlliBuck
Illinois-Ohio State since 1925

"IlliBuck" is—or was—originally a turtle, destined for a long life (it was hoped, anyway). The wear and tear of traveling between Champaign-Urbana and Columbus was too much, even for the hardy marine reptile. The original IlliBuck died in the spring of 1926 and his successor is now a wooden replica. Members of two junior honorary societies, Bucket and Dipper of Ohio State and Atius-Sachem of Illinois, annually meet at halftime of the Fighting Illini-Buckeye game to present the "IlliBuck" Trophy to the previous year's winning school.

One of the most thrilling IlliBuck games was in 2007 when Illinois upset the No. 1–ranked Buckeyes in Columbus, propelling the Illini to the Rose Bowl following the season. From 1983 to 1994, Illinois took possession of IlliBuck for eight of 12 seasons, including five in a row from 1988 to 1992.

Scores from each game are carved into the back of the wooden turtle. Once space has been filled, the last winner of the trophy retains possession and a new IlliBuck is made for the next season.

The Land of Lincoln Trophy/Tomahawk
Illinois-Northwestern since 1945

Illinois and Northwestern play annually for the "Land of Lincoln" Trophy, which is relatively new to the series. An administrative decision in 2008 to retire the 62-year-old "Sweet Sioux" Tomahawk Trophy that had been in place since 1945 allowed the move to the Land of Lincoln Trophy, since these were the two Big Ten schools within the state boundaries. Both schools agreed that no matter the outcome of the 2008 game, the Tomahawk would remain in Evanston. Alas, the Wildcats took that last Tomahawk game.

The story of the Tomahawk Trophy dates to 1945 when the staff members of the two student newspapers conceived of the idea of a wooden Native American trophy. "Sweet Sioux," the Tomahawk Trophy, was inaugurated in 1947 to replace the wooden Native American.

The two schools agreed in 2008 to have sculptor Dick Locher, who was a Pulitzer Prize–winning editorial cartoonist famously known for producing the artwork for the Dick Tracy comic strip series, produce a copy of Abraham Lincoln's famed stovepipe hat as the trophy.

A favorite Illini win in the series came on November 20, 2010, at Wrigley Field. In front of more than 41,000 fans at The Friendly Confines, the Fighting Illini rode the legs of star running back Mikel Leshoure to a 48–27 victory. Leshoure rushed for a school-record 330 yards in the game on his way to 1,697 yards on the season.

Illinois also clinched the outright Big Ten title in 2001 with a Thanksgiving Day 34–28 win over the Wildcats that would eventually send the Illini to the 2002 Nokia Sugar Bowl in New Orleans. Fighting Illini fans also enjoyed a series win in 1983 when the victory gave Illinois a perfect 9–0 conference mark. It remains the only season in Big Ten history when one school defeated every other conference team in the same season. Fighting Illini fans tore down the Dyche Stadium (now Ryan Field) goal posts in the north end zone, eventually carrying them to Lake Michigan, where they were tossed into the cold waters.

42 Pizza Popularity

Visitors and citizens of Champaign-Urbana are fortunate to have dozens of excellent eating establishments within the community, including several close to campus.

The pizza options give everyone a style they can love. For Chicago-style deep dish, there is really none better than Papa Del's Pizza Factory.

Owner Bob Monti opened the first Papa Del's on October 24, 1970, at 601 S. Wright Street after developing a recipe and making pizzas for his fraternity brothers at Phi Sigma Epsilon for several years. The name Papa Del's stemmed from Monti's fraternity brothers, who nicknamed him "Del Monte," after the popular brand of canned vegetables. The "Papa" part stemmed from the fact he had been at the fraternity six years and was president.

There were a couple of other locations before settling at 1201 South Neil Street, Champaign, in what was once the local Coca-Cola bottling factory.

The Original Sicilian Pan Pizza remains a customer favorite, but the All American Thin Pizza has been steadily gaining in percentage of orders. Give yourself plenty of time as the pan pizzas can take 45 minutes or so to bake. An order of Fried Garlic Butter Doughnuts will help fill the time until the piping hot pizza is delivered to your table.

The Papa Del's menu offers many other items as well, but the pizza is king.

For thin and crispy pizza, there are several options in Champaign-Urbana. Monical's Pizza, which originated in Tolono, a few miles south of Champaign-Urbana, remains popular as the chain has spread throughout Central Illinois. Other local options for thin crust include Jupiter's Pizza (both downtown Champaign and at The Crossing), Manolo's Pizza and Empanadas, next to Krannert Fine Arts Center, and several other pizzerias in town. A hidden gem, though, is the Old Orchard Bowling Alley in Savoy, which purchased the original Monical's Pizza recipe many years ago and serves from its kitchen.

Anyway, there is no shortage of great local pizza in Champaign-Urbana.

43 Foodie Delights

Illinois alumni, fans, and visitors who consider themselves foodies can enter good food overload with all the options Champaign-Urbana, and the surrounding area, can offer.

Campustown has several excellent options up and down Green Street. Longtime favorite Murphy's has terrific burgers and fresh-cut fries on their bar food menu. Legends is home to one of best fish sandwiches in town in addition to an outstanding collection of Fighting Illini sports history on display. Shawarma Joint offers a top-notch Mediterranean menu.

Maize established itself in the tiny corner restaurant at First and Green (also home to Ye Olde Donut Shop many years ago) to the point that it opened a second, much larger, version in Maize at the Station in the old train station at University and Chestnut.

For a little more upscale on campus, the legendary Timpone's on South Goodwin near Krannert is an Italian restaurant with a rotating menu of local, organic dishes, plus an extensive wine list. This is where you might find an Illini celebrity returning to campus. Timpone's also has an excellent thin crust pizza.

Downtown Champaign is always lively on the weekends. Farren's Pub and Eatery has been rated as having one of the Top 10 burgers in the state of Illinois. The Russell Burger at the top of the menu is there for a reason. Incredible.

Seven Saints offers a wide range of sliders along with custom-made sandwiches and salads. Their cheese curds may be the best in area. Watson's Shack and Rail is known for its outstanding fried and rotisserie style chicken, while featuring their Nashville hot chicken.

Black Dog Smoke and Ale House is located where Main and Chestnut Streets intersect in the original train station that was completely renovated into a fantastic environment. The BBQ at Black Dog quickly earned legendary status, and for good reason. If you are lucky to arrive before they are gone, the burnt ends are out of this world.

Neil St. Blues has a Southern-style menu and features live music several nights a week. Nando Milano Trattoria is a high-end Italian restaurant that rivals any in cities much larger.

Big Grove Tavern is a farm-to-table restaurant with a changing menu that is always popular. It offers outdoor seating for some great people watching.

Hamilton Walker's features a retro vibe in a circa-1880s building and is a classy American steakhouse with specialty cocktails. You'll want to make reservations for this place on the weekend.

Kofusion is an Asian fusion restaurant known for its incredible sushi. This restaurant moved into an old bank building, so check out the large safe that is still intact.

As most college campuses feature a wonderful selection of food trucks, one of Champaign-Urbana's most popular has also set up shop inside the Collective Pour Tuesday through Saturday. Smith Burger Co. crafts fresh burgers smashed to order with incredible topping options. Combined with all the beer options at Collective Pour, Smith Burger Co. is an outstanding complement when one is looking for something more casual.

Downtown Urbana has a great vibe as well. The Courier Café is located in the building that once housed the *Champaign-Urbana Courier* newspaper and has a menu full of tasty options from breakfast through late night.

Across the street and down the alley one will find Bunny's Tavern, with lunch specials each day and perhaps the best fish sandwich in Champaign-Urbana. The fish comes with one bun but could easily fill three. Another great Friday fish option is Boomerangs Bar and Grill on East Washington.

Silvercreek is just down Race Street and is a traditional American casual fine dining style restaurant. Broadway Food Hall offers many great options and is terrific for a lunch stop with a large bunch with so many menus to choose from.

If Thai food is your fancy, you won't go wrong with Siam Terrace, located on Main Street in downtown Urbana. From spicy to mild, you can't try all the options!

A hidden treasure a little off the beaten path is Baldarotta's Porketta and Sicilian Sausage, located in the center of the Lincoln Square Mall, a block south of the downtown area. Not sure there is a better Italian beef option in Champaign-Urbana, along with a plethora of other fresh menu items and pizza. This place is worth finding.

44 Drawing a Local Cold One

Champaign-Urbana has become the home of several local brewing companies if craft beer is to your taste.

Triptych Brewing in Savoy is away from campus a bit, but worth the few minutes. They often have food trucks for food and snacks, and an outside seating patio. Triptych is always experimenting with new recipes, so there are often new selections to choose from. Dank Meme is probably the most popular and can be found in many local bars and restaurants.

Blind Pig Brewery is, at the time of this writing, in the midst of relocating following an ownership change. The new Blind Pig Brewpub will be located at the corner of North Neil Street and West Church Street in Downtown Champaign, and will continue to offer a great selection of beers. The "U of IPA" is Blind Pig's most popular brew.

Riggs Beer Company is located on Rte. 130 just east of Urbana. With several acres of space, the outdoor seating area is huge and busy Thursday through Sunday. Riggs is closed Monday-Wednesday. Food trucks are parked in the lot each night for a rotating offering of food that can be carried in. Live music and several different festivals scheduled throughout the year make this a great place for large groups. The Riggs Hefeweizen is poured in many local restaurants and bars. Super area for kids to play and dog friendly.

The 25 O'Clock Brewing Company is located on Griggs Street just a block north and west of downtown Urbana and is open Thursday through Sunday. The brewers here have no problem trying new things and offer many different flavors and styles. Food can be carried in since none is offered on-site.

For the widest selection of beers, two spots in downtown Champaign have something for everyone's taste buds.

Pour Bros Taproom, located inside a former two-story car dealership, has a row of taps that can seem overwhelming, but the ability to search through the options with your personal pouring card allows one to find exactly what you are looking for. They also have ciders, mead, and wine on tap as you "pour your own." The live music out back when weather allows makes for a great meeting spot for friends.

Collective Pour is on the north side of downtown and features Smith Burger Co. as a fantastic food partner. This is a large taproom with around 60 ales on tap, so the options are nearly endless. Another wonderful place to meet with friends.

45 Dr. Harold Osborn Earns "World's Greatest Athlete" Status

Legendary Fighting Illini track and field coach Harry Gill developed some amazing athletes during his time at Illinois, but perhaps the star at the top of the list is Harold Osborn.

Osborn won two gold medals in the decathlon and high jump at the 1924 Paris Games and remains the only athlete to ever win gold in the decathlon and an individual event in the same Olympics. That performance resulted in worldwide media coverage calling him the "world's greatest athlete" after setting world records in both events.

A native of Butler, Illinois, and graduate of Hillsboro High School, he attended UI and competed in track and field from 1919 to 1922, earning a degree in agriculture. Osborn helped Gill and the Illini win Big Ten team titles indoors and outdoors all three years at Illinois. Osborn went on to teach agriculture in the small town of Lewistown, about 40 miles southwest of Peoria, when he shocked the world with his Olympic performance.

Osborn developed a unique jumping style using an efficient side-to-the-bar clearance that was known in that era of track and field as the "Osborn Roll." This modification of the Western roll resulted in more height and consistency. A childhood accident left him with very little vision in one eye, which gave him depth perception problems and forced him to carefully measure his distances and strides to the high jump bar.

His 6'6" high jump at the Paris Games remained the Olympic record for 12 years, while his decathlon score of 7,710.775 points set a new world record. That 10-event decathlon was marked by 113-degree temperatures in Paris that year.

Osborn and two fellow Illinois alums, Dan Kinsey and Horatio Fitch, scored more track and field points than any other nation at those 1924 Games. Fitch set a record in the semifinals of the 400 meters, but an hour later he finished second in the finals behind Scotland's Eric Liddell, a scene that was immortalized in the movie *Chariots of Fire*.

Earlier that spring at an AAU meet held on the UI campus, Osborn set the high jump record of 6'8" on May 27, 1924. He would go on to compete in the Olympics again in 1928, finishing in a four-way tie for second and officially credited with a fifth-place finish after the jump off tiebreaker.

Osborn won 17 United States titles and set six world records during his career. He held world indoor records in the standing hop, step, and jump; the 60-yard-high hurdles; and the running high jump. His longest standing world record was in the standing high jump of 5'5¾", which he achieved at the age of 37 and remains a record today since the event is no longer held. Osborn won NCAA and AAU high jump titles in 1922, AAU outdoor high jump titles in 1925 and 1926, the indoor title four years in a row from 1923 to '26, and was the AAU decathlon champion in 1923, 1925, and 1926. Osborn also won two Canadian titles, one British title, and several European titles.

After his international competition career, Osborn received his Doctor of Osteopathic Medicine in 1937 and returned to Champaign, where he practiced osteopathic medicine, continued to compete in athletics, coached and taught at Champaign High School, and then assisted with the Illini track program into the 1940s.

Osborn was enshrined as a charter member of the National Track and Field Hall of Fame in 1974 and as a member of the initial University of Illinois Athletics Hall of Fame in 2017. Dr. Osborn died in 1975 at the age of 75.

46 Two-Sport Illini Jerry Colangelo Becomes Arizona Legend

The legacy left by Illinois alum Jerry Colangelo will no doubt be extensive. From humble beginnings in the Hungry Hills neighborhood of Chicago Heights, Illinois, on the far south side of the city, through starring at Bloom High School, to attending the University of Kansas as a true freshman before transferring to Illinois, and then establishing himself as one of the nation's foremost sports leaders, Colangelo has been a winner at each stop.

He grew up in a house that his grandfather constructed with wood from railroad cars and often left home with a salt shaker in his pocket. When his stomach growled, he would swipe a tomato from a neighborhood garden and fix himself lunch.

While sitting out his year of residency as a true freshman at Kansas, Colangelo's locker was next to the legendary Wilt Chamberlain. At the end of the 1958 season, when Chamberlain told Jerry he would be leaving KU to play for the Harlem Globetrotters for a year and then move on to the NBA, Colangelo immediately looked to transfer back home to Illinois.

Colangelo lettered in three seasons with the Fighting Illini from 1960 through '62, serving as team captain as a senior. An Illinois teammate his first two seasons was Mannie Jackson, who would one day own the Harlem Globetrotters and also establish himself as one of Phoenix's most prominent citizens. Colangelo also played baseball for two years at Illinois.

Following his collegiate career, Colangelo would start his professional sports career in 1966 with the NBA's Chicago Bulls as a marketing director, scout, and assistant to the president of the team. His first big break came two years later in 1968 when he was hired as the first general manager of the expansion team, the Phoenix Suns, becoming the youngest GM in professional sports.

His unluckiest moment likely came after the 1969 season when the NBA held a coin flip between the Suns and Milwaukee Bucks to win the rights to UCLA superstar Lew Alcindor (who became Kareem Abdul-Jabbar). The Suns had the call and Colangelo, at the urging of Suns fans, said "heads" over the phone call with NBA commissioner Walter Kennedy and the Bucks.

Kennedy flipped the 1964 Kennedy half-dollar into the air with his right hand, caught it, and turned it over onto the back of his left hand.

The coin showed tails. The future all-time leading scorer would start his NBA career with the Bucks.

Colangelo didn't let the coin flip slow down his passion for a championship, though. He set a goal of one day owning the Suns and, nearly 20 years later in 1987, coordinated a group of investors that purchased the club for more than $44 million.

As a hands-on owner, Colangelo used his unique skillset to head all business and basketball facets of the franchise from selling tickets to coordinating sponsorships and brokering media deals. He served as chairman and CEO, general manager, and head coach during his 40 years with the Suns.

Among his many accomplishments, Colangelo built two state-of-the-art sports facilities and brought Major League Baseball to the Phoenix area with the Arizona Diamondbacks expansion team. Additionally, he won a World Series championship with the Diamondbacks and returned the once-tarnished U.S. Olympic Men's Basketball Team to glory. As chairman of USA Basketball, Colangelo created a team that brought home the gold medal in the 2008 Beijing Olympics, another in the 2012 London Olympics, again at the 2016 Rio Olympics, and a fourth at the 2020 Tokyo Olympics. He retired following the Tokyo games.

In addition to owning the Suns and Diamondbacks, Colangelo also owned the Phoenix Mercury, Arizona Sandsharks, and Arizona Rattlers. A four-time NBA Executive of the Year, he was named the Most Influential Sports Figure in Arizona for the 20th Century. He was a member of the first University of Illinois Athletics Hall of Fame class in 2017 and was elected to the Naismith Basketball Hall of Fame in 2004.

47 Glasnost Bowl Turns into Pivotal Illini Win at L.A. Coliseum

John Mackovic had been named the Illini head football coach in February of 1988 following Mike White and inherited a young and loaded roster. After not playing in a bowl game the previous two seasons, the Illini were invited to play Florida in the 1988 All-American Bowl in Birmingham. With nearly the entire core group returning in 1989, expectations were extremely high.

While the 1988 season was playing out, Illinois was negotiating with Raycom Sports and Entertainment, which was based in North Carolina, to play Southern California in the first-ever Glasnost Bowl, scheduled for Labor Day weekend 1989 in Moscow. The game was named after the policy of glasnost ("openness") introduced by Soviet lead Mikhail Gorbachev in 1985.

Raycom, which was looking to expand from a regional television production to something national, had added Big Ten Conference games to its portfolio after acquiring Rasmussen Communications in 1988.

At the end of the 1988 season, Mackovic had taken on athletic director duties after Neale Stoner was forced to resign in the wake of allegations of misuse of Athletic Association personnel, funds, and equipment. One of Mackovic's first issues to deal with was the Glasnost Bowl, which included a trip to Moscow to check out the 50,000 seat Dynamo Stadium, site of the proposed game.

"One of the things I've always dreamed of is to take American-style football around the world," Mackovic said at the time.

The trip proved to be eye-opening to the travel party, as the teams would need to bring nearly everything needed to prepare a team with them when they traveled in late August. Teams would need to bring enough food for the entire travel party, extra staff to prepare, all the practice equipment, sideline chains, towels, toilet paper, electrical converters, medical equipment, and even ice machines. The teams would need to find goal posts or locate a welder in Moscow to assemble some. It was going to be a monumental task.

The Russians were not exactly knowledgeable about American football, asking Mackovic how many ambulances would be needed for the game. He told them Illinois always had one on hand as a precaution.

"They said, 'Well, you'll need to take away the dead.' I said, 'Well, we're not counting on anyone dying.' They thought the game was vicious like that, that we killed off players. They assured us a hospital was close by."

The Glasnost Bowl, which would have been televised worldwide, fell through in midsummer when the field conditions, accommodations, and logistics couldn't meet the standards of major college football. So the game against USC, ranked No. 1 in many preseason polls, was rescheduled for Labor Day at the Los Angeles Coliseum.

Blue Illinois football jerseys made for Gorbachev, former U.S. President Ronald Reagan, and President George H.W. Bush, who had succeeded Reagan earlier that year, would be stored in the Illini football equipment room.

"It was a nice opportunity to show that maybe Americans and Russians were getting along better," Mackovic told the *Chicago Tribune*. "As we met with Russian reps, nobody said, 'This would be good for the two countries.'

"What I was telling players was: 'This is a once-in-a-lifetime chance. You may never get a chance to visit Russia again, for one thing.' Just to open their eyes to the rest of the world. I always wanted them to explore and know more about our world."

A novel idea, but impossible to execute. Both schools decided it was too much to pull off. In exchange, Mackovic was determined to make the best of it and took the players to California for the week, a lengthy trip that the NCAA likely wouldn't approve today.

"We turned lemons into lemonade and booked the whole week," Mackovic said. "We took the team to Disneyland. We treated it like a mini bowl trip. They loved it."

The game on Monday was televised nationally by ABC and set the tone for a 10-win season. USC led 13–0 midway through the fourth quarter when Jeff George connected with Shawn Wax, who grabbed a tipped pass and ran to the end zone for a 53-yard touchdown play.

After forcing a USC punt, George and the Illini took over with 4:18 remaining in the game. The cool junior QB moved the Illini 80 yards and finished the drive with a 20-yard touchdown pass to Steven Williams to give Illinois a 14–13 victory. The Fighting Illini would go on to finish 10–2 on the season with a final ranking of 10th in the nation. USC would go on to beat Michigan in the Rose Bowl and be ranked eighth nationally.

48 The Small Family and Big Ten Championships

There have been several multi-generational families who competed in the Orange and Blue at the University of Illinois, but one family has taken the crown for Big Ten championships ... in three different sports!

Bill Small was recruited to Illinois by Harry Combes after an outstanding high school basketball career at West Aurora, where he led his teams to consecutive fourth- and second-place finishes in the state tournament in 1958 and 1959. He was joined in his class by Bill Burwell and future Illini Hall of Famer Dave Downey, and the three would start for three seasons.

Since freshmen weren't eligible at that time, Small and his classmates sat out the 1960 season before becoming fixtures from 1961 through the '63 season. Joining Small, Burrell, and Downey in the starting lineups in 1961 and 1962 was future National Basketball Hall of Famer Jerry Colangelo.

During his three years at Illinois, Small scored a career total of 963 points for a 13.6 average and set the career free throw shooting record after leading the Big Ten in free throw shooting in 1961 and 1962. He was named Third-Team All-Big Ten in 1962 and Second-Team in 1963 with that '63 squad winning the school's only Big Ten title between 1952 and 1984. That senior season was also when the Illini moved from historic Huff Gym to the cavernous Assembly Hall for the final two games of the regular season.

The Fighting Illini defeated Bowling Green in the opening round of the 1963 NCAA Tournament but lost to eventual national champion Chicago Loyola in the regional finals.

Bill Small's graduation wasn't the end of his connection to the University, though.

Mike Small, oldest son of Bill and Kay, fell in love with golf as a youngster and was a four-year letter winner at Danville High School, where he helped the Vikings to a state championship before matriculating to the University of Illinois.

As an Illini player under coach Ed Beard, Small was a senior member of the 1988 Big Ten championship team, where he finished second behind teammate and longtime PGA Tour member Steve Stricker and added a second Big Ten title to the family mantle. Mike won medalist honors twice his final year, including the prestigious Butler National Intercollegiate.

While Mike was starring on the golf course, over at Illinois Field another Small was making a name for himself as a shortstop for the baseball team. Andy also starred at Danville High School, only on the basketball court and baseball diamond until a torn ACL kept him sidelined his senior baseball season. He was prepared to go to Illinois as a student when new baseball coach Augie Garrido called and offered him a chance to return to the diamond.

Andy redshirted as a freshman and started eight of the 19 games he played in his first year. As a sophomore, he started 32 games at several infield positions. Then, as a junior and senior Andy cemented himself as the starting shortstop for coach Itch Jones in his first two years at Illinois, ranking among the national leaders and setting Illini season and career records for hit by pitch.

Andy helped the Fighting Illini to Big Ten championships in both 1989 and 1990 under Garrido to move the family total to four. That would be enough for most families, but Mike had a different idea when he returned to his alma mater as the head golf coach in 2000.

Mike had turned professional in 1990 and played on various tours before joining the PGA Tour in 1995. After traveling around the continent for several years and leaving his wife, Ann, at home with two young boys, Mike thought it was time to add some normalcy to his life.

If it was only that easy.

First, there is nothing normal about being a collegiate head coach. Leading a team is a daily task in addition to all the recruiting that is required to build a program. And no coach has built a Big Ten and national powerhouse against more odds than Mike.

Collegiate golf powers have normally resided in the south and western parts of the nation. Mike bucked that trend by winning 14 of 15 Big Ten titles from 2010 through 2024 and leading the Illini to finishes in the top five nationally in nine of 13 postseasons from 2012 through 2024.

Mike has continued to play professionally on a part-time basis while coaching and has won enough state and national tournaments to be placed in several halls of fame as a player.

Through the 2024 golf season, the Small family totaled 17 conference championships and with several years remaining on his contract, that number could grow.

49 Illini in the Pro Football Hall of Fame

The Fighting Illini football program may not be one of the top 10 all-time winningest programs, but the list of outstanding individuals who played on the field at Memorial Stadium will compete with just about any school.

Illinois ranks 10th among all colleges with six members of the Pro Football Hall of Fame in Canton, Ohio, alongside some of the nation's elite historic programs.

Harold "Red" Grange and George Halas were both members of the inaugural Hall of Fame class in 1963. The stories of these two have been well documented as Grange has often been noted as a

Schools with the most Pro Football Hall of Famers (as of 2024)

Notre Dame (14)	Miami—Florida (9)
Southern California (14)	Alabama (8)
Michigan (11)	Syracuse (8)
Ohio State (10)	Minnesota (7)
Pittsburgh (10)	Illinois (6)

savior of the National Football League after playing in a nationwide barnstorming tour shortly after his Illini career ended in 1925.

Halas was credited as one of the primary founders of the National Football League during the initial meeting of franchise owners in the Canton auto showroom in 1920. His Chicago Bears teams won six NFL titles, three other divisional titles, and finished second 15 times. Only six of Halas' 40 teams as coach finished below the .500 mark.

Ray Nitschke was the heart of the great Green Bay Packers defense of the 1960s, earning either First- or Second-Team All-NFL honors seven times in eight years from 1962 to '69. He was the first defensive player from the Packers' dynasty years to be elected to the Hall of Fame when he was inducted as part of the class of 1978. At Illinois, he played both fullback and linebacker before being drafted as a linebacker by the Packers.

Dick Butkus may be the only linebacker to surpass Nitschke as the game's greatest linebacker during the era both roamed the gridiron, although Nitschke played on better teams. The two had a healthy respect for each other, and Butkus even said that Nitschke was his idol. But as rivals each was fiercely proud of their spots in the history of the game.

When Butkus was enshrined in 1979, he said, "There's only one thing I've ever wanted to do: Play pro football. Everyone seems to be made for something, and I've always felt that playing football was the thing I was supposed to do. I love the game."

The versatile halfback/wide receiver Bobby Mitchell, who teamed with Nitschke at Illinois from 1955 to '57, was blessed with exceptional speed, uncanny faking ability, and balance. How he lasted until the seventh round of the NFL Draft will always be a mystery, but the Cleveland Browns were the lucky beneficiaries. Mitchell, who won multiple Big Ten sprint championships and once set the world record in the 70-yard low hurdles, used that speed to combine with Jim Brown for one of the most dynamic backfields the NFL had ever seen.

After four years with the Browns, Mitchell was traded to Washington, where he became the first Black player for that organization, as well as one of the game's most productive flankers. Mitchell was inducted into the Hall of Fame in 1983.

The first five Illini Hall of Famers are well documented and well known. It's the sixth, though, that is often the answer to sports trivia questions because his impact on the game was off the field and behind the scenes.

Hugh "Shorty" Ray entered the Hall of Fame in 1966 as a contributor in his role as the League's Supervisor of Officials from 1938 to 1952. During that period, he not only worked tirelessly to improve the techniques of officiating, but he also spent countless hours studying ways to streamline the rules, improve the tempo of play, and increase safety for the players.

Ray was only 5'6", 136 pounds, but he played baseball, football, and basketball at Illinois and was a captain of the 1906 Illini basketball team, the school's first year of varsity hoops. He would officiate Big Ten football, basketball, and baseball games in the 1920s and '30s before being urged by Halas to bring his officiating expertise to the NFL in 1938. He became known as pro football's "unknown hero" who helped save an often-unexciting game from extinction with rule changes and insisting his officials become absolute masters of the rules book.

50 Lou Henson

When Gene Bartow left Illinois after just one season to become John Wooden's successor at UCLA, Illini fans and the basketball world wondered who would take his place. Just three days later, athletic director Cecil Coleman was ready to name his new head coach ... and the announcement shocked the media group that had gathered on April 5, 1975, at the press conference.

Several names had been discussed in the media including Bartow's assistants, Tony Yates and Leroy Hunt, plus Virginia Tech's Don DeVoe and Kansas State's Jack Hartman. Never mentioned, though, was the head coach/athletic director at New Mexico State who had taken the Aggies to a Final Four and six NCAA Tournaments in his nine seasons when the tournament field was much smaller. In fact, the Urbana *Courier* newspaper, along with several others around the state, was printed that morning stating DeVoe would be named head coach.

Coleman had other ideas and started Lou Henson on a 21-year coaching career at Illinois that elevated the program to among the nation's best.

It wasn't a slam-dunk decision at the time for Henson as Oklahoma had also offered him the Sooner coaching position on the same date, and Henson was a native of that state. Illini fans can probably thank Lou's wife, Mary, for the decision to come to Champaign-Urbana. Mary was a native of Illinois and much of her family was within an easy drive.

Henson's first year in the 1975–76 season, the Illini posted a 14–13 record. The season his team burst on the national scene came in 1978–79 when Illinois started out with a 15–0 record, including a significant two-point win over No. 1-rated Michigan State and Magic Johnson.

His 1980–81 team qualified for the NCAA Tournament for the first time since 1963. Henson's other major accomplishments include an NCAA Final Four appearance in 1989, 11 seasons with 20 or more victories, and 12 NCAA Tournament appearances.

Henson retired as coach following the 1995–96 season and accumulated a record of 423–224 in his 21 seasons to set the school record for victories. He was inducted into the National Collegiate Basketball Hall of Fame in 2015 after leading both New Mexico State and Illinois to Final Four appearances and setting career wins records at both schools. Henson's name adorns the home court at both institutions.

Lou and Mary Henson established themselves as pillars of the Champaign-Urbana community after Lou was named Fighting Illini head coach in 1975. Lou finished his 21-year coaching career at Illinois with a school-record 423 victories and was inducted into the National Collegiate Basketball Hall of Fame in 2015. His name adorns the court at State Farm Center.

After retiring from Illinois at the end of the 1996 season, Henson was coaxed back to his alma mater when the Aggies made a coaching change just before the 1997–98 season started. He would spend eight full or partial seasons at NMSU before retiring with an all-time coaching record of 779–412. His total number of wins ranked among the top 16 of all time and he was one of only four NCAA coaches to have amassed at least 200 total wins at two schools.

Henson's players knew he would hold them accountable on both ends of the court, in the classroom, and in life away from the game. His players who would go on to play professionally credited Henson with preparing them as players and for life after college and remained loyal to the end.

Lou is credited with breaking the color barrier at Hardin-Simmons University, insisting that the team and school be racially integrated when he took that job in 1962.

It wasn't just Henson's coaching record, though, that made him so popular with fans and supporters at both schools. Mary and Lou were active in the community, socializing with friends at dinner, playing cards, or at any number of events.

A native of Okay, Oklahoma, Lou was a stellar athlete in several sports and played basketball at Connors State Junior College and New Mexico State. He honed his considerable checkers and dominoes skills against the seven siblings in his family and became an accomplished bridge card game player later in life. Henson enjoyed playing bridge until the end of his life.

While in college, Lou spent three summers working for the Jolly Green Giant canning factory in Lanark, Illinois, where Mary lived. They met in the final month of the final summer Lou would work in Lanark, and the love affair would last the rest of their lives.

Lou and Mary continued living in the original house in Champaign they moved into when he was hired at the UI in 1975. Both were always approachable and would strike up a conversation with just about anyone. Lou was inducted into the Illinois Athletics Hall of Fame in 2018. After fighting cancer for nearly 20 years, Lou passed away in the summer of 2020 at the age of 88.

51 The H Boys with Rice

Illinois has been considered "Linebacker U" by many informed followers for many years, dating back to the 1950s when Chuck Boerio, Ray Nitschke, and Bill Burrell wore the Orange and Blue, through the 1960s when Dick Butkus, Don Hansen, Ron Acks, and Terry Miller roamed Zuppke Field, and on through the 1970s with Tom Hicks, Scott Studwell, and John Sullivan racking up tackles. The 1980s featured Jack Squirek, Mike Weingrad, and Darrick Brownlow, who would garner Big Ten Defensive Player of the Year honors.

But it was the early 1990s when the best grouping of linebackers came together for the Illini. Brownlow was a three-time First-Team All-Big Ten pick from 1988 through 1990. As a senior, he tutored a young linebacker from East St. Louis who was sitting out the season as a redshirt. In 1991, that linebacker, Dana Howard, anchored the middle linebacker position for what would be the first of four seasons. Howard was joined in the starting lineup by classmate John Holecek from 1992 through '94.

Those two were joined by freshmen Kevin Hardy and Simeon Rice in 1993, forming what many still consider the greatest collegiate linebacker group ever seen in the Big Ten and possibly the nation.

Each brought their own special skillset to the team, and head coach Lou Tepper knew exactly how to incorporate them into the lineup.

Howard was the unquestioned team leader and toughest player on the Illini defense. Holecek was a great complement with his toughness and ability to cover from his weakside position. Hardy was a superior athlete with size who could cover running backs to receivers with his ability to run, while also being able to pressure the quarterback if needed.

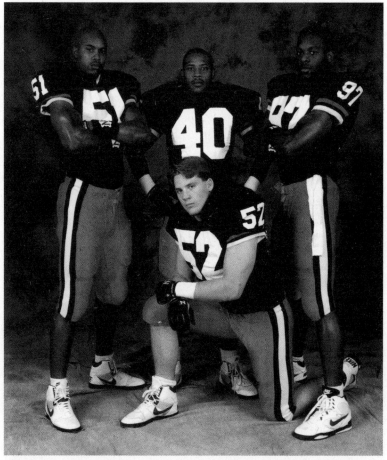

Illinois boasted arguably the greatest group of linebackers in college football history when Kevin Hardy (51), Dana Howard (40), Simeon Rice (97), and John Holecek (52) were teammates in 1993 and 1994. Howard and Hardy both won the Butkus Award as the nation's top collegiate linebacker in 1994 and 1995, respectfully.

Rice brought his own story and special level of athleticism to Tepper's defense as the rush linebacker, which was a glorified defensive end. Rice, who was 6'5", came from the powerhouse program at Mt. Carmel High School in Chicago and wanted to play running back.

Caravan head coach Frank Lenti Sr. saw something else in Rice's game despite not getting much of a look from college coaches. Lenti strongly suggested to Tepper that Rice had an incredible upside on the defensive side of the ball and the Illini head coach offered him a scholarship in the final weeks before the signing period. That decision would prove to be one of the best late recruiting decisions in the history of the program.

Howard and Holecek had a special relationship as great friends off the field and played in perfect harmony on the field. Howard earned Second-Team All-Big Ten honors as a freshman, then First-Team recognition his sophomore, junior, and senior seasons. Holecek was named honorable-mention All-Big Ten as a sophomore, then First-Team as a junior and Second-Team as a senior in 1994.

Howard was a First-Team All-American in both 1993 and 1994, earning consensus All-America recognition and the prestigious Butkus Award as a senior. He would go on to earn induction into the College Football Hall of Fame in 2018 after becoming the Big Ten's all-time tackles leader. Holecek proved to be a wonderful teammate by helping Howard handle several obligations during the Butkus Award campaign.

Following the 1994 season, both Hardy and Rice had major decisions to make as both were identified as top NFL prospects with the chance to be highly drafted after their junior seasons. After consulting with each other, both decided to return for their senior seasons. Following Howard's recognition path, Rice would earn Second-Team All-Big Ten honors as a freshman in 1992 and First-Team All-Big Ten honors his final three seasons. Hardy was

First-Team as a junior and senior. Rice would earn All-America honors as a junior and senior, while Hardy was a consensus All-American as a senior in 1995 when he would follow Howard by stacking another Butkus Award that season.

The group likely cannibalized much of the recognition with Holecek likely getting the short end of all-league honors. All four had significant NFL careers, with Hardy and Rice going second and third overall, respectively, in the 1996 Draft. As NFL players, Howard had a three-year career, Holecek played eight years, Hardy spent nine years as a pro, and Rice had a 12-season career that included a Super Bowl victory with the Tampa Bay Buccaneers in 2003.

52 Favorite Campus Haunts

No matter when an Illini was on campus, either as a student, returning alum, as a townie, or just a fan attending a game, there was likely a favorite hangout.

Campus bars on Green Street, Sixth Street, Daniel Street, or Fourth Street are ingrained in the memories of many, with a more recent crop of watering holes (some using traditional names) hosting long lines of students awaiting entrance.

The Illini Inn, originally located on Fourth Street between Daniel and Chalmers, has been an Illini tradition since 1970 and is home to the Mug Club. Membership to the Mug Club topped 100,000 students, alumni, Champaign-Urbana residents, visitors to the University, and even Bill Murray.

Anyone 21 and over can walk up to the bar and complete a challenge in order to receive their membership card and officially be part of the tradition. An applicant is given a card with a number.

They must remember that number as they chug a beer, and then drink their next one normally. Afterward, they recite their card number back to the bartender, receive their card, and gain Mug Club membership for life.

For instance, the author may have waited until one of his children was about to graduate before earning the right to be assigned No. 100,611.

Another longstanding tradition at the Illini Inn was for hockey fans to scoot down the street from the UI Ice Arena in between periods of the Illini Hockey Club games and then back before the next period started.

The White Horse Inn on Green Street was another favorite spot with a great outdoor beer garden and Tuesday night wing specials. That was where the author was sitting when the nation started following the low-speed chase of O.J. Simpson in the white Ford Bronco down a Los Angeles freeway on June 17, 1994.

Perhaps the most iconic bar was, and remains, Kam's, "Home of the Drinking Illini." It's not in the same place as it was for decades when it opened to Daniel Street, as it moved near the corner of First and Green when a high-rise apartment building was built where it and other establishments once stood.

The stories from Kam's are pretty consistent since it opened in 1931. Many Greek events, pregame parties, postgame celebrations, and jam-packed most weekend nights. It was always a center of campus social life. A few things that visitors will never forget are the distinct smell and the stickiness of the floor. Safe to say that the new location didn't carry over those parts of the original.

To help keep a couple of traditional campus spots no longer in business alive, the owners of Kam's joined two additional bars, Stan's Gridiron and Second Chance, to the property. Kind of a "three-in-one" for bars.

Next door to Kam's was C.O. Daniel's, which stood for Cochrane's on Daniel. For many years, students would move back and forth from one bar to the other. Cochrane's was also the name of a bar near the corner of Wright Street and Green Street, thus the need for differentiation. That location would later become Orchid and Tonic, but those were nothing like the dance floor offered at Cochrane's.

The Champaign-Urbana music scene was especially hot from the 1960s through the '80s.

Mabel's was located on the south side of Green Street and hosted some incredible music acts in the day. Some of the featured artists included Alice in Chains, Cheap Trick, and Joan Jett, along with hundreds of other local and regional acts. It later became Brothers Bar and Grill.

The Red Lion opened in 1966 and the list of bands who regularly graced its stage reads like a catalog of 1970s Midwestern rock, including Head East, Dan Fogelberg, Cheap Trick, the Ramones, and Champaign's own REO Speedwagon. Other regional bands who frequented the Red Lion included One Eyed Jacks, Starcastle, Appaloosa, and the Finchley Boys.

Red Lion closed in 1981 and was operated by several owners under many different names until 2010, when it was renovated and dubbed the Red Lion once again.

Chester Street Bar, also known as C-Street, was the top campus dance bar for everyone, but also a center of the LGBTQ community. There was never a lack of energy as the floor was always hopping with dancers from campus and the Champaign-Urbana area.

Before the campus high-rise apartment craze cleared out several establishments on campus, the Clybourne and Firehaus sat side by side on Sixth Street just south of Green. Famous for fishbowls, Firehaus was more casual than Cly's.

O'Malley's Pub, in the basement of the mansion located on the corner of Fourth and Green Streets, was where people gathered for "Pie at Midnight." The tradition of singing Don McLean's

"American Pic" every night at midnight was a rite of passage for many on the UI campus.

Along with Kam's and Red Lion, current campus bars that are still popular include Joe's Brewery on Fifth Street along with Legends and Murphy's Pub on Green Street. Many names and dates have been chiseled into the wooden booths at Murphy's. All three have great food options as well.

As with most college campuses, the bar scene is part of the tradition of the school and alumni. Many marriages and lifetime relationships started with conversations in these iconic spots. These are only several of the dozens of great drinking spots around campus over the decades.

53 Fighting Illini at the Friendly Confines

When Northwestern, located in the northern Chicago suburb of Evanston, came to an agreement with the Ricketts family to play a Big Ten football game at Wrigley Field in 2010, the choice of opponent was Illinois.

The Friendly Confines of Wrigley Field regularly hosted football games from 1920 to 1970, including around 400 National Football League games. The primary tenants were the Chicago Bears, owned by Illinois alumni George Halas, who called the park home from 1921 (as the Chicago Staleys) through 1970. The Chicago Tigers (1920) and Chicago Cardinals (1920, 1931–1939) also played professional football games at Wrigley.

Games at Wrigley weren't limited to the pros as the park also hosted high school and collegiate football games, including a 1923 battle between Northwestern and Illinois. On October 27,

1923, the Fighting Illini defeated the Wildcats, 29–0, in front of 32,000 fans. The game was moved to Wrigley Field—then named Cub Park—after Illinois ticket requests for the game at Evanston exceeded 10,000. Northwestern's stadium held approximately 17,000 fans.

On that date, the Illini led 19–0 at halftime after three touchdowns by sophomore sensation Harold "Red" Grange, the second score on a 90-yard interception return. Earl Britton kicked a field goal in the third quarter and Clarence "Stub" Muhl caught a fourth-quarter TD pass to finalize scoring at 29–0.

Prior to the game, there was concern that Cubs Park wasn't big enough to hold a regulation football with NU head coach Glenn Thistlethwaite measuring the field in late August and declaring that the field wasn't large enough unless the field was oriented southwest-to-northeast (home plate to centerfield). That particular field layout would make it difficult for fans to watch the game.

In early September, UI athletic director George Huff and head coach Bob Zuppke agreed to play the game with reduced end zones, stating that playing the game on a slightly smaller field was preferred in order to allow more fans to attend the game.

Fast forward to 2010 when Northwestern and Illinois were again scheduled to play at Wrigley. It was clear the field would be a tight fit running east-west from home plate toward right field. So tight that the east goal post was fastened to the right field wall, allowing just a few feet from the back of the end zone to the brick wall.

An early week visit by Big Ten Commissioner Jim Delany made him question the safety of the field with the corner of the field being less than two feet from the wall in the right-field corner. The back of the center of the end zone was just six inches from the right-field wall. The west end zone had some additional space to the covered and padded third-base dugout.

Both schools had signed off on the layout, and the configuration had been made public. But once Delany refused to sign off, a phone call with the commissioner, both athletic directors, and both head coaches was arranged to come up with a solution.

It had already been decided that both teams would occupy the north sideline so that players and staff would not block sightlines from the main stands down the first base side of the field. After several ideas were bandied about, Wildcat leader Pat Fitzgerald suggested that both teams would run all their offensive plays in one direction, toward the western end zone. Every time the ball changed hands, the players would be turned around, so the action headed west and away from the tight right-field wall.

After questions about the fairness of which end each team stood on the sidelines, it was decided that the teams would switch ends at halftime with a 10-yard open zone in between the teams.

The unique plan was a national media story, overshadowing the event's main attraction as the first football game to be played there in nearly 40 years. ESPN's *College GameDay* show originated from a stage set up across Clark Street with the famous Wrigley Field marquee in the background.

Once the game started, however, even though the marquee and much of the outside of Wrigley was painted or decorated in purple, it was the Orange and Blue that dominated the crowd and the action on the field.

Junior running back Mikel Leshoure had a day for the ages, breaking the Illinois school and Wrigley Field records with a career-best 330 rushing yards. He ran for a whopping 153 yards in the first quarter on only 10 carries with two touchdowns. Illinois' 519 rushing yards was the most by an Illini team since setting the school record with 562 against Illinois-Normal (now Illinois State) in 1944.

54 Chief Illiniwek

The halftime performance of Chief Illiniwek thrilled generations of Fighting Illini fans from his first appearance at a football game against Pennsylvania on October 30, 1926, to his final farewell during a basketball game against Michigan on February 21, 2007.

Following years of debate pitting political correctness against tradition, the UI Board of Trustees made the decision to end the tradition of 80 years when the NCAA announced in 2006 that it would bar the University from hosting national tournament play on campus if Chief Illiniwek was allowed to perform.

Chief Illiniwek was always identified as a campus symbol during his long run and not a mascot, even though many media accounts called him that regarding the controversy.

The origin of Chief Illiniwek dates to 1926 when Ray Dvorak, the assistant director of bands at the UI, conceived of the idea of having a Native American war dance performed during halftime of Illinois football games. The first performance was on October 30, 1926, at Memorial Stadium at halftime of the game against Penn. Following his performance, Chief Illiniwek was met by a drum major dressed as Penn's Quaker mascot, offered a peace pipe, and walked off the field arm-in-arm. Student Lester Leutwiler, an Eagle Scout, created the original costume and performed the dance based upon his experience as a Boy Scout.

The expression "Illiniwek" was first used in conjunction with the Illinois football team by coach Bob Zuppke and referred to the Illinois Confederation of Native Americans who historically had inhabited much of present-day Illinois.

Another student, Webber Borchers, was the only Chief to ride on horseback around the field, continuing the performances and soliciting contributions for a permanent costume in 1930. A total of 36 different students officially portrayed the role of the Chief and all but one were men. Adelle (Stith) Brooks, the only woman to portray the tradition, served in 1943 because of the shortage of male students during World War II and was called "Princess Illiniwek."

The controversy surrounding the Chief percolated on campus primarily starting in 1989, although he had been the subject of debate since the mid-1970s. The student portraying Chief Illiniwek also began performing at halftime of the men's and women's basketball games as well as at volleyball matches. His dance corresponded to the music and lyrics of the "3-in-1" performed by the Marching Illini and basketball bands, which is an arrangement of three original songs titled "The March of the Illini," "Hail to the Orange," and "Pride of the Illini."

Chief Illiniwek did not appear on the sidelines or on the field other than during his performance at halftime.

The final ruling on the Chief's future really came from the NCAA in August 2005 when the governing body of collegiate athletics instituted a ban on schools that use what they call "hostile and abusive American Indian nicknames" from hosting postseason games beginning in early 2006. The University appealed the ban in October 2005, but the NCAA ruled that no new information had been added to the original submission and the ban was upheld. The UI appealed again in January 2006, but the Executive Committee denied that one as well and indicated no further appeals would be entertained.

On February 16, 2007, the board of trustees issued a unilateral ruling retiring Chief Illiniwek. The Chief's last performance, portrayed by Dan Maloney, took place just five days later on February 21, 2007, at the last men's home basketball game against Michigan. The official UI BOT vote to retire Chief Illiniwek's name, image, and regalia came on March 13, 2007.

The story of the controversy and different resolutions and rulings is long and, depending on your opinion, still not totally resolved. It's safe to say that Chief Illiniwek will not officially perform at a University of Illinois event ever again. His performance can be found archived on many internet videos and seared into the memories of many who saw him in person.

In an effort to resolve the controversy, Chancellor Robert Jones included the work of a committee that issued a report in 2019 of its "critical conversations" that included more than 600 participants representing all points of view. He appointed a Commission on Native Imagery: Healing and Reconciliation to implement the recommendations of the committee, including four goals:

1. Provide closure, healing, and reconciliation for stakeholders.
2. Facilitate the establishment of new traditions.
3. Remember the history of the Chief with a focus on both the intent and impact of the tradition.
4. Honor and partner with the Native Nations for whom Illinois is their ancestral home.

In December 2020, Chancellor Jones announced the Implementation Plan on Native Imagery, a set of reforms including an expansion of the UI's American Indian Studies program, repatriating sacred artifacts to indigenous people, offering in-state tuition to students from federally recognized tribal nations, having a campus historian develop an accurate history of the school's use of Native American symbols, and creating a council to develop new traditions for the student body.

There has never been an indication of possible change to the Fighting Illini nickname.

55 Tonja Buford Bailey— World-Class Hurdler

Former Fighting Illini women's track and field coach Gary Winckler earned the reputation as one of the world's best coaches of hurdlers, and many of his students helped lead Illinois to 11 Big Ten championships.

The list of champion and All-America sprinters and hurdlers includes Celena Mondie-Milner, Renee Carr, Aleisha Latimer, Yvonne Harrison, Benita Kelly, Tonya Williams, Dawn Riley, Susanna Kallur, Yvonne Mensah, and Perdita Felicien.

But one of the best and most decorated female student-athletes to ever step on campus was Tonja Buford-Bailey, who not only won more individual Big Ten track titles than any other Illini athlete, but also more titles than any other women's or men's athlete in the history of the conference. Her total of 25 championships broke the record of 23 by Wisconsin distance star Suzy Favor.

From 1990 to '93, Buford-Bailey dominated hurdles competition at Big Ten track and field meets. Her eight individual titles and two relay championships as a senior may never be broken.

Buford-Bailey was a four-time Big Ten Track Athlete of the Year selection and was named Athlete of the Championships three times. She shared Illinois' Female Athlete of the Year award in 1992 and won it outright in 1993.

A native of Dayton, Ohio, Buford-Bailey became the first Illini women's track runner ever to compete in the Olympic Games when she qualified for the 400-meter hurdles at the 1992 Summer Games in Barcelona, Spain. At the 1996 Atlanta Games, Buford-Bailey won a bronze medal in that event. She also won silver in the 400m hurdles at the 1995 World Championships in Gothenburg.

Buford-Bailey even earned a spot on the 2000 Olympic squad after becoming a mother.

Her best result came at the 1995 World Championships, where she earned silver behind fellow-American Kim Batten by just 0.01 seconds. Both athletes went under the former world record and Buford-Bailey's time of 52.62 would remain her personal best, and still ranks among the 10th fastest of all time at the time of printing.

After her running career concluded, Buford-Bailey returned to coach the Illini in 2004, first as an assistant under Winckler then replacing him as head coach from 2008 to 2014 and winning the Big Ten Indoor Championship in 2013.

She left Illinois after the 2014 season for the University of Texas, where she would be head women's coach and earn the 2016 USATF Nike Coach of the Year. She competed as Tonja Buford until she married former NFL wide receiver Victor Bailey in 1995. Their son, Victor Jr., played major college basketball at Oregon, Tennessee, and George Mason.

Buford-Bailey was a four-time state hurdles champion at Meadowdale High School in Dayton, and at the age of 12 met the legendary Wilma Rudolph.

Buford-Bailey has coached athletes to Olympic Games in 2012, 2016, 2020, and 2024.

56 World Champion Hurdler Perdita Felicien

The list of Fighting Illini All-American sprinters and hurdlers is long and illustrious under Coach Gary Winckler. But only one earned world champion status.

Canadian native Perdita Felicien was recruited to Illinois by Winckler as the program's next superstar, and Felicien certainly delivered.

Born in Ontario, she began running track at age seven, and during her elementary years won numerous regional competitions. Felicien began hurdling at age 14 but found it mentally taxing and preferred the sprints. In high school she took national titles and set several provincial hurdles records before matriculating to Illinois for the 1999–2000 school year.

Felicien's story is not complete without some background on her mother, Cathy Felicien Browne.

"Who I was and who I am as a woman, as a world-class athlete, was only because of my mother's story and because of who my mother is," Felicien said.

Felicien Browne's story begins on the Caribbean island nation of Saint Lucia. Money was tight when she was growing up, so she often had to skip classes to help her mother. She also sold seashells and other trinkets at beachside hotels.

She saw a man by a pool with a little baby, so she walked up to him, introduced herself, and asked if she could be the child's babysitter. He and his wife were Canadian, and they told her when she turned 20, they would bring her to Canada to work as a full-time childcare provider.

Felicien Browne never expected to hear from the Canadian couple again, but they followed through and her parents encouraged her to seize the opportunity. She worked for several families—cooking, cleaning, and looking after children. It was not an easy life.

Perdita watched very closely as her mother overcame difficulties time after time, observing how she had sacrificed so much to give her children a chance at success in life.

"Through my life, my mother would say things as I was young and growing, you know, 'When you came into my life, Perdita, you gave me hope,' or 'You gave me purpose and a reason.' And I didn't really understand what she meant," Felicien said in an interview in advance of her book, *My Mother's Daughter: A Memoir of Struggle and Triumph.*

"It wasn't until I started to write, and I pieced my mother's life together, I saw all the things that she had to endure to give me the experience and the richness of the life that I have," Felicien said.

As an Illini, Felicien was a ten-time All-American and won three NCAA titles, one in the 60-meter hurdles in 2002 and two in the 100-meter hurdles in 2002 and 2003, setting national marks in both events.

Felicien won four Big Ten championships and was a three-time Illini Female Athlete of the Year in 2001, 2002, and 2003.

Her collegiate success carried over to the professional tour, winning gold in the 100-meter hurdles at the 2003 IAAF world outdoor championships and taking the 2004 IAAF world indoor title. Felicien represented Canada at five world championships and a pair of Olympic Games in 2000 and 2004. She was named for the third time to the Canadian team for the 2008 Olympics, but just prior to competition was forced to withdraw from the team due to a stress fracture.

After winning a silver medal at the 2003 Pan-American Games, she was named the Outstanding Canadian Athlete of the Year for track and the NCAA Female Track Athlete of the Year. In 2010, Felicien won a silver medal at the world indoor championships. Her 2011 gold medal at the Canadian Nationals was her tenth Canadian championship.

In 2016, Felicien was inducted into the Athletics Canada Hall of Fame. She was inducted into the inaugural University of Illinois Athletics Hall of Fame in 2017 and into the Ontario Sports Hall of Fame in 2023.

Felicien retired from competition in 2013 and went back to school to study journalism. She was part of the broadcasting team for the Toronto 2015 PanAm Games coverage and the CBC TV network broadcast teams for the Winter Olympics in South Korea and later the Summer Olympics in Tokyo in 2021. Since 2020, Felicien has been the host of *All-Round Champion*, a TV series produced by Marblemedia for TV Ontario and BYU TV.

57 Illini Part of Record-Setting Victories as Final Victims

At the end of the 2023 college football season, there were 18 major college coaches with 200 or more wins, four with at least 300, and just one with more than 400 career wins. Illinois was part of two record-setting wins at the end of legendary coaching careers 29 years and 844 miles away from each other.

In 1982, Mike White's Fighting Illini football squad would be remembered for many things. Illinois played its first night game at Memorial Stadium in the season opener on September 4. Quarterback Tony Eason would set an all-time Illini record for passing efficiency. And it was the year that Illinois went "bowling" for the first time in 19 years since the 1963 Big Ten championship season and subsequent Rose Bowl appearance.

But it was the invitation to the Liberty Bowl in Memphis that would be most monumental as coaching icon Paul "Bear" Bryant announced the bowl game would be his last as head coach of the Crimson Tide as he would be putting away his houndstooth hat and retire.

That announcement took what would be a mid-level bowl game to the national spotlight since Bryant was the game's winningest coach with 322 victories after the regular season.

The night sky was clear, and the 34-degree temperatures possibly favored Alabama's wishbone offense. Illinois trailed the Tide by 7–6 at the half, as Alabama defenders repeatedly pummeled Eason with a ferocious pass rush, knocking him out of the game three times.

Each of the three plays Eason was sidelined, the backup who entered the game tossed an interception, thwarting several Illini scoring opportunities. Despite a record 423 yards passing by Eason, Illinois dropped a 21–15 decision, giving Bear his 323rd victory to retire as the game's winningest coach. Bryant would die just a few weeks later on January 26, 1983, from a massive heart attack.

As the years passed, Penn State's Joe Paterno and Florida State's Bobby Bowden both passed Bryant's mark in the early 2000s. Bowden retired following the 2009 season with 357 victories in his 40 years as a head coach.

In State College, Paterno continued his amazing run as the head man with the Nittany Lions and had six additional seasons over Bowden to build his record-setting career. On October 29, 2011, when Illinois traveled to Happy Valley, a freak snowstorm had dumped several inches of the white stuff on top of Beaver Stadium. Seats were filled with snow and only around 60,000 fans in a stadium that held more than 100,000.

Paterno would be forced to coach that game from the press box because he was still recovering from an accidental hit on the sidelines during a preseason practice. Coaching in his 46th season as head coach at Penn State, Paterno entered the game tied with Eddie Robinson with 408 collegiate victories for most ever at the Division 1 level. Robinson had coached 56 years at Grambling State until his retirement in 1997, had incredible success as head coach of the Tigers, and is a Hall of Famer in his own right.

In a tightly fought contest, the Nittany Lions took the lead on a touchdown with just 1:08 remaining in the game. The Fighting Illini drove from their own 17 to the Penn State 25-yard line with just five seconds remaining in the game. A 42-yard field goal attempt by Derek Dimke would send the game into overtime.

However, as fate would have it, the snow possibly played a part in the finish as a snowball thrown from the Nittany Lion student section landed at the feet of Dimke during the attempt and the ball bounced off the right upright to give Penn State and Paterno a 10–7 victory.

The victory was Paterno's 409th to move him into the top spot among all-time Division I head coaches. What no one could foresee were circumstances that would become public the following Monday when the Jerry Sandusky scandal broke and Paterno would be fired just a week later.

There are six known individuals who attended the final games of both Bryant and Paterno as they were played 29 years apart and more than 525 miles from Champaign-Urbana, including the author, a photographer, a former television reporter, a radio network engineer, and two longtime fans and alums.

58 Illini Tennis Tradition Rockets Under Tiley

The Illinois men's tennis program was an early Big Ten power, winning conference titles six times between 1917 and 1932 and finishing no worse than second place. But from that 1932 season until Craig Tiley was named head coach in 1993, the Illini won only the 1946 conference championship and rarely competed for the top spot.

A native of South Africa, Tiley's hiring in the summer of 1992 by athletics director Ron Guenther changed the trajectory of the program and moved Illinois among the nation's elite.

It might not have shown that first season in 1993 when the Illini were 4–23 and finished 11th, but it only went up from there.

It took until 1996 before Illinois was selected to compete in the NCAA championships after finishing second in the Big Ten. But the 1997 season started a streak of nine consecutive Big Ten championships through the 2005 season, including five trips to at least the quarterfinal round of the NCAA Tournament and a national championship in 2003.

The 2003 national championship squad will always set the bar for the greatness of the Illini tennis program. Worth noting that season is that the roster consisted of all Americans, a rarity among tennis powers around the country.

Illinois swept to a 32–0 record on the season. Leading the way on that squad was Amer Delic, who became the only Fighting Illini tennis player to win an NCAA title in singles after posting a 36–5 singles record on the season. Delic twice reached the national semifinals in doubles and earned All-America honors three times. Following the 2003 season, Delic was named the Jesse Owens Big Ten Male Athlete of the Year and the Illinois Male Athlete of the year.

In the championship match against Vanderbilt, Illinois dropped the doubles point and two of the first three completed singles matches to fall behind 3–1 with the first team reaching four wins earning the victory.

First, junior Michael Calkins prevailed at No. 5 singles to narrow the deficit to 3–2. On the No. 4 singles court, junior Phil Stolt won in three sets to tie the match at 3–3 with all eyes turning to a winner-take-all match between Chris Martin and Vanderbilt's Lewis Smith. The score was tied at one set apiece, and Martin led the third set at 5–4. Martin rifled match point past Smith, but Smith called the ball out. But the chair umpire overruled Smith and the NCAA championship belonged to the Orange and Blue. The Illini rushed the court and swarmed Martin for his clutch play with a massive dog pile.

It was the first time since 1972 that a team other than Georgia, Southern California, UCLA, or Stanford earned the title.

In 2005, Tiley was offered the opportunity to be the director of player development for Tennis Australia, which is the governing body that oversees tennis in Australia. In his 12 seasons at Illinois, Tiley had won nine Big Ten titles, the school's first national championship, an indoor national title, and set a national-record 64-match winning streak.

Few coaches had as big an impact on Illinois athletics as Tiley. He was honored for his work when he was inducted into the ITA Men's Collegiate Tennis Hall of Fame in 2010 and in the inaugural University of Illinois Athletics Hall of Fame in 2017.

Tiley was elevated to CEO of Tennis Australia in 2013. He became Director of the Australian Open in 2006, one of the four Grand Slam events in professional tennis.

During his time at Illinois, Tiley coached six players who went on to play professionally with the Association of Tennis Professionals (ATP) including Kevin Anderson, Ryler DeHeart, Delic, Graydon Oliver, Rajeev Ram, and Brian Wilson.

Anderson, Delic, and Tim O'Connell, who won Big Ten singles titles three times and two doubles titles from 1926 through '28, are the first three men's tennis players inducted into the UI Athletics Hall of Fame.

Anderson, known for his big serve, was a two-time Grand Slam runner-up having reached the 2017 U.S. Open Final and the Wimbledon Final in 2018. At Illinois, Anderson earned All-America honors five times and won the 2006 national doubles championship with partner Ryan Rowe. In 2007, he helped lead the Illini to a national runner-up team title.

59 Terrence Shannon Jr. Stars in Final Season

There have been many incredible seasons posted by Fighting Illini basketball greats during the 120 years of the storied program, including National Player of the Year honors bestowed on Ray Woods (1917), Chuck Carney (1922), Andy Phillip (1943), Dee Brown (2005), and Ayo Dosunmu (2021). But none may match what Terrence Shannon Jr. posted during the 2023-24 season, especially during the postseason run when the Illini reached the NCAA Elite Eight and totaled 29 wins, third most in program history.

Never has someone with the speed and power of the 6'6", 225-pound Shannon worn the Illini uniform. In addition to his hard charging offensive style, he shot nearly 40 percent from three-point range and usually guarded the opponent's top offensive player.

Expectations were already at a high mark when Shannon decided to return for his bonus senior year. Every basketball player who played during the 2020–21 season that was interrupted by COVID-19 was given an extra year of eligibility and Shannon took full advantage of his fifth season.

He averaged 23.0 points per game on the season to rank third nationally, but his three-game total of 102 points while helping the Illini to the Big Ten Tournament championship was a totally different level of domination. After scoring a tournament record 40 points in a semifinal win over Nebraska, Shannon followed up with a 34-point effort in the championship victory over Wisconsin to earn the tournament's Most Outstanding Player honors.

He followed that with 26 points in the NCAA Round 1 victory over Morehead State, 30 points in the Round 2 win over Duquesne, and 29 in the Sweet 16 victory over Iowa State. His season total of

736 points in 32 games broke the Illinois single season record of 668 points set by Don Freeman 58 years earlier in 1966.

In addition to Freeman's best season when the Illini posted a 12–12 mark, other great season-long performances include Nick Weatherspoon in 1972–73 when he averaged 25.0 points and 12.3 rebounds when the Illini were 14–10 and when center Johnny "Red" Kerr averaged 25.3 points in 1954 when the Illini finished 17–5 and ranked No. 19 nationally. But it was just a different era.

The greatest teams in Illini history were incredibly balanced, including the Whiz Kids of the 1940s, the Flyin' Illini of 1989, and the 2005 squad that finished as national runner-up. Illinois' all-time leading scorers Deon Thomas, Kiwane Garris, Malcolm Hill, and Dee Brown were incredibly consistent during their four-year collegiate careers, but none had a season that stood above all others.

More recently, the All-America seasons of Ayo Dosunmu and Kofi Cockburn have to rank just behind Shannon. In Dosunmu's final season of 2021, he averaged 20.1 points, 6.3 rebounds, and 5.3 assists in what many consider the best all-around season up to that time in a year he won the Bob Cousy Award as the nation's best point guard. Cockburn was a double-double machine in his final year of 2022 after averaging 20.9 points and 10.6 rebounds. No Illini player ever had the size and strength of Cockburn.

The Illini have had several players move on to productive pro careers including Nick Anderson, Kendall Gill, Derek Harper, Kenny Battle, and Ken Norman, but only Norman's senior season of 1987, when he averaged 20.7 points and 9.8 rebounds, would come close to matching Shannon's season. Unfortunately, the Illini squad of 1987 had their season end in a first-round upset to Austin Peay to tarnish that year.

That being said, with all the great players and seasons since 1906, Terrence Shannon Jr. posted the greatest single season in Fighting Illini history.

60 A Spaceship on the Prairie

In the mid-1950s, as graduating classes at the University of Illinois continued to grow and popularity of the basketball team at Huff Gym had that facility busting at the seams, talk began on campus about building a larger assembly space.

The University Auditorium, now known as Foellinger Auditorium, was too small to host the large graduating classes and gatherings. Basketball at Huff Gym was so popular that students had to use split season tickets so that everyone who want to attend could see at least half the games.

Around 1958 plans were started to construct a building to assemble the student body and serve as a multi-use facility. The student enrollment has a little under 19,000 in 1959 and predicted to reach more than 24,000 by 1965 and 34,000 by 1970.

The site of new building was chosen just south of Memorial Stadium, and noted Illinois alumni Max Abramovitz was selected as architect. The moniker "Assembly Hall" was given to the project at the start and once the project was completed, it was kept as the building's name despite ideas for naming it after famous UI alums or dignitaries.

Beginning on May 25, 1959, construction of Assembly Hall was carried out by structural engineers Othmar Ammann and Charles Whitney, general contractor Felmley-Dickerson Co., and architect Abramovitz, taking almost four years of construction before its dedication on May 3, 1963. The building's price tag was $8.7 million and paid for with student fees and issued bonds.

Weighing over 4,000 tons from only the roof, the concrete dome of Assembly Hall spans a 400 feet diameter, is 128 feet tall, and was built with a folded plate design about 3.5 inches thick. Despite the dome's massive size and weight, the dome was self-supported and was the largest dome structure in North America until the Houston Astrodome opened in 1965.

It was considered an engineering marvel, and during the $160 million renovation project that was completed in the fall of 2015, the vast majority of the building's structure was considered in pristine condition. The unique roof continues to be supported by 614 miles of one-quarter inch steel wire wrapped at the base of the dome under intense pressure.

The building was renamed "State Farm Center" in 2013 when naming rights were sold to the insurance giant for $60 million over 30 years. State Farm Center now lists a capacity of 15,544 and, in the spirit of the original plans, hosts not just sporting events but many performances and events during the year.

The first basketball game played at Assembly Hall was on March 4, 1963, when the Fighting Illini hosted Northwestern while still battling for a Big Ten championship.

Illinois had played basketball at Huff Gym starting in 1925 after moving from Men's Gym (now known as Kenney Gym). The 1963 team had one practice at the new arena prior to game number one.

A capacity crowd of 16,137 was in attendance that day and were awed by the sight of the huge arena and a bit apprehensive over reports that it might collapse under the incredible weight.

Northwestern's Rick Falk, who would one day coach the Wildcats, is credited with the first basket in a game at the building when he knocked down a baseline jumper.

The immense space behind the baskets and around the floor made for a much different playing atmosphere than the players were used to, and the shooting statistics showed. The Illini shot 36 percent for the game while Northwestern checked in at 30 percent for the game and an ice-cold 22 percent in the second half.

The Illini outscored the Wildcats by nine in the second half on their way to a 79–73 win to keep their Big Ten title hopes alive.

One historical note from that game was when Dave Downey broke Johnny Kerr's career scoring mark five minutes into the game when he sank two free throws.

Another fun fact about the building was that two Illini basketball players, Bill Burwell and Jay Lovelace, worked construction on Assembly Hall as laborers, including pouring concrete for the domed roof.

The Fighting Illini would clinch a share of the Big Ten title with a win over Iowa at Assembly Hall five days later on March 9. The team would win its first game in the NCAA Tournament over Bowling Green before losing to eventual national champion Loyola-Chicago in the second round.

61 Braggin' Rights

The Illinois-Missouri basketball series reaches back to 1932 when the Illini posted a 36–24 victory in Columbia, and the neighboring state schools played each other seven times from that first matchup until 1955. The Illini head coach in 1932 was Craig Ruby, who was a former star and coach at Missouri.

Norm Stewart had coached the Tigers since 1967 while Lou Henson started in the 1975–76 season, and an agreement was made for the teams to begin playing the "Show-Me Classic" in December 1976 at Columbia and alternating home games, with the teams splitting the first four games.

To take the series a step farther, the schools agreed to split the difference in the travel and play in St. Louis at the Checkerdome (before the name changed to St. Louis Arena in 1984). Starting in 1994, the holiday treat has been played at the Enterprise Center, as thousands of fans from both schools split the arena with black and gold on one half, and orange and blue on the other half of the seating areas.

Since the date normally falls just before the Christmas holiday, and St. Louis is in easy driving distance of both schools, it remains one of the toughest tickets on the Illinois basketball schedule each season.

There have been some amazing performances from both teams, as well as some incredible finishes and several memorable fan interactions.

Two notable occurrences that included fans were after Quin Snyder's final series appearance as coach of the Tigers and during a performance by Chief Illiniwek at halftime.

In 2005, after Illinois posted an 82–50 drubbing on the Tigers, a Mizzou fan threw a full tub of popcorn on Snyder as he was exiting the arena floor.

As for the Chief Illiniwek incident in 2001, it started out as just a normal halftime of the Chief performing to "3-in-1" as he had done for decades. However, Matt Veronie, who was portraying the Chief that season, would experience something that had never happened before.

Veronie described what happened to the *Champaign News-Gazette* in 2014. During his performance, he glided toward the baseline when "out of the corner of my eye I could see it coming," he said. A man, wearing Missouri black, busted through a line of Illinois students and alums who had surrounded the court and tackled the Chief.

"He knocked me down hard, really stunned me," Veronie said. "I shoved him off me, popped up and said, 'All right, I might as well finish my dance,'" he said. "The place went crazy."

It all happened right in front of the Illini cheer squad, who jumped into action, giving the attacker the business and subduing him until security made it to the scene.

The inebriated Tiger fan was arrested and hauled off to jail, where he was found to be wanted on additional charges.

Heading into the 2024–25 season, Illinois leads the intense rivalry, 34–20, which includes a nine-game winning streak from 2000 through '08. During an eight-game winning streak in the series in the 1980s, Mizzou coach Stewart tried several different things to break up the string, including traveling the day of the game. He even tried to end the series, but the athletic directors at both schools recognized all the positives, including huge ticket sales, a presence in St. Louis, and excitement among fans of both teams.

Memorable finishes include the final game at the St. Louis Arena in 1993, when Illini star guard Kiwane Garris was fouled with no time remaining at the end of the second overtime. One of the greatest free throw shooters in Illinois history, making 83 percent from the line in his 116-game career, Garris missed 10 from the charity stripe that night, including two with no time remaining and the game tied at 97 at the end of the second overtime. Stewart, who figured the game was over with Garris at the line, had rushed to midcourt to complain to the officials, yet no technical foul was called. Despite the missed free throws, Garris scored 31 points that night in the 107–106 Mizzou victory.

In 1988, the Flyin' Illini trailed by 18 points at one point in the first half before battling back behind Kenny Battle and his teammates for an 87–84 Illinois victory. Battle led the way with 28 points, while Lowell Hamilton added 21, Kendall Gill scored 11, Nick Anderson followed with eight and 10 rebounds, and Marcus Liberty scored nine points.

The largest margin in the series came in 2005 when Dee Brown and James Augustine led the Illini to an 82–50 victory. Brown had 17 points, seven assists, and two steals, while Augustine added 12 points, eight rebounds, and three steals.

The breathtaking finish in the 2014 classic will always rank as one of the series' best. Illini guard Rayvonte Rice held the ball for the last shot, then hit a fadeaway three-pointer over two defenders as the final horn sounded for the last of his 19 points to give Illinois a thrilling 62–59 victory.

The series is an absolute must for Illini fans as there is no other game where the 22,000-seat arena is split nearly 50/50. No matter who is winning, more than 10,000 fans are screaming, making it one of the best atmospheres of any game on the schedule.

62 "Mr. Illini" Ray Eliot

There may never have been a more passionate Illini than former football coach Ray Eliot. He earned the "Mr. Illini" nickname for all the right reasons.

Born Raymond Eliot Nusspickel in New York City in 1905, he grew up in Brighton, Massachusetts, before establishing himself wearing No. 38 as a guard on Bob Zuppke's football teams of 1930 and 1931. He also lettered for the Illini baseball team.

Many families changed their surnames in the early to mid–20th century to avoid discrimination, and Ray began using his middle name of Eliot as his surname.

Following his graduation from the University of Illinois, Eliot became an assistant football coach and head baseball coach at Illinois College in Jacksonville during the 1932–33 academic year, then head coach of the Blueboys from 1934 to '36, compiling a record of 15–7–1. He coached the college's baseball team until 1937.

Zuppke and Illinois gave Eliot an opportunity to return to Champaign-Urbana in 1937 as the Fighting Illini line coach and Illinois' first head ice hockey coach. He was Zuppke's line coach the final five seasons of Zup's Illini coaching career and the hockey coach from the fall of 1937 to the spring of 1939, compiling a record of 3–11.

When Zuppke resigned as head football coach in 1941 after a 29-year career at Illinois, many of the nation's top coaches wanted the Illinois job. After nearly two and half months of searching for Zup's replacement, athletic director Doug Mills walked down the hallway at Huff Gym to Eliot's office and offered him the job. On January 12, 1942, Eliot was tabbed as his mentor's successor at a salary of $6,000 annually. It certainly wasn't an easy time to take over a collegiate football program as U.S. participation in World War II would soon start taking throngs of college-age men into military service.

Then, as the Illini entered the 1943 season with high expectations, several prominent players were ordered to report to other campuses for military training. So, Eliot lost Alex Agase, Tony Butkovich, Joe Buscemi, John Genis, Frank Bauman, Mike Kasap, and Art Dufelmeier. In all, more than 100 eligible athletes were called away between spring drills and the 1943 season as the team became known as "the Disappearing Illini."

Illinois won just three games that season, with its most unusual loss coming to rival Purdue, where many of Eliot's players were sent for training. Agase, Butkovich, Buscemi, Genis, Bauman, and Kasap all wore Boilermaker uniforms, with Agase and Butkovich eventually earning All-America status.

The Illini won the first of Eliot's three Big Ten titles that season and became the first Big Ten team to participate in the brand-new Rose Bowl agreement to pit the champions of the Big Ten and Pacific Coast Conference in the New Year's Day classic. Illinois rocked the Bruins, 45–14, in that milestone contest.

Eliot would lead his 1951 Illini squad back to the Rose Bowl, where they would defeat Stanford 40–7 and earn a piece of the mythical national championship with a 9–0–1 record, Illinois' first undefeated record since 1927. His 1953 team tied Michigan State for the Big Ten title, but the Spartans earned the trip to the Rose Bowl by vote of conference athletic directors.

After Eliot coached his final game in 1959, he was carried off the field by his players. He would move into an administrative role as an associate athletic director from 1960 to 1973, and as honorary associate athletic director from 1973 to 1980, including a stint as interim athletic director in 1979 prior to the introduction of Neale Stoner. Eliot would pass away in 1980.

Eliot would win 83 games and three Big Ten championships during his 18-year career at Illinois, but it was his ability to instill pride and belief in his players that stood out. The way he delivered speeches is legendary. Those who heard and knew him will always remember him as "Mr. Illini."

The passion exhibited in his speeches made him one of the most requested motivational speakers in the nation. Eliot's famous "Proper State of Mind" speech was given to hundreds of audiences around the state and nation and a recording can be found on YouTube or at FightingIllini.com.

63 1946 Football Champions and First Rose Bowl

Eliot won the first of his three Big Ten titles in 1946 after an influx of former soldiers returned to American college campuses and began participating once again in athletics. Eliot and his staff had more than 300 men show up for football tryouts prior to the 1946 season, many who were hardened by their time fighting a war.

Alex Agase returned with a Purple Heart. Art Dufelmeier came back 60 pounds lighter after spending 11 months in a German prison camp. Running back Tony Butkovich, killed in Okinawa in

1945, didn't come back at all. Yet insiders thought this might be the most powerful Illini football team in school history.

Former Illinois Sports Information Director Chuck Flynn recounted in the book *Hail to the Orange*: "The '46 team was a very difficult team for Ray to coach. In the first place, the majority of them now were married; they drank, they caroused, they carried on and they weren't used to the kind of discipline that going to college and observing training rules and so on required."

Some of the returning players were in their upper twenties and many had been shot at during the war. Returning to college life and football practice was not an easy transition.

The season didn't begin in a great way. Illinois started the '46 season with a 2–2 record that included wins over Pittsburgh and Purdue and losses to Notre Dame and Indiana. Losing to the powerful Johnny Lujack–led Irish was disappointing, but not nearly as much as the loss at Indiana two weeks later.

Eliot even offered to resign. Instead, though, he turned practice the following Monday into a long, and sometimes loud, gripe session that cleared the air and brought the team together.

The Fighting Illini then rolled to five straight conference victories, including wins over ranked squads from Wisconsin, Michigan, and Ohio State, to earn the Big Ten's first invite to play in the Rose Bowl in the brand-new agreement with the Pacific Coast Conference to match champions in the venerable bowl game.

The victory over Ohio State was Illinois' first over the Buckeyes since 1934, while the 20–0 shutout of Northwestern clinched the conference title.

Eliot needed something to help motivate the Illini, many of whom weren't crazy about spending four weeks and the holiday season in California, far away from wives and family. They spent several days riding the Illinois Central Railroad, west via New Orleans, thanks to UI Board of Trustees President Wayne

Johnston, who also happened to serve as president of the Illinois Central.

The long train trip got the team to Pasadena two days later than expected, and to make matters worse, it rained nearly every day until New Year's Day. Nor was the team pleased when the Rose Bowl Committee gave each player $5 and a box of dried fruit for Christmas. Trips to a Hollywood movie studio helped when the players rubbed elbows with Bob Hope and Big Crosby while watching them film one of their famous *Road* movies.

West Coast sportswriters were not supportive of the agreement with the Big Ten and wanted Army and California native Glenn Davis to play PCC champion UCLA on New Year's Day instead of the Illini, who were ranked fifth in the nation.

Eliot made sure each Illini football player had a copy of the local newspapers delivered to their hotel room each day as the sports section was filled with stories on what the Bruins would do to the underdog Illini.

The psychological ploy worked like a charm as the Illini rolled past UCLA by a 45–14 score with Buddy Young and Julie Rykovich each gaining 103 yards as Illinois outrushed UCLA 320–62. All-American guard and defensive lineman Agase beat up the Bruins' center so badly that, in the third quarter, the official asked him to take it easy.

Agase would earn consensus All-America honors in 1946 and is a member of the College Football Hall of Fame Class of 1963. He earned All-America honors at both Illinois and Purdue after spending the 1943 season in West Lafayette in military training.

Young would also earn induction into the College Football Hall of Fame.

64 Dr. Karol Kahrs, Title IX Pioneer and Leader

The United States Congress passed Title IX regulations in 1972, mandating equal opportunities for women and leading the way to major changes within collegiate athletics programs around the nation, including the University of Illinois.

At their May 1974 meeting, the UI Board of Trustees approved the Athletics Association's recommendation to add women's sports to the varsity athletics offerings. Just a few days later, athletic director Cecil Coleman hired Dr. Karol Kahrs from the UI physical education department to oversee Illinois' seven-sport women's program with an initial budget of $82,500 for the 1974–75 school year.

Interestingly, women were the first to form a basketball team on the UI campus in the 1890s, several years before the first men's team in 1905. Women's teams competed as club teams until becoming varsity sports in 1974. The women's track and field team, coached by Hall of Famer Dr. Nell Jackson, won the 1970 national championship.

Kahrs joined several colleagues around the nation as leaders within the Association for Intercollegiate Athletes for Women (AIAW) to coordinate national championships since women's sports were not competing under the NCAA governance.

In fact, it took until the 1981–82 season before the Big Ten Conference incorporated the women's programs with the existing men's programs.

Kahrs never backed down from a challenge and immediately went to work in hiring coaches and establishing competitive programs, including the addition of soccer and softball to the original offering of seven sports.

First Fighting Illini Women's Coaches

Basketball: Steve Douglas, 1974–75
Cross Country: Jessica Dragicevic, 1977–80
Golf: Betsy Kimpel, 1974–78
Gymnastics: Kim Musgrave, 1974–75
Soccer: Jillian Ellis, 1997–98
Softball: Terri Sullivan, 2000–15
Swimming and Diving: Jeanne Hultzen, 1974–75
Tennis: Peggy Pruitt, 1974–75
Track and Field: Jerry Mayhew, 1975
Volleyball: Kathleen Haywood, 1974–75

In 1988, Kahrs served as director of internal affairs for the Athletics Association, helping with its merger into the University in 1989 as the Division of Intercollegiate Athletics (DIA). In 1992 the National Association of College Women Athletic Administrators recognized Kahrs' contribution to intercollegiate athletics and named her NACWAA Administrator of the Year for District V. She served as the first chairperson of the Big Ten Women's Athletic Administrators from 1974 to '76 and was a member of the committee that submitted the initial proposal to add women's athletics to the conference in 1981. In 2014, Dr. Kahrs was given the Lifetime Achievement Award by NCAWAA and in 2006 was inducted into the National Association of Collegiate Directors of Athletics (NACDA) Hall of Fame.

The UI commemorated the 50th Anniversary of the Title IX legislation on September 9, 2022, with a summit on campus themed, "How it Started, How it's Going" that included panels, speakers, reunions, and incredible stories of how the initial varsity athletes had to overcome many challenges.

The keynote address was delivered by Sheila Johnson, Illinois alumna and successful businesswoman, whose accomplishments include co-founding Black Entertainment Television (BET), partner of three professional sports franchises, and business developments in hospitality and real estate.

A special tribute for Dr. Kahrs led off the luncheon for championing female student-athletes as her name was placed on the Dr. Karol Kahrs Hall of Fame Room at the Bielfeldt Athletics Administration Building.

65 Women's Basketball Resurgence

When Title IX opened the door for many collegiate women's sports programs to be elevated to varsity status in 1973, Karol Kahrs, who worked in the Physical Education department at the University of Illinois, was tabbed to hire coaches and get the teams organized.

Steve Douglas was an associate professor of political science in the spring of 1974 when Kahrs, who had taken the title of women's athletic director, chose him to be head coach of the inaugural Illini women's basketball team. He was paid $1,000 for the season. Douglas earned the women's coaching job for two primary reasons: He'd coached the women's national team in Malaysia, and he was team captain for Tex Winter's top-ranked Kansas State Wildcats, playing in the 1958, '59, and '60 seasons when K-State won three Big Eight championships and advanced to the 1958 NCAA Final Four.

His tenure as an Illini coach was always meant to be brief, and after two seasons Douglas handed the job off to full-time coach Carla Thompson before returning to his focus on Malaysian and Indonesian political studies.

The NCAA's 1981 vote to include women's sports under its governing structure basically ended the Association for Intercollegiate

Sports for Women (AIAW). Illinois earned a spot in the inaugural NCAA Women's Basketball Tournament in 1982 under Jane Schroeder after finishing second in the Big Ten and finished with a 21–9 record. Laura Golden led back-to-back squads to the tournament in 1986 and 1987, but the hiring of future Hall of Fame coach Theresa Grentz in 1995 set the stage for the best run in Illini women's basketball history.

Grentz was already the seventh-winningest women's basketball coach in NCAA history and had been the head coach for the 1992 U.S. Olympic Team when she was hired as Illini coach in 1995. She had been head coach at Rutgers for 20 seasons, leading the Lady Knights to the 1982 AIAW national championship and nine consecutive NCAA Tournament appearances from 1986 to 1994. As a player, she helped establish the first national power in women's collegiate basketball at Immaculata, where the Mighty Macs won 74 games and captured three consecutive national titles in 1972, 1973, and 1974.

In 1996–97, Grentz's second season at Illinois, she led the Fighting Illini to their first Big Ten women's basketball championship with a 24–8 mark and advanced to the NCAA Sweet Sixteen. The Illini followed up with another NCAA Sweet Sixteen appearance in 1998 as part of four consecutive NCAA Tournament appearances. Illini fan excitement reached such a level that the team outgrew Huff Gym and moved down Fourth Street to State Farm Center (then known as Assembly Hall).

After Grentz left Illinois in 2007, it was a long dry spell as the 2002–03 season would be the last NCAA Tourney appearance for nearly 20 years until Shauna Green did so in her first season in 2022–23.

Green made the move to Champaign-Urbana after a terrific run at Dayton, where her teams captured five Atlantic 10 regular season championships and qualified each season of her tenure for postseason play, including four appearances in the NCAA Tournament.

Year one at Illinois saw Green lead the program to new heights, finishing 22–10 overall and 11–7 in the always tough Big Ten before the team's first NCAA Tournament appearance in 20 seasons. It was the largest turnaround in program history after the 2022 team posted a 7–20 record.

The transfer backcourt of Makira Cook and Genesis Bryant earned a quick following of Illini fans as attendance skyrocketed to nearly 3,500 per game after being at 1,200 the season before. The swelling crowd really began to grow after knocking off eventual NCAA runner-up Iowa and their superstar Caitlin Clark, 90–86, in Champaign on January 1, 2023. The Illini jumped into the Top 25 for multiple weeks during the season and set the foundation for success moving forward. Four Illini underclassmen (Cook, Bryant, Kendall Bostic, and Adalia McKenzie) earned All-Big Ten recognition and returned for the 2023–24 season when the Illini were ranked in the Top 25 to start the year. The popularity of Illini home games has grown quickly with season ticket sales showing a significant increase.

66 Edwardsville Duo Breaks Barriers

When discussing their Illini basketball legacies, one cannot separate Govoner Vaughn and Mannie Jackson as their names will always be connected from their time as stars at Edwardsville High School then at the University of Illinois.

Growing up together in Edwardsville, they got their first taste of Huff Gym as high school sophomores when their high school team earned a trip to the state basketball tournament, where they finished fourth.

Two years later in 1956, the senior duo led Edwardsville all the way to the championship game before falling to West Rockford when the two combined for 49 of their team's 65 points.

"Right after the championship game and presentation of the trophies, Coach Combes and Coach Braun ushered Mannie and I along with our former high school teammate Don Ohl into his office," remembered Vaughn in *A Century of Orange and Blue*.

"They said they would like to offer us a four-year athletic scholarship to Illinois, and I was just amazed," Vaughn said.

In a time of change sweeping across college athletics, Braun and Combes were aware no Black athlete had lettered in Illinois basketball, and they were willing to take a chance on Vaughn and Jackson.

Walt Moore had been the first Black player on the Illinois basketball roster and on the court in a 1952 contest against North Carolina, but his stay in Champaign was short-lived as he left the university at the semester break because of grade issues. After a stint with the military, Moore would return to school at Western Illinois, where he would become a Hall of Fame athlete as one of the school's all-time greats.

Vaughn and Jackson would be the trailblazers for Illinois basketball, but the trail would not be smooth. They faced intense pressure to succeed and racial prejudice on the road. One place their race was never an issue was with their teammates, and it didn't take long for the players to blend right in.

"Mannie and Gov were the type of guys you wanted to have on your team," said guard Lou Landt. "They were really humble and always conducted themselves in a first-class way."

At just 6'3", Vaughn played most of his Illini career as a center, matching up with opposing big men like Indiana's Walt Bellamy and Ohio State's Jerry Lucas.

Jackson was a quick 6'2" guard known for his leaping ability and shooting touch.

"Mannie Jackson was like Doctor J before there was a Doctor J," said sportswriter Bill Lyon, who covered the Illini in those years for *The News-Gazette*. "He just floated through the air, tucked his legs up under him, and shot a jump shot that was unstoppable."

Traveling and hotel accommodations in those days were not easy for Black players, and it was never more evident than on a road trip to Kentucky in 1958. While trying to attend a movie with White teammates the night before the game, Vaughn and Jackson were denied entrance because of their skin color.

The next day during the game, both were heckled from the crowd, and when Jackson fouled out near the end of the game, the band played "Bye Bye Blackbird."

Vaughn received a more overt threat after missing a 25-foot shot at the buzzer that would have won the game for Illinois.

"As we were leaving the court, two White guys were standing nearby and one of them said, 'Hey, boy, it's a good thing you missed, or we'd have cut off your ears and send them back to your folks up north.' Believe me, I was glad to get back home," Vaughn said.

Their story didn't end following their final collegiate game in 1960. Vaughn would earn team MVP honors and scored 1,001 points for his career. Jackson was team captain as a senior and finished with 922 points. Both still rank among the top 60 scorers in Illinois basketball history.

Both played for the Harlem Globetrotters after graduating from Illinois before going their separate ways in the business world. Jackson would purchase the Globetrotters in 1993 and hired Vaughn to be director of alumni relations.

For their trailblazing efforts and excellence as Fighting Illini, both players have their jersey banners hanging from the rafters of State Farm Center. They grew up together, played high school basketball together, broke the color barrier at Illinois together, and years later continued to work with each other.

Vaughn and Jackson were the first two Black players to start a game for Illinois and letter for the Illini, and Jackson was the first Black team captain. The two were more like brothers than just teammates and their names will be linked forever at Illinois.

67 The Wright Family— Four-Generation Illini

When John Paddock made the move from Ball State to Illinois prior to the 2023–24 school year, he joined a family legacy unmatched in Fighting Illini history.

He joined great-grandfather Robert Wright, grandfather John Wright Sr., and uncle John Wright II to form four generations of Fighting Illini football players.

Robert lettered as an end for Bob Zuppke in 1935 and was a member of the varsity team during the 1934 season. John Sr. became the leading pass receiver in Illinois history during his career in 1965, 1966, and 1967. John II lettered as a wide receiver from 1990 to '92. And, most recently, Paddock earned a spot in Illini football lore after leading the Illini to victory at Minnesota on November 4, 2023, in his most meaningful playing time as quarterback for the Orange and Blue.

Robert lettered in football and track at Illinois prior to his graduation in 1936. He ran hurdles and relays in track and played end and halfback for the football team. He was a member of the 480-yard shuttle hurdle relay team that won the Drake Relay title in 1936, setting a record. In the 1936 Big Ten meet, he was third behind world record holder Jesse Owens of Ohio State.

After college, Robert became one of the nation's most successful track coaches during a 38-year career at the high school and collegiate levels. In 19 years at Oak Park-River Forest High School, he led his track teams to 14 suburban league championships and finished in the top five at the state meet nine times, including the 1947 state championship.

His final nine years of coaching came at Illinois, where he produced eight Big Ten champions and had 23 other athletes place in the championship meet before retiring in 1974.

John Sr. played split end for the Illini and set Big Ten and Illinois records of 159 catches for 2,284 yards, more than twice the previous UI record totals of Rex Smith (70 catches) and John "Rocky" Ryan (1,041 yards). He was named Second-Team All-Big Ten as a junior and First-Team All-Big Ten as a senior in 1967. He also lettered twice in track as a hurdler. Academically, John Sr. earned even more honors, including Academic All-America recognition in 1966.

After college, John Sr. played for the NFL's Detroit Lions but had his career cut short in his third season by an injury.

John II joined the Fighting Illini program under John Mackovic before finishing it with Lou Tepper as head coach. In two bowl game performances, Wright had nine catches for 94 yards in the 1991 John Hancock Bowl against UCLA and seven catches for 82 yards and two touchdowns in the 1992 Holiday Bowl against Hawaii. He was a team captain of the 1992 squad.

In 1992, Illinois made the claim of having both a father and a son earn First-Team Academic Football All-America honors. When John II was honored with that distinction, he joined his father, John Sr., who was a 1966 recipient. John Sr. was also a three-time Academic All-Big Ten honoree, while John II was honored in the same way four times.

John Paddock, whose mother, Ashley, is John Sr.'s daughter and John II's brother, began his career at Ball State, where he started all 12 games in 2022 while throwing for 2,719 yards and 18 touchdowns.

Paddock established a special spot in the hearts of Illini fans when he entered the 2023 Minnesota game at Minneapolis for the first time with 1:25 remaining and facing a fourth-and-11 from the Gopher 15-yard line and Illinois trailing by five points. He needed just 35 seconds to drive the Illini 85 yards on three straight completions, including a 46-yard game-winning touchdown throw to Isaiah Williams to give Illinois a stunning 27–26 victory. Paddock finished the game 3-for-3 passing for 85 yards, and a 448.0 passer rating in one of the most stirring performances by an Illini backup quarterback in program history.

The legacy got even better the following week when Paddock threw for 507 yards and four touchdowns in a 48–45 Fighting Illini overtime victory against Indiana on November 11, 2023. The 507 yards was a Memorial Stadium record and second-most in Illini history behind Dave Wilson's 621 yards against Ohio State in 1980.

This amazing quartet is the first four-generation family in Fighting Illini history, with each member making a major contribution to success on the field.

68 The Football Law Firm of Newton and Randolph

The list of great defensive tackles at Illinois is impressive with two College Football Hall of Famers in Alex Agase and Morris "Moe" Gardner, and another Big Ten Silver Football Award winner in Don Thorp, but the pair of Jer'Zhan "Johnny" Newton and Keith Randolph in the 2022 and 2023 seasons is as good a tandem as Illinois fans may have seen.

Nicknamed "the Law Firm," Newton and Randolph earned national attention in 2022 when the Fighting Illini defense ranked among the nation's best.

As a junior, Newton was a Second-Team All-America selection by the Walter Camp Foundation and Associated Press, while being named First-Team All-Big Ten. Randolph earned Third-Team All-Big Ten honors as a junior in 2022. Both were named preseason All-Americans by multiple outlets prior to the 2023 season, and Newton was Illinois' first-ever Preseason Associated Press All-American.

Newton led the nation in quarterback hits (19) and ranked sixth in quarterback pressures (54) in 2022. Combined, the Law Firm led the nation in tackles-for-loss (27.0) and QB pressures (81) among defensive-line duos in 2022. The two were second and third in the Big Ten in TFLs (14.0 and 13.0, respectively) to rank first and second among interior defensive lineman in 2022.

A native of Clearwater, Florida, Newton was signed by the Illini by coach Lovie Smith after flipping from an earlier commitment to Maryland. He was ranked as the 1,063rd player in the nation. On the 2024 NFL Draft Board, he was ranked much higher … like Top 10.

"I never took it to heart," Newton said in a media interview. "I've always been the underdog because of my size. But I knew I had to be better than a lot of those guys."

After his outstanding junior season, he considered entering his name into the NFL Draft, but didn't see it listed in the top two rounds by the mock drafts and returned for his senior season determined to barge his way into the first round.

He did just that while earning consensus All-America honors after being named the Big Ten Defensive Player of the Year.

"I've been around some great ones, some first-round draft picks," Illini head coach Bret Bielema said during the 2023 season. "For me, at the interior defensive tackles position in college, he's by far the best player I've been around. Last year, I knew he was a really good player and when Johnny decided to come back, he wanted to come back with the idea that he was going to play as good as he possibly could and put a one [first round] on his back for draft day."

As the other half of the Law Firm, Randolph has done more than establish himself as one of the best to wear the Orange and Blue at the position.

A native of Belleville, Illinois, he helped Belleville West win a pair of Illinois state basketball titles, teaming with future pro basketball player E.J. Liddell to form one of the best high school basketball front courts in state history.

Prior to his junior year in high school, he had never played football, but his family pleaded for him to try it, and Randolph gave it a shot.

Turned out to be a pretty good move. Randolph became a highly sought-after recruit and an All-State high school player who eventually chose the Illini over multiple other Power Five offers.

Randolph was a key in-state recruit for Illinois and his strong play played a key role in helping the Illini defense rank among the nation's best in several categories as a junior. He had a chance to leave early as well but knew there was an opportunity to put himself in a much better draft position by returning for his senior season.

He finished the 2022 season with career highs in nearly every statistical category, including games played (13), tackles (53), tackles for loss (13), and sacks (4.5), while earning All-Big Ten honors.

"When you're getting guys drafted over and over again, how can you say no to that?" Randolph said before his senior season in 2023. "And especially for in-state guys, this is your home."

Returning for his fifth season at Illinois allowed Randolph to be voted a team captain and earn a spot on nearly every possible award watch list for a defensive lineman.

"I want to leave a legacy here," Randolph said. "I want to be able to come back in 20–30 years and people know who I am. I want to leave the school in a better place than I found it. That was my plan. That was my goal, and I feel like I've done that."

69 New Sheriff in Town

In 1985, as Illinois football coach Mike White was finishing his six-year run with California quarterbacks calling the signals for the Illini, the nation's No. 1 prep quarterback was just two hours east at Indianapolis Warren Central High School.

Jeff George was recruited by every heavyweight college in the nation after receiving the Dial Award for the national high school scholar-athlete of the year and was the first Gatorade National Player of the Year.

Out of high school, George made the decision to stay close to home at Purdue to play for the Boilermakers. When coach Leon Burtnett was let go after George's first year and was replaced by Fred Akers, who favored a run-heavy offense, Jeff made the decision to transfer.

After first committing to Miami and Jimmy Johnson, George made a late change and made the quick drive to Champaign-Urbana to play for White and follow the Illini QB lineage of David Wilson, Tony Eason, and Jack Trudeau. He would even pay his own way as rules at the time limited transfers within the Big Ten to non-scholarship status and sit out a year in residence.

It took one practice for his teammates to witness his rifle arm. It also took that first day for someone to mention that a new sheriff was in town. His nickname of "the Sheriff" was established.

Things almost went sideways after the 1987 season George sat out. White was removed as coach after a recruiting infraction.

Illinois athletic director Neale Stoner knew the reputation White had built as Illinois being a passing program and he knew the Illini had a superstar at the quarterback position. He quickly dipped into the NFL coaching ranks and hired John Mackovic, who had just led the Kansas City Chiefs to a playoff appearance and had the reputation as an offensive-minded coach.

George took the field as the starter in 1988 and led the Illini to a 6–5–1 record and All-American Bowl appearance against Emmitt Smith and the Florida Gators, Illinois' first bowl appearance since 1985. Included in the 1988 season was an amazing comeback victory against Indiana when George engineered two touchdown drives in the final three minutes.

After trailing 20–9, George led the Illini 80 yards in 1:27, culminating with a fourth-down, 21-yard TD pass to Shawn Wax. Moments later, cornerback Chris Green met IU quarterback Dave Schnell head on at the 30-yard line, popping the ball into the air, where it was grabbed by Illini linebacker Julyon Brown. George took full advantage and floated a five-yard touchdown pass to Mike Bellamy in the final seconds for an amazing 21–20 Illinois victory.

George and his team returned in 1989 with a Big Ten championship and the Rose Bowl as the goal. After opening with another incredible comeback win at Southern California, an amazing come-from-behind win at Michigan State, and a six-game winning streak, the Illini found themselves in position for the conference crown in mid-November against powerful Michigan. The 24–10 loss to the Wolverines dampened Rose Bowl hopes but wins against Indiana and Northwestern gave the Illini a 9–2 record and earned the team an invitation to the New Year's Day Citrus Bowl against Virginia.

Illinois handled business against the Cavaliers by the score of 31–21, with George having one of his best games with 321 yards and three touchdown passes. After leading Illinois to a 10–2 mark, George had a major life decision in front of him as word from the NFL had him near the top of the draft board.

After studying the options and some of the best workouts many NFL scouts ever saw, on March 20, 1990, George made the emotional decision to enter his name into the NFL Draft.

"The decision to stay at the U of I for one more year or to enter the 1990 NFL Draft was a very complicated decision," George said that day. "There were many factors to consider … I considered heavily some personal goals that I have, also the national championship, the Rose Bowl, and winning the Heisman Trophy. Another factor considered was finances. I also considered the potential wage scale for rookies in the NFL in the future. I have decided that it is in my best interest to forego my last year of eligibility as the University of Illinois and petition the NFL to enter the 1990 Draft."

And with that, the decision was made. Just over a month later, on April 22, the Indianapolis Colts selected George as the No. 1 pick in the 1990 Draft, the highest pick in Illinois football history. He would sign a $15 million contract.

During his 14-year NFL career, George played with seven different teams and completed 2,298 passes for 27,602 yards and 154 touchdowns.

70 Victory to Vandalism … Memorial Stadium Turf Fire

In September 1989, the Fighting Illini football team had already experienced a roller coaster of emotions. After having the Glasnost Bowl game against Southern California in Moscow, USSR, canceled because of major logistics issues before a terrific comeback win over the Trojans at the Coliseum to open the season, the Illini were knocked around at Colorado by the score of 38–7.

The Fighting Illini returned to Memorial Stadium the next week and took out any frustrations on Utah State by the score of 41–2 in Illinois' first home game of the season. For a bit, it also looked like it might be the last for a while.

Overnight after the Utah State game, a few vandals broke into the stadium and attempted to burn some words into the Zuppke Field artificial surface. However, a strong breeze took a small flame at around the north 10-yard line and spread the fire across midfield, burning an area 20 to 40 feet wide at its biggest point.

One break was that the next game against Ohio State, scheduled for national television, was two weeks away. But the burned area of the field could not be repaired. The entire surface from goal line to goal line would need to be replaced.

Astroturf Industries, the installer of the surface, was called to Champaign on short notice to survey the damage and help UI officials come up with a plan. The task of replacing an entire field on such short notice would be a tall order, but one that all parties took on.

Many discussions were held on alternatives, including possibly moving the Ohio State game to West Lafayette since it was the closest large stadium to Champaign and the Boilermakers didn't have a home game conflict.

Work on replacement started almost immediately, with the luck of good weather helping the process. In a time when turf only came in green, all the lines and any graphics on the field needed to be painted.

The midfield graphic was a large Chief logo that was very complicated to paint. Once the field was installed and the lines had been painted, the artist began work on the logo. The cool evenings in early October were not ideal for quick drying and a tent with fans and heaters was constructed over the midfield area to help with drying.

An intense Friday night of finishing touches allowed for the game to be played in front of a home crowd of 69,088. Five

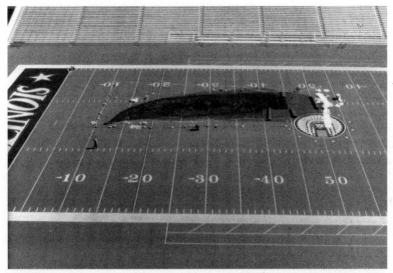

Vandals broke into Memorial Stadium overnight following a game in late September 1989, and started a fire that quickly spread from the 11-yard line to nearly midfield. The entire field from goal line to goal line was replaced over 12 days in time for the next game on October 7.

minutes into the game, quarterback Jeff George didn't get up after a sack by Ohio State's Aaron Spellman. Redshirt freshman Jason Verduzco entered the game and completed nine of 14 passes for 126 yards while leading the Illini on two scoring drives that gave Illinois a 10–7 lead at half.

George returned for the second half and completed 12 of 20 passes for 130 yards while Howard Griffith ran for 117 yards in a 34–14 Fighting Illini victory.

The real heroes during that two-week period, though, were the AstroTurf installers who replaced the entire field in around 12 days.

One of the more humorous moments during the incident came a few days after the fire when representatives of the surface manufacturer participated in a press conference to try and explain what happened.

After initially stating that barrels of accelerant would have been required to burn such a large area, a demonstration on a small piece of turf went awry when, after applying a small amount of lighter fluid, the sample piece burst into flames.

Two weeks after the fire, two members of the Illinois fencing team and a third student were arrested for the arson that caused nearly $600,000 in damage after using lighter fluid to burn the word "foo" into the turf.

71 The Williams Bros.

When Mike White was named the Illinois football coach in 1980, he made it clear he was bringing the West Coast passing game with him to the Midwest. He started by recruiting California quarterbacks David Wilson, Tony Eason, and Jack Trudeau.

But to incorporate a passing game, you also need players to catch all the passes, and one family combined for more catches than any other in Illinois history.

Oldest sibling Oliver Williams was one of Tony Eason's top targets in 1981 and 1982 after starting his collegiate career at Los Angeles Harbor College. After the transfer to Illinois, Oliver earned Second-Team All-Big Ten honors when he caught 38 passes for 760 yards and six touchdowns in 1981, followed by 35 receptions for 523 yards and six more TDs in 1982.

Oliver helped lead the 1982 squad to the Liberty Bowl against Alabama, the Illini's first bowl appearance since 1963. He was selected by the Chicago Bears in the 12th round of the 1983 NFL Draft and spent his rookie season on the injured list. After spending various amounts of time with the USFL Chicago Blitz, the St. Louis Cardinals, and USFL San Antonio Gunslingers, he signed with the Indianapolis Colts in 1985. Oliver would play in the final eight games that season, catching nine passes for 175 yards and one touchdown. He played three more games with the Colts in 1986 before joining the Houston Oilers during the NFL players' strike the following season. He had 11 receptions for 165 yards and one touchdown in three games.

David Williams followed Oliver at both L.A. Harbor College and Illinois, playing one season at the junior college before becoming a three-year star for the Fighting Illini.

As a sophomore in 1983, he joined with classmate Trudeau to form the most productive QB/WR duo in Illini history. Illinois posted one of the best seasons in school and Big Ten history in 1983 by becoming the only team in conference history to defeat all other league schools in the same year with a perfect 9–0 record. As Big Ten champions that season, the fourth-ranked Illini advanced to play UCLA in the Rose Bowl.

David caught 69 passes for 958 yards with six touchdowns and will always be remembered for his clinching touchdown catch while diving into the south end zone at Memorial Stadium in the key 16–6 victory over Michigan in late October of 1983.

David became the first Big Ten player, and second NCAA receiver, to top 100 catches in a season in 1984. His 101 receptions and 1,278 reception yards still rank atop the Illinois single season charts as he became an unstoppable force.

As a senior, David caught 92 passes, which is still second best in school history, for 1,156 yards, which is third most. He ended his career with a school-record 292 catches, 3,392 reception yards, and 24 career touchdowns, while his 16 catches at Purdue in 1985 remains the Illini standard for single-game receptions.

David was a two-time consensus First-Team All-American and First-Team All-Big Ten pick after earning Second-Team All-Big Ten honors as a sophomore. He was inducted into the College Football Hall of Fame in 2005 and the University of Illinois Athletics Hall of Fame in 2019.

After being drafted in the third round of the 1986 NFL Draft by the Chicago Bears, he ended up playing for the Tampa Bay Buccaneers in 1986 and the Los Angeles Raiders in 1987.

But it was the Canadian Football League where David's pro career would really shine. He played seven seasons in the CFL, winning the league's Outstanding Player Award in 1988, and was inducted into the Canadian Football Hall of Fame in 2019.

Steven Williams came along and joined the family legacy in 1985, playing one season with David before lettering the next three seasons and leading the Illini wide receivers with 38 catches for 523 yards as a senior when he was named Second-Team All-Big Ten. Steve ended his Illini career with 52 catches for 657 yards and two touchdowns.

As a trio, the Williams brothers combined for 437 receptions, 6,018 reception yards, and 45 touchdowns over 10 combined seasons in the 1980s.

72 2001 Big Ten Champs ... and the Sugar Bowl

In 1999, Ron Turner's third year as head coach, his team made a big jump by winning eight games, including five wins in the final six games of the season. Included in that stretch was an incredible 35–29 comeback win at Michigan and a 46–20 victory at Ohio State. The capper was a 63–21 rout of Virginia in the MicronPC. com Bowl in Miami.

Led by sophomore quarterback Kurt Kittner, a productive receiving corps, and a developing offensive line, the future looked very positive as pieces were in place at many of the key positions.

The 2000 season, however, didn't play out to expectations. The 19th-ranked Illini opened that season with three straight wins and were in position to host ESPN's *College GameDay* on September 23 for the Michigan game, except the third-ranked Wolverines lost 23–20 at UCLA the week prior and producers took the show elsewhere.

Events in that Michigan game would lead to a major change in collegiate football policies after two backward officiating calls that involved turnovers on fumbles, with both going against the Fighting Illini. Official reviews were already in place at the NFL level, but the game-changing misses in this game strongly shoved the Big Ten to move forward with reviews in the college game.

The Illini limped home that year by winning only two of the final eight games, with four of the losses coming by four points. Injuries added to the challenges faced that season when the Illini finished 5–6.

Despite the tough finish, the Illini entered the 2001 season confident that talent and experience at key positions would put them in position for success. After opening with three non-conference wins, Illinois lost the Big Ten opener at Michigan on September 29. The Illini would catch fire by sweeping to seven straight wins in October and November and clinch the outright Big Ten championship with a 7–1 conference record and No. 10 national ranking.

One by one, Illinois defeated Minnesota, Indiana, Wisconsin, 15th-ranked Purdue, Penn State, 25th-ranked Ohio State, and Northwestern. Two days after an exciting 34–28 victory over Northwestern on Thanksgiving Day at Memorial Stadium to clinch a share of the title, the Illini got some help from Ohio State when the Buckeyes defeated the Wolverines in Ann Arbor. The OSU victory gave Illinois its first outright Big Ten title since 1983.

Kittner passed for 3,256 yards and a school-record 27 touchdowns and was protected by the offensive line of All-Big Ten

First-Teamers Tony Pashos (tackle), Jay Kaluga (guard), and center Luke Butkus. Future longtime pro receiver Brandon Lloyd caught 10 touchdown passes. Stars on the defensive side of the ball included linebacker Jerry Schumacher, lineman Brandon Moore, cornerbacks Eugene Wilson and Christian Morton, and safety Bobby Jackson.

The Big Ten title meant Illinois would be playing in the Bowl Championship Series for the first time, but not necessarily where the traditional conference champion would normally go. Since the Rose Bowl was scheduled to host the BCS Championship game (Miami vs. Nebraska), Illinois was sent to the 2002 Sugar Bowl to play LSU in New Orleans on New Year's Day. Despite tens of thousands of Illini fans descending on the Big Easy, the game was as close to a home game for LSU as if it were in nearby Baton Rouge. The Tigers jumped out early and held on to a 47–34 win over the Illini.

The Fighting Illini finished with a 10–2 record and No. 12 national ranking.

A monumental event in 2001 changed life for everyone in the United States when the 9/11 terrorist attacks turned everyone's attention to the events in New York City, Washington D.C., and Pennsylvania. The Illini were originally scheduled to play Louisville just four days later on September 15, but the sports world shut down for nearly a week to allow for a reset. Instead of a football game at Memorial Stadium that day, the campus hosted a patriotic community gathering in remembrance for those who had lost their lives earlier that week.

Since both Illinois and Louisville had a bye week scheduled for September 22, the game was moved back a week and the 11:00 a.m. kickoff was the first college football game to start play after that fateful day.

73 The Juice Williams Drive to Defeat No. 1 Ohio State

Illinois was having a fine season in 2007 during Ron Zook's third year as head coach of the Fighting Illini program, especially after combining for a 4–19 record in his first two seasons in Champaign.

The Illini lost a 40–34 heartbreaker to Missouri in St. Louis in the opener when backup quarterback Eddie McGee was intercepted at the 1-yard line inside a minute to play after mounting a huge comeback in the second half. But after that setback, Illinois ran off five straight wins including two monumental wins over No. 21 Penn State and fifth-ranked Wisconsin in back-to-back Saturdays at Memorial Stadium.

Zook next took his team into a showdown at Iowa City against the Hawkeyes in what would be a low-scoring slugfest. A couple of fortuitous penalties helped Iowa to the 10–6 win that day. The first came when the Hawkeyes were called for an illegal formation on third-and-2 when running back Albert Young was stopped short of the first down. Rather than forcing Iowa to make a decision to go for it on fourth down or punt, Illinois took the penalty to repeat the down. Given a second chance, the Hawkeyes completed a 20-yard touchdown pass to give them the 10–6 lead.

With 8:51 remaining, McGee found an open Joe Morgan for an apparent 82-yard touchdown pass, but the Illini were flagged for an ineligible receiver downfield and eventually had to punt. With less than 90 seconds remaining in the game, McGee was intercepted at the Iowa goal line to seal the Hawkeye victory.

Another loss the following week to Michigan moved the Illini to 3–2 in league play and seemed to stifle any momentum the team had built during the Penn State and Wisconsin victories. But the Illini bounced back with wins over Ball State and Minnesota to improve to 4–2 in Big Ten play before traveling to Columbus for a showdown against undefeated and top-ranked Ohio State.

The Buckeyes were eyeing a shot at the BCS Championship game and were heavy favorites despite Illinois winning two of the previous three games in Columbus.

But there are reasons they play the games, as the favorites don't always win. This was one of those.

The stingy Ohio State defense had held their previous 10 opponents to two touchdowns or less, including only five total touchdown passes. Illini sophomore quarterback Juice Williams wasn't going to be intimidated, though. Using an effective running game, including 106 yards by Daniel Dufrene, 88 yards by Rashard Mendenhall, and 70 by himself to set up Illinois' passing game, Williams tossed touchdown passes to Michael Hoomanawanui, Jacob Willis, Brian Gamble, and Marques Wilkins.

The "Legend of Juice Williams" was really built on the last drive of the game. There was no trickery. There was no sleight-of-hand. It was just good, physical, pound-it-at-you Big Ten football.

With Illinois leading 28–21 and Ohio State driving to possibly tie the score, Marcus Thomas intercepted a deep pass by Buckeye quarterback Todd Boeckman to give the Illini the ball at the OSU 18-yard line with 8:09 remaining. Thomas was subbing for injured star cornerback Vontae Davis.

The 16-play drive that followed is the stuff of legends. The first series left Illinois in a fourth-and-1 and probable punt. That is, until Buckeye coach Jim Tressel called timeout and allowed Williams to plead his case to Zook for going for it at the OSU 33-yard line. Zook looked Williams in the eye and said, "You'd better get it," or something close to that.

Williams plowed two yards for the first down and kept the drive alive. From there, Williams and Mendenhall methodically crushed any Buckeye hopes for victory. Illinois ran out the clock, literally, by converting three third downs with a combination of runs.

Williams rushed six times for 32 yards, but three of the runs converted third downs into Illini first downs and kept the sticks moving, and clock running. Once they were out of timeouts, the Buckeyes could do nothing but watch the seconds disappear from the game clock.

The drive was only 42 yards, and no points were scored, but the 16 plays took the entire 8:09 off the clock and a wild Illini celebration on the field ensued after one of the greatest wins in Illinois football history. It was the Fighting Illini's first win over a No. 1–ranked team since 1956.

A win over Northwestern in the regular season finale on November 17 moved Illinois into a second-place tie and into a two-week waiting period to see how the bowl situation would play out. The Illini were ranked 17th in the BCS, needing to move to at least 14th for consideration for a BCS bowl opportunity.

But sometimes crazy things happen.

The Illini needed help from conference favorites Ohio State and Hawaii to get out of the way. After sitting out a week once the Big Ten season was over, Illinois moved to No. 15 in the BCS standings. Illini eyes were watching No. 1 Missouri against No. 9 Oklahoma and No. 2 West Virginia against Pitt. LSU and Kansas had been No. 1 and 2 the week before, but both lost to Arkansas and Missouri, respectively, moving Ohio State to No. 3. A move by the Buckeyes into the national championship game would give Illinois a path to the Rose Bowl.

There were eight games on the final day of the season with a potential effect on the final BCS pairings. If the Illini didn't jump into the Rose Bowl picture, it was likely the Capital One Citrus Bowl or the Champs Sports Bowl, both in Orlando.

With both Missouri and West Virginia losing their final games, the Buckeyes and LSU were elevated into the BCS Championship game, and the Illini moved to No. 13.

It was now time to wait and see what the Rose Bowl would do with the first pick of the BCS bowls.

As everyone around the Illini program anxiously awaited the bowl invite, it became very clear as soon as Zook walked into the team meeting room with a rose in his hand. A huge roar ensued. The Fighting Illini were headed to Pasadena for the first time since 1983.

"We were all in there for a while and Coach Zook walked in with a rose and everyone was like, 'What is he doing?' Then we all started celebrating," All-America linebacker J. Leman said. "The company line before today was that we were happy with any bowl game, but we are just ecstatic about going to the Rose Bowl."

Senior All-American offensive lineman Martin O'Donnell showed up a little late and walked into the room to see his teammates with roses in their hands.

"What a way to come full circle," he said. "We go 1–11 in our first year here, barely beating a I-AA team at home, through a lot of bad seasons with no bowl games before this year, and now we finish with the Rose Bowl."

74 From Rags to Rose Bowl and the Kennedy Assassination Game

To understand the significance of the biggest game of the 1963 regular season, one needs to know how the Fighting Illini got there.

The legendary Ray Eliot had retired from coaching after the 1959 season. Three days before Christmas, UI President David Henry announced that 33-year-old University of California coach Pete Elliott would become the youngest coach in the Big Ten.

Eliot had left some talent on the field including quarterback John Easterbrook, fullback-linebackers Bill and Jim Brown, end Ed O'Bradovich, and tackle Joe Rutgens, who would earn All-American recognition. The lack of talented underclassmen would be felt down the road, though, when Elliott started spring drills in 1961 with only 14 lettermen, with three of them leaving the team before the fall.

A losing streak reached 15 games from the final game of 1960 until a 14–10 upset over Purdue in 1962. That victory gave a talented corps of young players a boost of confidence. One of those players, Dick Butkus, was already establishing himself as one of the Big Ten's premier players during his sophomore season.

After the Purdue upset, Illinois lost two more games before upsetting Michigan State, 7–6, in the season finale to provide a springboard into 1963.

Butkus was one of 26 returning lettermen, and the bruising center-linebacker had caught the national media's eye as a star.

"Before he's through," Elliott prophetically said in 1963, "He'll be the greatest linebacker anybody ever saw."

Butkus and future pro Don Hansen made a fearsome linebacking duo. Tackle Archie Sutton anchored the line. On the offensive side of the ball, Elliott leaned on several sophomores including quarterback Fred Custardo, quick halfback Sam Price, and fullback Jim Grabowski. The team would be molded around a rough and solid defense and a conservative offense.

The Illini opened with a 10–0 victory over California and all-star quarterback Craig Morton, who tossed three interceptions in the game.

Fourth-ranked Northwestern, who were Big Ten favorites, were next. In what was called one of the greatest hitting contests at Memorial Stadium, Butkus totaled four quarterback sacks, forced a fumble, and was credited with seven solo tackles and 12 assists in a 10–9 Illini victory. A 20–20 tie at Ohio State moved the Illini into the Top 10 as Illinois would improve to 5–0–1 before a 14–8 loss to Michigan that dropped the Illini into third place behind Michigan State and Ohio State.

Illinois came back to beat Wisconsin while Ohio State lost to Northwestern to set up a season-ending showdown in East Lansing with fourth-ranked Michigan State. The winner would represent the Big Ten at the Rose Bowl.

On Friday, November 22, 1963, shortly after noon, the Illini team and travel party boarded a charter flight at Willard Airport just like a normal road trip. Upon their arrival around 90 minutes later in Lansing, Michigan, the team was apprised of President John F. Kennedy's assassination in Dallas, Texas.

"Hearing about President Kennedy was a deep, emotional blow to all our players," Elliott recalled in author Lon Eubanks' book *The Fighting Illini*. "I can't think of anything that would even be comparable."

Discussions between campus leaders initially led to an agreement to play the game as scheduled on Saturday. However, as information and emotions became more clear, political pressure eventually moved the game to the following Thursday, Thanksgiving Day.

As Illinois players were getting taped for the game at their hotel, word was shared that they would be returning to Champaign.

The game matched Michigan State's "80 yards and a cloud of dust" offense—a reference to MSU's ground attack led by All-America halfback Sherman Lewis—against a strong Illini defense that hadn't allowed any team that season to score more than 21 points.

Butkus set the tone on MSU's first play from scrimmage when he smothered Lewis behind the line of scrimmage for a loss. It would be that type of day for the Spartan star, who gained just 58 yards on 13 carries. The Illini defense had seven takeaways during the game with four interceptions and three fumble recoveries in a 13–0 shutout victory.

Newspaper headlines shouted "Illini Go From Rags to Roses" after the whitewash and Illinois would be making its first trip to Pasadena since the 1951 season.

The Fighting Illini used the same style of rock 'em' sock 'em football to defeat Washington 17–7 in the Rose Bowl game. Grabowski joined fullbacks Julius Rykovich and Bill Tate as Rose Bowl MVPs.

75 Illini Media Coverage

Since the very early days of University of Illinois varsity athletics, media coverage of Fighting Illini sporting events has been a critical part of keeping fans informed about their favorite teams.

Illinois boasted the very first full-time athletics publicity director when Michael Tobin took the position in 1922, just as Harold "Red" Grange was entering school as a freshman. There have only been 10 people in that position from Tobin through Derrick Burson, the present-day sports information director.

Newspapers ruled the media world for decades as sportswriters became the conduit between the players and coaches and their readers. How games, players, and coaches were portrayed by the mostly men who covered the contests was just about the only way information was shared until radio and television started to proliferate the airwaves.

Some of the nation's most well-known reporters and announcers have covered Fighting Illini games and events. National announcers such as Keith Jackson, Brent Musburger, Verne

Lundquist, Gary Danielson, Joe Tessitore, Gus Johnson, Dick Enberg, Dick Vitale, Curt Gowdy, Al McGuire, Bob Griese, Billy Packer, Todd Blackledge, Ron Franklin, Brad Nessler, and Kirk Herbstreit all called Fighting Illini games on the major television networks over the years.

Daily Illini alumni include Will Leitch, Gene Shalit, and Roger Ebert. National sportswriters from coast to coast have frequented the Illini media areas. The names read like a who's who of historical sportswriters—Ring Lardner, Damon Runyon, Dick Young, Red Smith, Grantland Rice, Jim Murray, Edwin Pope, Sid Hartman, Christine Brennan, Mitch Albom, and Sally Jenkins.

The *Chicago Tribune, Chicago Sun-Times,* and *St. Louis Post-Dispatch* once covered the Illini with their most talented beat writers and columnists. In addition to the *News-Gazette* and *Daily Illini,* each daily paper in the state had a beat writer following the Fighting Illini, including Decatur *Herald and Review,* Danville *Commercial News,* Bloomington *Pantagraph,* Springfield *State Journal-Register,* Peoria *Journal-Star, Rockford Register Star, Daily Southtown,* Arlington Heights *Daily Herald, Quad-City Times,* Galesburg *Register-Mail, Rock Island Dispatch Argus,* and Mattoon *Journal Gazette and Times-Courier.*

Times have changed as newspaper staffs were cut and the number of reporters fell. Today's press box has more of an online presence than at any time in history. Illinois fans can get a great flavor of coverage from several different outlets like IlliniInquirer.com, OrangeandBlueNews.com, IlliniGuys.com, and IlliniBoard.com, or even from the official UI website of FightingIllini.com.

But there is one sportswriter and announcer who has seen more Fighting Illini sporting events over the decades than anyone else—Loren Tate. His name has been familiar to Fighting Illini fans since taking over as *News-Gazette* sports editor in 1966. He has been writing his column, "Tatelines," for nearly 60 years. In fact, he was the sports editor, columnist, and Illini beat writer for much of that time before retiring from full-time work in 1997. If there were competing teams, a score was being kept, and a winner was determined, you could count on Tate covering the event.

"Retirement" doesn't really represent Tate's life, though. He continued to write three columns a week for many years until cutting back to one Sunday column each week when he was in his late '80s. He helped introduce and has co-hosted *Saturday Morning SportsTalk* each Saturday on WDWS-AM radio since 1979. Tate also served as the color analyst for Illini football and basketball games for nearly 30 years.

Born in 1931 in Kentucky, Tate grew up in Monticello, Illinois, and was introduced to the newspaper business by working summers at the *Piatt County Republican*, a weekly paper run by his stepfather. A member of both the Monticello High School and Sports Hall of Fames, Tate was an outstanding baseball and basketball player. He went to college at Illinois, spending his first year on both the basketball and baseball freshman teams. After two years in the Army, Tate landed a position as sportswriter, and eventually the sports editor, at the Hammond, Indiana, *Times* for 11 years before coming to the *News-Gazette*. He even spent several years reporting sports for local television station WICD-TV.

The number of trees processed to make the paper Tate has used taking his immaculate notes over the decades would fill a forest. He has used just about every means possible in filing his stories or reporting on the game.

As good reporters do, Tate wrote and called it as he saw it. That wasn't always the way everyone wanted to read or hear it, but Illini fans were better off for getting it straight. We'll never have another like him.

76 Take in a Fighting Illini Road Game

Every Fighting Illini fan who enjoys games at Memorial Stadium or State Farm Center should strongly consider taking a road trip and seeing their favorite team compete at an enemy stadium or arena.

Inside the Big Ten Conference footprint, visits to Evanston, West Lafayette, Bloomington, Iowa City, Madison, Ann Arbor, East Lansing, or Columbus are all within around a five-hour drive from Champaign-Urbana.

Football tickets for these games are sometimes much easier to obtain since the Fighting Illini ticket office gets a limited number of tickets for each road game. Road basketball game tickets are much harder to come by since the ticket allotment is considerably smaller and mostly used by players and coaches for their families and friends.

Every stop around the Big Ten has an entertainment and dining area near campus that can be fun to visit and experience. If you were to make a major trip to one of the East or West Coast schools, there are myriad things to do in addition to the game.

For the new schools out west, UCLA and USC are both in Los Angeles, with Hollywood, Disneyland, beaches, and countless other activities. Seattle is close to Mount Rainier, has a wonderful music scene and beautiful scenery, Pike Place Market, Puget Sound, and the area near campus at Husky Stadium on Lake Washington where many fans ride their boats to the football games. Eugene, Oregon, has incredible micro-brew options along with many outdoor activities.

Rutgers is located a short trip from New York City by car or train and has a cool monument next to SHI Stadium signifying the birthplace of college football on November 6, 1869, when Rutgers hosted Princeton.

College Park, Maryland, is a short Metro ride from Washington, D.C., and all it has to offer. Personal favorite next to campus: Looney's Pub.

Evanston is a northern suburb of Chicago, so everything the Windy City has to offer is nearby. When attending a ballgame, though, it's never wrong to visit Mustard's Last Stand. Personal favorite: Soul and Smoke BBQ. Hidden but delicious.

State College, Pennsylvania, is beautiful in the fall with the foliage in full color blanketing the rolling mountains in the region. There are plenty of choices along College Avenue near Old Main. The Tavern holds a special place in my heart for a wonderful meal and the Penn State Berkey Creamery offers some incredible ice creams, yogurts, and sherbets. You don't want to skip this spot.

Madison is the capital of Wisconsin and downtown is located between two lakes. The weekend hot spots can be found near campus on State Street or many of the areas in the Capitol area. It's hard not to find fun. Football parking here is among the worst in the Big Ten since Camp Randall is locked in with campus buildings and a residential neighborhood. Personal favorites: The Great Dane, Jordan's Big Ten Pub, and The Old Fashioned (for an Old Fashioned, of course).

Campus activity in Columbus, Ohio, centers around High Street in the University District. Football game weekends are packed in that area. Ohio Stadium is one of the best places in the nation to catch a football game with thousands of knowledgeable fans who are used to winning. Personal favorite: Varsity Club, located very near Ohio Stadium.

Lincoln, Nebraska, boasts the Haymarket District in downtown, just blocks from Memorial Stadium and Pinnacle Ban Arena. The traditional campus bar area is down O Street, but much of the activity on game weekends is centered around the Haymarket. Personal favorites are Harry's Wonder Bar and Zoo Bar.

When visiting Iowa City, the bar scene near Washington and Clinton Streets is as good as any in the Big Ten. Some of the bars have been around for decades, so plenty of tradition for visitors and students. Personal favorites are The Airliner and The Fieldhouse.

Minneapolis is a major metropolitan area, so visitors really have their choice. The Dinkytown area next to campus is the primary student hangout area, but Downtown Minneapolis has a lot to offer in both restaurants and sports bars. Depending on the season, the Vikings, Twins, Timberwolves, or Wild may be in town. Personal favorite for breakfast: Al's Breakfast in Dinkytown. Be prepared to wait. Extremely small space, but wonderful view of the grill.

Bloomington, Indiana, is a beautiful campus with lots of limestone buildings. The gameday scene is pretty good around Memorial Stadium. Personal favorites are Kilroy's or The Dunnkirk Library. Terrific place for good steaks is Janko's Little Zagreb.

West Lafayette is the closest Big Ten school to Champaign-Urbana and is around a 90-minute drive. Of course, many fans of both schools stop at the legendary Beef House near Covington, Indiana, since it is about halfway between the schools. In West Lafayette, Harry's Chocolate Shop is the traditional campus hangout. Don't be fooled by the name. Personal favorites: Triple XXX Family Restaurant, an old-school spot for hamburgers and root beer, and Bruno's Pizza and Big O's Sports Room with their incredible Boilermaker memorabilia collection.

East Lansing is connected to Michigan capital Lansing and features many dining and drinking options. Personal favorites: Hopcat and Red Cedar Spirits.

Last but not least is Ann Arbor, located a short drive from Detroit. Parking around Michigan Stadium can be a nightmare. Despite topping 100,000 fans, the Big House isn't as loud as several other stadiums around the conference. Personal favorites: Zingerman's Delicatessen and The Grotto in Ann Arbor; Sidetrack Bar and Grill in Ypsilanti.

Taking in a road game is a great way to engage with other Illini fans since we will likely be outnumbered at the game, unless you take in the game at Northwestern, when orange and blue often dominates the seating areas.

77 A One-Time Feat—Illini Defeat Every Other Big Ten Team in 1983

Only once in Big Ten football history has one team defeated all other conference schools in the same season. And with the number of schools moving from 10 at the time to 18 (in 2024) it won't happen again.

After playing in the 1982 Liberty Bowl, Mike White's Fighting Illini football program was on an upward trajectory with high expectations entering the 1983 season.

Despite losing record-setting quarterback Tony Eason and several good pass catchers, a rock-solid defense returned to help the young offensive stars learn their roles on the team.

The rugged defensive line was anchored by Don Thorp, Mark Butkus, and Mike Johnson. Mike Weingrad, Archie Carter, and Clint Haynes were the primary linebacker corps. Mike Heaven, Keith Taylor, Dave Edwards, and Craig Swoope comprised the defensive backfield.

On offense, Jack Trudeau moved into the starting quarterback role and had two terrific running backs in Dwight Beverly and Thomas Rooks to set the tone for the rushing attack. The offensive line may have been the best position group on the team that season with Bob Stowe, Rick Schulte, center Bob Miller, Chris Babyar, and Jim Juriga serving as starters.

Future college football Hall of Famer David Williams and Cam
Benson were starting wideouts. With tight end Tim Brewster, they
gave Trudeau plenty of good targets to throw to.

The season got off to an inauspicious start, though, with a
28–18 road loss to Missouri before bouncing back with a 17–7
win over Stanford in the home opener. In 1981 and 1982, eight
of the 10 Big Ten schools played a nine-game conference schedule before all teams played a nine-game Big Ten slate in 1983
and 1984. Illinois opened conference play in 1983 with a 20–10
victory over Michigan State, holding MSU to just 42 yards
rushing.

Fourth-ranked Iowa was next up at Memorial Stadium and
came into the game with the league's best offense, averaging 38
points and 507 yards per game.

The Hawkeyes never had a chance that day.

The Illini defense stifled the Iowa running game to just 15
yards on the ground and quarterback Chuck Long was sacked seven
times while completing just 12 of 27 passes, the only time he would
be at less than 50 percent in his college career. The capper was an
inspiring goal-line stand that kept Iowa out of the end zone in the
33–0 shutout victory. The nation was alerted that a new power was
emerging in the Big Ten.

After a 27–15 win at Wisconsin, it was sixth-ranked Ohio
State's turn at Memorial Stadium. The Illini had come very close
to beating the Buckeyes in 1980 behind David Wilson's record-
setting 621 yards and six touchdowns, and again in one-score losses
in 1981 and 1982.

The Buckeyes led 13–10 when the Illini drove to the Ohio
State 11-yard before Trudeau was intercepted. That started a long
OSU drive to the Illinois 19 where the Buckeyes faced a fourth
down and 4. Instead of kicking a field goal, Coach Earle Bruce
chose to go for the clinching first down with under two minutes
to play. The Illini defense rose to the occasion when Vincy Osby

bumped OSU quarterback Jim Karsatos out of bounds at the 17, two yards short of the first down with 1:43 remaining.

On the first play of the Illini drive Trudeau fired a sideline pass to little-used walk-on Scott Golden that was good for 24 yards. Next snap: same play, same combination, virtually the same result for a gain of 22 yards. After an incomplete pass, Trudeau scrambled for 16 yards to the OSU 21. Before the Buckeyes knew what hit them, Trudeau audibled a pitch to Rooks on a sweep, who followed blocks by Juriga and Brewster into the end zone. It was a breathtaking drive that clinched a 17–13 victory, and after the final gun, the fans rushed the field and dismantled both goal posts—a first at Illinois.

The Illini made a trip to Purdue and posted a 35–21 victory over the pass-happy Boilermakers to extend the Illini winning streak to six games and set up a showdown in Champaign with co-Big Ten leader, the No. 8 Michigan Wolverines.

Every major newspaper from around the country requested credentials to the game. CBS was carrying the game to viewers from coast-to-coast. The game was played in front of a stadium-record crowd of 76,127 on Halloween weekend on the UI campus. The winner would have the inside track to the Rose Bowl, and it was no secret that Michigan coach Bo Schembechler was not fond of White and the Illini after Illinois fired his assistant coach Gary Moeller following the 1979 season.

Both defenses were locked in for the game with Michigan scoring a field goal in the first half and Trudeau combining with Rooks on a 9-yard touchdown pass for a 7–3 lead. The Wolverines added a field goal in the third quarter to close within one point before the Illini pulled off one of the iconic plays in school history.

Trudeau found Williams in a crossing pattern and, catching the pass in stride, took it all the way to the house in the southeast corner of the end zone for a 46-yard touchdown play to increase the lead to 14–6. Later, as the clock was winding down, Joe Miles captured Michigan's punt returner in the end zone for a safety and the final 16–6 Illini victory.

The Memorial Stadium goal posts never had a chance. Within seconds, both were pulled down by the delirious crowd. Roses were shared in the Illini locker room as the biggest hurdle had been overcome.

The Illini made quick work of the Minnesota Gophers with a 50–23 win at Minneapolis for their eighth win in a row. Now, only Indiana stood in the way of Illinois clinching a trip to the Rose Bowl.

Final score: Illinois 49, Indiana 21. Again, the goal posts never had a chance. For the third straight game, fans stormed the field and tore them down in celebration.

Still on the line, though, was a chance at history. A victory at Northwestern would be the first time one Big Ten school defeated all other nine teams in the same football season. The sold-out Dyche Stadium crowd was mostly wearing orange and blue as the Illini rolled over the Wildcats 56–24. And to the dismay of Northwestern fans, the north goal posts came down as Illini fans swarmed the field, tore them down, and carried the steel poles to Lake Michigan.

Thorp, Swoope, and Jurigan would all be named All-Americans, with Thorp earning First-Team status. Thorp also was named winner of the Big Ten Silver Football as the league's MVP. The Illini had 13 players earn First- and Second-Team All-Big Ten honors.

For the first time since 1963, the fourth-ranked Fighting Illini were Big Ten champions and heading to Pasadena to face Pac-10 champ UCLA. The final score of the 1984 Rose Bowl didn't end up the way Illini fans wanted in the 45–9 loss, but the memories of that special season will remain forever.

78 Mike Small and Illini Golf Excellence

The Illinois men's golf program had a smattering of success prior to 1988, winning six Big Ten titles between 1923 and 1941, but it had been a dry spell until Coach Ed Beard led his squad to the championship at the Orange Course in Savoy.

And it would be 20 more seasons before the Illini would hoist the championship trophy again. In that 1988 tournament, long-time pro Steve Stricker and his teammates Mike Small, Don Edwards, Kevin Fairfield, and Heath Crawford broke a streak of six straight conference titles by Ohio State.

Stricker would go on to a long and extremely successful professional career, and Edwards became the CEO of his own private equity firm before becoming chair of the UI Board of Trustees. When Small joined the professional ranks in 1990, the landscape was quite different compared to now. With fewer opportunities to play in the U.S. before breaking onto the PGA Tour, Small had to play in various tours around the world before earning his PGA Tour card in 1998.

With no guarantees, the physical and mental grind can be strenuous. With a young family, Small decided he needed a change. The timing happened to coincide with the end of Beard's coaching career and UI athletics director Ron Guenther offered the coaching opportunity to Small with the offer to let him continue playing when it didn't interfere with his coaching.

It was one of the greatest hires in Fighting Illini history.

After being named head coach in June 2000, Small immediately began building a program meant to sustain success. It took 10 seasons before winning that first Big Ten title, but there are only a few blips since, winning 13 of 15 conference tournaments through the 2024 season. Following another Big Ten title in 2023, Small has been named Big Ten Coach of the Year a conference-record 13 times. His teams have finished in the top five in nine of the 13 NCAA championships through 2024, including second-place finishes in 2013 and 2024.

Since 2010, Small has mentored two NCAA individual champions—Scott Langley (2010) and Thomas Pieters (2012)—and coached 13 Big Ten Player of the Year honorees. His list of conference players of the year is impressive with James Lepp (2003), Langley (2010), Luke Guthrie (2012), Thomas Pieters (2013), Brian Campbell (2014), Thomas Detry (2015), Charlie Danielson (2016), Dylan Meyer (2017), Nick Hardy (2018), Adrien Dumont de Chassart (2021, 2022, and 2023), and Jackson Buchanan (2024).

Small's success as a player while still coaching has played a large role in the growth of the program. His professional experience has proven to recruits and players that he has the knowledge of being successful at the next level. Small's playing accolades are almost too many to mention, but they include playing in 10 PGA championships (making three cuts), 14-time Illinois PGA champion, three appearances in the U.S. Senior Open, making 15 of 24 PGA Tour cuts from 2003 to 2015, the 2017 PGA OMEGA Senior PGA Professional Player of the Year, and member of the Illinois Golf Hall of Fame. The list just goes on and on.

Small's impact at Illinois after turning the Fighting Illini into an annual national contender cannot be underestimated. Schools from around the country have looked at Champaign-Urbana and tried to copy what he's done.

The Demirjian Indoor and Lauritsen/Wohlers Outdoor Golf Practice Facility is the envy of college golf, using the experience from Illini on the pro tour to help design the very best practice facility possible.

The Atkins Golf Club, formerly Stone Creek Golf Club, was gifted to the university by The Atkins Group and has been redesigned to allow for some of the most challenging golf in the Midwest.

79 The First Farm Aid Concert at Memorial Stadium

For those who were on campus in the mid-1980s, or at least lived in Central Illinois, the memory of the initial Farm Aid benefit concert at Memorial Stadium on Sunday, September 22, 1985, will never be forgotten.

More than 80,000 concertgoers listened to an incredible lineup of musicians that day. The idea for the concert was conceived after Bob Dylan made comments to a worldwide audience of more than one billion people about U.S. family farmers being in danger of losing their farms through mortgage debt.

Those comments inspired fellow musicians Willie Nelson, John Mellencamp, and Neil Young to organize Farm Aid. In cooperation with Illinois Governor Jim Thompson and University of Illinois officials, less than a month after the Live Aid comments, Nelson hosted a press conference at Memorial Stadium to announce the benefit concert and promising a terrific lineup of entertainers.

The lineup was a mix of rock, country, blues, and just about everything in between, and will go down as the greatest collection of music artists to appear at the same time on the UI campus.

The 14-hour concert carried on through intermittent rain, but you won't find anyone who regrets being in attendance, except maybe the man who was in the port-a-toilet that was tipped over.

*In perhaps the greatest lineup of music entertainers ever assembled, the
University of Illinois Memorial Stadium hosted the first Farm Aid Concert on
September 22, 1985. More than 80,000 fans jammed to a wide-range of artists
during the 14-hour concert with tickets costing $17.50.*

The Memorial Stadium artificial surface was brand new in 1985,
with only two games played on it before the concert (which was to be
held before the Illini played at Nebraska that weekend). An untold
number of plywood sheets protected the new surface from damage
as fans filled the field, with the stage at the north end of the field.

The lineup for Farm Aid: Alabama, John Anderson, Hoyt
Axton, The Beach Boys, The Blasters, Bon Jovi, Jimmy Buffett, Glen
Campbell, Johnny Cash, June Carter Cash, David Allan Coe, John
Conlee, Ry Cooder, Shirlie Collie, Lacy J. Dalton, Charlie Daniels
Band, John Denver, Bob Dylan, John Fogerty, Foreigner, Vince
Gill, Vern Gosdin, Arlo Guthrie, Sammy Hagar, Merle Haggard
and the Strangers, Daryl Hall, Emmylou Harris, Don Henley, The
Highwaymen, Waylon Jennings, Bill Joel, Randy Newman, George
Jones, Rickie Lee Jones, B.B. King, Carole King, Robbie Krieger,
Kris Kristofferson, Huey Lewis, Lone Justice, Loretta Lynn, Delbert
McClinton, Roger McGuinn, John Mellencamp, Roger Miller, Roy
Clark, Joni Mitchell, Nitty Gritty Dirt Band, Willie Nelson, Roy
Orbison, Tom Petty and the Heartbreakers, Charley Pride, Bonnie

Raitt, Wade Ray, Lou Reed, Kenny Rogers, Johnny Rodriguez, John Schneider, Brian Setzer, Southern Pacific, Sissy Spacek, Tanya Tucker, Eddie Van Halen, Debra Winger, Neil Young and the International Harvesters, Dave Millsap, Joe Ely, Judy Rodman, Dottie West, The Winter Brothers, and X. From a historical note, it was the first public appearance of Hagar on stage with Van Halen shortly after Hagar replaced David Lee Roth with the group.

Bob Dylan and Tom Petty were two of more than 60 major musical artists who performed at the first Farm Aid Concert held at Memorial Stadium in 1985. The event raised more than $9 million in support of farmers across the nation.

The talent in Memorial Stadium that day will never be matched. It had live television coverage on multiple networks. More than $9 million was raised in support of U.S. farmers in 1985 and the annual music festival continues today.

80 Volleyball Golden Girls

The Fighting Illini volleyball program has a rich history of success since Mike Hebert was named head coach in 1983. Within two seasons, he led Illinois to a 38–2 record and its first NCAA Tournament appearance.

The Illini followed with three straight Big Ten championships in 1986, 1987, and 1988, advancing to the NCAA national semifinals in both '87 and '88. Hebert's Illini were the first team east of the Mississippi River to earn a No. 1 national ranking.

The Fighting Illini continued the run of success on an annual basis with 19 NCAA Sweet Sixteen appearances and advancing to two more Final Fours in 2011 under Kevin Hambly and again in 2018 under Chris Tamas. In the 2011 semifinal match against USC, match point is considered by many longtime volleyball viewers as arguably the greatest rally ever played. Some 55 touches, 18 over-the-net volleys, and 68 seconds of electric play earned a spot on ESPN *SportsCenter*'s "Top 10 Plays" as the Illini completed a five-set win over the Women of Troy.

The list of Fighting Illini All-Americans is long and impressive, including 1988 Honda Broderick Award winner Mary Eggers as the 1988 National Player of the Year, Nancy Brookhart, Laura Bush, Kirsten Gleis, Tina Rogers, Erin Borske, Laura DeBruler, Colleen Ward, Ali Bastianelli, and Jacqueline Quade. Eggers is the most accomplished player in Illini volleyball history, as in addition to her Honda Broderick Award, she was a three-time First-Team All-American and four-time First-Team All-Big Ten honoree.

Two additional All-Americans would go on to star on the international stage at the 2020 Tokyo Olympic Games, which were actually held in 2021 after being delayed by the COVID-19 pandemic.

Michelle Bartsch-Hackley, who wore the Orange and Blue from 2008 to 2011, helped lead Illinois to the 2011 national championship match before embarking on a professional career. She joined the U.S. National Team in 2016.

Jordyn Poulter is not only one of the best setters in Illini history, but also Big Ten and NCAA history. She was a major catalyst in guiding Illinois to the program's fourth NCAA National Semifinal appearance in 2018 when she earned First-Team All-America status after totaling the second-most assists in the NCAA and leading the Big Ten with 1,521 on the season.

Together, the pair of Illini alums helped lead the U.S. team to the Gold Medal in Tokyo. Bartsch-Hackley was named "Co-Best Outside Hitter" of the Olympics while Poulter was named "Best Setter" of the Games.

Former Illini Erin Virtue, who played from 2001 to '04, also played a part in the Gold Medal as an assistant coach, making UI history as the first Illini women to capture gold in any sport at the Olympic Games. Poulter and Virtue would return with the team at the Paris Games in 2024, helping the U.S. to a Silver Medal.

When the program started in 1974, matches were played on campus at the Intramural and Physical Education Building, better known as IMPE, before moving to Kenney Gym. Sold-out crowds in the late 1980s precipitated a move to historic Huff Hall in 1990, where the Illini have played since. The UI program also holds the distinction of having the first Black volleyball head coach when Illinois alum Terry Hite coached the Illini to a 40–28 record in 1975 and 1976.

81 Illini Wheelchair Athletics and the "Father of Accessibility"

Tim Nugent was simply a visionary who changed the world for people with disabilities. He started a small program at the University of Illinois a few years after World War II that would advocate for wheelchair-accessible buses, curb cuts, and other amenities that would be adopted around the nation and even around the world.

Nugent started the UI's Department of Rehabilitation Education Services (now the Division of Disability Resources and Educational Services, or DRES) in 1948 to help those returning from World War II. He recognized early in his career that his students with disabilities needed the same options for recreation as everyone else—which led to the founding of the UI's wheelchair athletics program.

Nugent helped start up the National Wheelchair Basketball Association in 1949, as well as wheelchair football, track, archery, and square dancing. He served as commissioner of the NWBA for its first 25 years.

In 1948 the UI was the first college in the United States to establish a collegiate wheelchair basketball team, the Gizz Kids, a play on the name of Illinois' famous men's basketball team the Whiz Kids, who won Big Ten titles in 1942 and 1943. In 1970, the UI formed the Ms. Kids, the first women's wheelchair basketball team in the nation, several years before Title IX was passed.

Nugent helped present the UI as a national leader in wheelchair sports, with Illinois student-athletes participating in every Paralympic Games since the inaugural event held in Rome in 1960. From 1960 through 2024, 172 Illinois athletes competed in the Paralympic Games, including Jack Whitman, who won the first gold medal ever awarded in the 1960 Rome Games.

Whitman was inducted into the U.S. Wheelchair Sports Hall of Fame in 1971 and was regarded as "America's Father of Wheelchair Archery."

Over the decades, Illinois has won 15 national men's wheelchair basketball championships and 14 women's wheelchair national titles. In just the last four Paralympic Games, in wheelchair track, through 2020, Illinois athletes won 54 medals, including 20 gold medals while setting 14 world records.

Since wheelchair track first appeared as a sanctioned event in the U.S. in 1956, UI athletes have consistently proven themselves among the world's best, winning nearly 150 medals in Paralympic competition and winning every prestigious road race in the world, including the Boston, London, Chicago, New York City, and Paris Marathons.

Illinois racer Ron Stein was the first international star with his eight gold medals in the 1960 and 1964 Paralympics topping the list among UI athletes until Tatyana McFadden matched him with her eighth gold at the 2020 Paralympics.

In the 1980s and '90s, Illinois wheelchair track athletes achieved incredible success. Sharon Rahn Hedrick won gold medals in both the 1984 and 1988 Games in the 800-meter event, Scot Hollonbeck began a streak of track dominance in the 1992 Games that stretched into the early 2000s, and Jean Driscoll won her first Boston Marathon in 1990, the first of her record-setting eight victories on that course.

Starting in the mid-2010s, McFadden dominated the women's division on both the track and the road, stretching from the 100 meters to the marathon, establishing herself as one of the greatest wheelchair racers of all time.

It's not unusual for people driving around the south end of campus or in the rural areas around Champaign-Urbana to spot the wheelchair racers training. They especially like any rises or hills they can find in the area since many road races around the world include some change in elevation, something that is rare in flat Champaign County.

In 2019, Nugent was inducted into the United States Olympic and Paralympic Hall of Fame as a special contributor, the only person to have such an honor. His legacy on the UI campus can be found in many different areas. Nugent was awarded the Chancellor's Medallion by the University, and the City of Champaign renamed Stadium Drive on campus Tim Nugent Way. In 2010, the campus opened Timothy J. Nugent Hall, replacing Beckwith Hall, a residence hall opened in 1981 for students with severe disabilities who require daily assistance. And, in 2011, Nugent was named a Lincoln Laureate by the state of Illinois.

82 Illini Baseball's Greatest Season

The Illinois baseball program has a long and storied history in the Big Ten Conference dating back to its first conference championship in 1900. The Illini won 17 Big Ten titles in the 38 seasons between 1900 and 1937, finishing in the top three every season except for five years.

Only 10 men have served as head baseball coach of Illinois, including Edward Hall, George Huff, George "Potsy" Clark, Carl Lundgren, Wally Roettger, Lee Eilbracht, Tom Dedin, Augie Garrido, Richard "Itch" Jones, and Dan Hartleb.

However, the 2015 Illini team stands above all others after becoming the first baseball squad in school history to reach 50 wins on the season and posting a 21–1 conference mark in winning the school's 30th regular season title. It was Illinois' first regular-season championship since 1998 and only the second since winning back-to-back titles in 1962 and 1963.

Hartleb had an idea his squad had a chance to be very good, but even he didn't know the level of play the Illini would exhibit. Illinois opened the season with an 18–5–1 mark prior to conference play, including taking two of three against tenth-ranked Oklahoma State in Stillwater.

Then, after splitting the first two games in the Big Ten opening series at Michigan State, the Fighting Illini became the talk of collegiate baseball by winning 27 straight games, just seven shy of the collegiate record. Illinois climbed to a school-record No. 2 national ranking and did not lose over a span of 52 days, including 15 wins at home, 10 on the road, and two at neutral sites. Twenty of those 27 came in Big Ten play as the Illini earned the overall No. 6 seed in the Big Ten Tournament, becoming just the second conference school to earn a Top 10 overall seed after Indiana and Kyle Schwarber were the No. 4 seed in 2014.

Not surprisingly, Illinois swept the Big Ten's individual awards with first baseman David Kerian earning Player of the Year, left-hander Tyler Jay being named Pitcher of the Year, and Hartleb named as Coach of the Year.

Jay would earn First-Team All-America honors while Duchene and Kerian were named Second-Team All-Americans.

Illini pitching coach Drew Dickinson, who was the Big Ten Pitcher of the Year himself in 2001, molded the pitching staff behind starters Kevin Duchene, John Krevetz, Drasen Johnson, and Rob McDonnell, while Jay was a lock-down, dominant closer out of the bullpen. Four members of the staff ranked in the Big Ten's top five ERA leaders. Jay led with 1.08 followed by Duchene (1.75) in third, Johnson (2.01) in fourth, and McDonnell (2.28) fifth.

The Fighting Illini were red-hot in home games at Illinois Field, posting a 25–4 record over the season, including three straight wins in the first-ever NCAA Regional hosted there with wins over Ohio, Notre Dame, and Wright State.

The regional victory earned the Fighting Illini their first-ever Super Regional with preseason No. 1 Vanderbilt making the trip to Champaign. The defending NCAA-champion Commodores were a tough draw for the Illini and swept two games at Illinois Field to advance to the College World Series before losing to Virginia in the championship game.

In one of the more surreal moments at Illinois Field, the Super Regional clinching win by Vanderbilt came on Monday, June 8, the same day as the start of the Major League Baseball Draft. As the Commodore players were celebrating and participating in the post-game press conference, shortstop Dansby Swanson was announced as the No. 1 overall pick by the Arizona Diamondbacks and right-handed pitcher Carson Fulmer was chosen eighth overall by the Chicago White Sox. Sandwiched in between was Illini closer Tyler Jay as the sixth overall pick by the Minnesota Twins. Three of the top eight draft picks that day appeared in the press conference at the Bielfeldt Athletics Administration Building within minutes of each other.

A record nine Fighting Illini players would go on to be drafted over the next three days.

83 Historic Wins Send Illinois Bowling in 2019

After starting the season with victories over Akron and at Connecticut, the Fighting Illini were in the midst of a four-game losing streak when sixth-ranked Wisconsin visited Champaign-Urbana for the Homecoming game.

The Badgers had closed as a 30.5-point favorite in the sports betting world and entered the game with a 6–0 record that included four shutouts. Wisconsin was led by talented running back Jonathan Taylor, while the Illini defense had been one of the nation's worst at stopping the run. In other words, it wasn't a very good matchup for the Fighting Illini.

The spirited Illini kept it close in the first half, surprisingly trailing just 13–7 at halftime. The Badgers extended it to a 20–7 lead early in the third quarter, but they missed a field goal, lost a fumble, and then had a late interception as Illinois continued to find the end zone.

First, Reggie Corbin dashed for a 43-yard touchdown run and then quarterback Brandon Peters threw a perfect pass to wide receiver Josh Imatorbhebhe in the end zone for a 29-yard touchdown, bringing Illinois within two points with just under six minutes remaining.

Wisconsin was driving to try and clinch their seventh-straight win, but Illini defensive back Tony Adams intercepted a Jack Coan pass on third-and-5 on the Badgers' 45-yard line with 2:32 remaining, the third Illini defensive takeaway on the day.

Two runs by Corbin and a third-down pass from Peters to Daniel Barker moved the ball to the Badger 40-yard line. After Corbin picked up two yards on first down, running back Dre Brown then had perhaps the key play of the drive with a 13-yard run to the Wisconsin 25 with only 34 seconds remaining. The Illini forced Wisconsin to burn their timeouts before Coach Lovie Smith used one to stop the clock with 0:04 remaining.

Enter Fighting Illini kicker James McCourt.

The Irish-born kicker, by way of South Florida, knocked through a 39-yard field goal as time expired to set off one of the greatest celebrations in Memorial Stadium history.

Final Score: Illinois 24, Wisconsin 23.

By point spread, it was one of the biggest upsets in college football history, and with campus landmark Kam's closing its doors on Daniel Street for good, many called it the "Kam's Miracle!"

That victory led into Fighting Illini victories over Purdue and Rutgers to move Illinois within one victory of becoming bowl eligible heading to Michigan State with a 5–4 record.

Smith had a good feeling about the trip to East Lansing and instructed the equipment staff to grab an orange No. 13 bowling ball from the lanes at the brand-new Smith Football Performance Center for the road trip.

But, after falling behind 28–3 in the second quarter, the bowling bowl didn't expect to make it out of the travel trunk.

On the final play of the second quarter, Peters threw a 46-yard touchdown pass to Imatorbhebhe to give the Illini a lift heading into halftime, but still trailing 28–10.

Fighting Illini placekicker James McCourt earned immediate legendary status by successfully kicking a 39-yard field goal as time expired to give Illinois a shocking 24–23 victory over sixth-ranked Wisconsin in what was noted as one of the biggest upsets in Big Ten history.

Down 31–10 after three quarters, Peters and Imatorbhebhe hooked up for an 83-yard catch-and-run for a touchdown on the first play of the fourth quarter. Corbin scored on a 6-yard run the next possession to make it 31–24. Things were getting interesting.

The Spartans fumbled and Illinois recovered at the MSU 8-yard line, only to have Peters' pass to the end zone intercepted. But the Illini were not done after safety Sydney Brown returned an interception 76 yards for a touchdown with 4:53 left to close within one point at 31–30. Ironically, McCourt, who was the hero three weeks earlier in the win over Wisconsin, missed the extra point and the Illini still trailed.

Michigan State took the ensuing kickoff and immediately moved into scoring territory after Elijah Collins ripped off a 40-yard run to the Illini 35-yard line. Three runs and two Illini timeouts later offered MSU kicker Matt Coghlin a 46-yard field goal opportunity that increased the Spartan lead to 34–30 with 3:17 remaining in the game.

Peters then started the Illini on a drive highlighted by an improbable and incredible fourth-down completion for 37 yards to Imatorbhebhe to set up Illinois at the MSU 19-yard line. A six-yard run and 12-yard reception by Brown moved the ball to the 1-yard line.

A fumbled snap moved the ball back three yards and was followed by a Peters run for no gain. On third down, Peters could not connect with Imatorbhebhe in the end zone to set up fourth down from the 4-yard line.

Peters' pass to Caleb Reams was broken up, but MSU was penalized for pass interference, giving Illinois a fresh set of downs at the 2-yard line. With both teams out of time outs, Brown was thrown for a three-yard loss, setting up one last play from scrimmage. Peters took the snap and rolled right as seconds ticked off the clock. Finally, Peters pulled the trigger and fired a bullet into the hands of tight end Barker for the game-winning score.

It was the biggest comeback in Fighting Illini history after trailing by 25 points in the first half. If McCourt didn't miss the PAT, Illinois likely would have kicked a game-tying field goal at the end of regulation to send it to overtime, but being down four points meant they had to go for the touchdown.

In the jubilant locker room, Smith pulled out the orange No. 13 bowling ball. The Fighting Illini were going bowling and would play a 13th game on the season.

Two historic victories played a critical role in placing the Fighting Illini into the Redbox Bowl, their first and only bowl appearance in Smith's tenure.

84 Fighting Illini Men's Track and Field Excellence

Track and field at the University of Illinois has been a proud program dating back to the early 1900s. With more than 50 combined indoor and outdoor team championships, and four NCAA championships for the men's teams, the program has featured many of the world's top athletes in their events.

Illini Olympians include some of the great names in UI athletics history. Avery Brundage competed in three events in the 1912 Games before becoming president of the U.S. Olympic Committee for 25 years and serving as the fifth president of the International Olympic Committee from 1952 to 1972.

Dike Eddleman is considered the greatest Fighting Illini athlete, winning 11 varsity letters combined in track, basketball, and football, helping the Illini to the 1947 Rose Bowl victory, the 1949 NCAA Basketball Final Four as the Big Ten's best player, and finishing tied for second in the high jump at the 1948 London Games.

Bob Richards and Don Laz dominated the pole vault in the 1950s after Richards competed in four Olympics, winning gold in 1952 and 1956 after earning bronze in 1948. Laz was the 1951 NCAA outdoor champion and 1952 Olympic silver medalist.

Harold Osborn became the only competitor in Olympic history to win an individual event while winning the decathlon during the same meet when he won the high jump and decathlon at the 1924 Games.

Herb McKenley was a four-time NCAA champion along with winning gold at the 1952 Olympics in the 1,600-meter relay and silver in the 100m (1952) and 400m (1948, 1952) as the first sprinter to ever medal in the 100m and 400m at the same Olympics.

Andrew Riley was a four-time NCAA champion and the first male athlete to win NCAA titles in the 100m and 110m hurdles during the same championship meet.

Sprinter Willie Williams won the right to be called "the World's Fastest Human" when he set the world record in the 100m with a time of 10.1 seconds, in the same stadium and very same lane that Jesse Owens had run as a gold medal winner at the 1936 Olympic Games.

But the 1970s are arguably the best stretch of Illini track and field performers. Under the legendary Gary Wieneke, Illinois middle and distance runners dominated the scene with Craig Virgin setting four Illini records in the 5,000m and 10,000m outdoors along with the two-mile and three-mile indoors that still stand from the mid-1970s. He was the first man to win four consecutive Big Ten cross country titles and the only American male to win a world cross country title, doing it twice in 1980 and 1981. Virgin was a member of the U.S. Olympic team in 1976, 1984, and on the 1980 team that boycotted the Moscow Games.

Teammate Michael Durkin was a middle distance star who won nine Big Ten championships, five in the mile and one each in the 1,000-yard, two-mile, 800m, and steeplechase. He was also on the 1976 Olympic team and part of the 1980 team that boycotted the Games.

Nigerian Charlton Ehizuelen was the greatest horizontal jumper in Illinois history, setting school records in the long jump and triple jump that still stand. In his first meet wearing an Illini uniform, he set the Big Ten long jump record of 25–9.5, one-half inch past the previous mark set by Jesse Owens 39 years earlier. That same day, he triple-jumped 53–11.75, setting Big Ten and NCAA records. Ehizuelen qualified for the Nigerian Olympic team in 1976, but the team boycotted after arriving in Montreal. A torn muscle kept him off the 1980 Olympic team.

Other middle-distance stars from the 1970s include Rob Mango, Dave Kaemerer, Ron Phillips, Lee LaBadie, Rick Brooks, Charlie White, Ben App, Tim Smith, Steve Schellenberger, and Jeff Jirele, who all earned All-America status.

LaBadie was the first Big Ten Conference undergraduate to break the four-minute barrier in the mile run during a dual meet with Southern Illinois on May 11, 1971. He was also a key member of a world record–tying two-mile relay squad with Mango, Kaemerer, and Phillips that was accomplished at the Astrodome in Houston in 1972.

85 Equipment Innovators

Just about anyone associated with track and field will recognize the name of Gill. But very few know that the company that produces much of the best track and field equipment was founded in Urbana, Illinois, in 1918 by longtime Fighting Illini track and field coach Harry Gill, who was determined to build better track equipment.

During a 29-year coaching career from 1904 to 1929, then again from 1931 to '33, Gill's Illinois track and field teams won an amazing 22 Big Ten championships and NCAA championships in 1921 and 1927. The 1921 NCAA title was the very first team championship conducted by the NCAA.

Born in Coldwater, Ontario, Canada, Gill began coaching track at the University of Iowa in 1901, then served two seasons at Beloit College before joining George Huff's Illini staff in 1904. He was still competing during his early coaching years, winning America's professional all-around championship in 1903 by clearing 6'2" in the high jump, throwing 145 feet in the hammer, 45–8 in the shot, 30 feet in the 56-pound weight, and running 16.8 seconds in the high hurdles. As an athlete at Harvard, Gill was a one-time holder of the discus world record.

At the 1924 Olympic Games, Gill's Illini track athletes scored 35 points, more than any other nation in those Games.

As an equipment innovator, Gill's company was manufacturing 90 percent of the equipment used in the United States by 1955 and continues to be a world leader in the industry. His breakthrough ash javelin was so well received, he expanded into other areas and by 1922 Gill was offering a full line of track and field equipment. Gill died in 1956 at the age of 80, but his company continued to grow and provide quality equipment.

Among the many firsts Gill has introduced over the years are the alloy vaulting pole (1932), L-type rocker hurdle (1937), automatic starting block (1956), official testing device for the high school discus (1963), the Rankin Method of pole testing (1966), the carbon vaulting pole (1991), automatic adjusting hurdles (introduced at the 1996 Olympic Games), and many other improvements.

Another athletics innovator associated with the UI is Henry V. Porter, who attended graduate school at Illinois and went on to be inducted into the Naismith Memorial Basketball Hall of Fame. In addition to a long and storied history as an athletics administrator at the state and national levels, Porter is credited as being instrumental in the development of the fan-shaped backboard and the molded basketball, which replaced the earlier laced model. He is also credited with originating the term "March Madness" through an essay he wrote in 1939. Gill Athletics purchased Porter Athletic Equipment Co. in 2006. Porter basketball systems are among the most popular in the industry.

Headquarters for Gill Athletics remains in Champaign and the company is the official equipment supplier of USA Track and Field.

86 Devon Witherspoon—Zero Stars to NFL Star

When football coach Lovie Smith brought Devon Witherspoon to the Illinois campus during fall camp in 2019, the Pensacola, Florida, native had zero recruiting stars next to his name and barely made it to Champaign in time to be admitted to school.

As a senior at Pine Forest High School, Witherspoon was the *Pensacola News Journal* Defensive Player of the Year and was drawing interest from only a limited number of colleges waiting on his academic eligibility status to be cleared. He had strong grades but still needed the qualifying test score. He didn't even start playing high school football until his junior year as he competed on the basketball court and as an outstanding track athlete.

Football offers came from Appalachian State, Georgia State, Massachusetts, Middle Tennessee, South Alabama, Southern Miss, Troy, Temple, and UAB. Zero Power Five offers.

In fact, Witherspoon had already reported to the football team at Hutchinson (KS) Community College when his qualifying test score came through in July. Then-Illinois secondary coach Keynodo Hudson, who was in his second year on Lovie Smith's staff, had remained in contact with Witherspoon and once the qualifying score was posted, immediately went into action to get him to the UI campus.

Witherspoon arrived a week into fall camp and university admissions staff worked quickly through the process and helped submit the proper information to the NCAA for clearance.

He checked in at a thin 153 pounds, but his athleticism was quickly evident, especially in one-on-one drills with the starting receivers. His first practice was the team's eighth of fall camp.

Witherspoon got to work in the weight room and on the practice field, earning his spot in the Illini defensive secondary. When the season started, there were several cornerbacks ahead of him on the depth chart, so he concentrated on special teams. Witherspoon quickly became the best gunner on the team and showed the ability to make open-field tackles. He certainly caught the eyes of special teams coordinator Bob Ligashesky and Smith.

With more reps coming his way, Witherspoon moved into the starting lineup at cornerback in the fifth game of the season and was the only true freshman to start on defense for the Illini that season.

The coaching change from Smith to Bret Bielema after the 2020 season allowed him to grow as a player and a person in making the adjustment to new coaches and a new system under defensive coordinator Ryan Walters and defensive backs coach Aaron Henry.

An incredible junior season in 2022 thrust his name into the national conversation for the nation's best defensive back and top defensive players. He was a finalist for the Jim Thorpe Award as the nation's top defensive back, semifinalist for the Bednarik Award as nation's top defensive player, was named the Big Ten's Defensive Back of the Year, and earned consensus All-America honors at the end of the year.

In his final season of 2022, Witherspoon graded exceptionally high in just about every category. He ranked second in the nation in forced incompletions (18) and fourth in the nation in forced incompletion percentage (28.6), according to Pro Football Focus. According to grading by ESPN, he allowed just 16 receptions on 54 targets as the primary defender on the season.

Illinois took a chance on a skinny kid from Florida with no stars next to his name as the last player in the recruiting class of 2019. Four years later, that chance turned into becoming the fifth overall pick in the 2023 NFL Draft by the Seattle Seahawks.

87 Dike Eddleman, the Greatest Illini Athlete

While attending Centralia High School in Southern Illinois, Dwight "Dike" Eddleman's name as a multi-sport superstar athlete was already spreading around the nation.

Eddleman played four years of varsity basketball at Centralia and led the Orphans to the 1942 Illinois state title after finishing fourth in 1939 and third in 1941. In the 1942 championship game, Eddleman cemented his legacy by leading a furious comeback from a 13-point deficit with five minutes remaining. He led the state in scoring as a junior and senior, with his junior season total of 969 points breaking the previous state record of 751 points. During his high school career, Eddleman scored 2,702 points, setting the state record for most points, and became the first Illinois high school player to average at least 20 points per game.

There wasn't a sport he didn't star in as he ran and jumped for the track team, played baseball, and was a football star. Eddleman won three Illinois state high jump titles.

With the famed Whiz Kids in the middle of their incredible run of basketball success at Illinois, Eddleman's decision to wear the Orange and Blue apparently ensured that the Illini would continue as a basketball power. In the fall of 1942, he enrolled at Illinois and played on both the freshman basketball and football teams.

His career was sidetracked, though, by being called to military duty in January 1943, weeks after the attack on Pearl Harbor drew the United States into World War II. As a member of the Army Air Corps, he was eventually stationed in Miami Beach, where he was assigned as a physical trainer for new cadets. A couple of military stops later, he ended at Wright Field in Dayton, Ohio, where he played for the Kittyhawks, a military all-star team. He ended up being named to the college all-star team made up of the best college players in the country and played in games around the nation before closing out his military career in 1946.

Eddleman returned to Illinois as a second semester freshman in the spring of 1947 and was immediately issued his Fighting Illini football and basketball uniforms and then flown to Berkeley, California, for two basketball games prior to the start of the spring semester. The Illini split the two games against the Golden Bears on December 20 and 21, 1946. Eddleman then boarded another flight to Pasadena in time to prepare for the New Year's Day Rose Bowl.

Eddleman played as a kick and punt returner in the Rose Bowl victory over UCLA and traveled back to Champaign with the football team on the train. As the war ended, many athletes who were called away were returning to campuses around the nation. Eddleman joined an Illini team with several reuniting Whiz Kids including Ken Menke, Gene Vance, and Andy Phillip, as well as All-American guard Walt Kirk. The team couldn't muster the magic of 1943 and finished second to Wisconsin in the Big Ten standings.

As a junior, Eddleman led the Illini in scoring and was named a Second-Team All-American and First-Team All-Big Ten in Harry

Combes' first season as Illinois head coach. Eddleman's senior season was spectacular as he led the Illini to the Big Ten title with a 21–4 overall record, then to an appearance in the NCAA Final Four, finishing third. He earned the Big Ten Silver Basketball award as the conference's Most Valuable Player while being named First-Team All-American and First-Team All-Big Ten.

As a three-year football letterman, Eddleman would set Illinois records for punting and punt returning, several of which remain, including the two longest punt returns (92 and 89 yards) in school history and the two longest punts (88 and 86 yards).

It was track and field where Eddleman left his biggest mark on the international stage. For the Illini, he would win three high jump titles in each appearance at the Big Ten Indoor Championships, the 1947 and 1948 conference titles at the Big Ten Outdoor Championships, and the NCAA Championship in 1948.

During the summer between his junior and senior years, Eddleman qualified with the U.S. Track and Field team to compete in the 1948 London Olympics. After cruising to England on the *SS America*, Eddleman competed in the high jump on the first day of competition. He finished in a three-way tie for second place after clearing 6 feet, 4.75 inches. It was the first Olympics that ties were broken by number of misses and Eddleman had one more than the other two, thus he was awarded fourth place. After returning to the U.S. on the *RMS Queen Elizabeth* and to Centralia by train to a huge celebration, Eddleman was back practicing football a week later.

Eddleman would play professional basketball for four seasons, then he worked in private business for many years before joining the UI as the executive director of the Grant-In-Aid program, the fundraising arm of the athletics department from 1969 to 1993.

During his amazing career, Eddleman won 11 varsity letters in three sports while competing in the Olympics, the NCAA Final Four, and a Rose Bowl, a legacy that will never be matched.

88 Cory Bradford's Amazing Three-Pointer Streak

When Lon Kruger recruited Cory Bradford out of Memphis, Tennessee, he knew he was getting a great shooter. Just how consistent he would be during his career was yet to be determined.

After redshirting as a true freshman, Bradford earned a spot in the starting lineup for the 1998–99 season, quickly becoming the team leader in scoring on an extremely young squad. Just as he had done so many times as a youth and high school player, Bradford just made shots.

After his 22nd game that season, though, he was informed that with a three against Minnesota in Minneapolis, he had tied Matt Heldman's Illini record for games with consecutive three-pointers.

"That was the first time I knew I had a streak going, but it never hit me to as how important it was going to become until the end of my sophomore year in the Big Ten Tournament," he said in the book *A Century of Orange and Blue*, which detailed the history of Fighting Illini basketball.

Bradford played in 37 games between that contest in Minneapolis and the 2000 Big Ten Tournament, and he made a three-pointer in each one to extend his streak to 59 straight. It had become a point of pride for everyone associated with Illini basketball, fans included, when Bradford made his triple each game.

But on March 10, 2000, in the first-round matchup against Indiana in the Big Ten Tournament, the intensity of the back-and-forth game seemed to distract everyone from the fact that Bradford had gone 0–5 from the three-point line and was in serious jeopardy of losing the streak.

With 7.3 seconds left and the game tied, it was Illini ball and Lon Kruger drew a play for point guard Frank Williams.

"They double-teamed Frank so Serg [Sergio McClain] couldn't get him the ball," recalled Bradford. "Serg drove the baseline and Coach Kruger taught us that every time a guy drives baseline, he has to have a bail out guy in the weak side corner. It was just a reflex for me to slide down to the corner."

A wide-open Bradford took the pass in the corner and smoothly hit nothing but the bottom of the net to send Illinois to the semifinals and extend his streak to 60. The record at the time was 73 straight games with a three by former Virginia Tech player Wally Lancaster. Bradford finished his sophomore season with a streak of 64.

Bradford entered his junior season feeling a bit of pressure from the streak since it was something that media and fans discussed and asked about each game. Even though there were a few games with just one during the early part of the 2000–01 season, the three-pointer was made early enough in the game that the streak was never thought to be in danger ... until the game that would tie the record.

On December 9, 2000, against seventh-ranked Seton Hall in front of a national television audience on CBS, Bradford would be shooting for a spot in the record books.

But things didn't go well as Bradford was clearly pressing and carrying the weight of the streak on his shoulders. He went 0–6 from the arc in the first half and struggled to the point that Coach Bill Self needed to take him out of the game and sit him the final five minutes of regulation while the Illini were making a furious comeback after trailing by 21 points late in the first half. Bradford would get another chance when Marcus Griffin missed a shot at the end of regulation to send the game into overtime.

The first set play of overtime was called for Bradford.

"Coach Self said, 'This is it,' and they ran a play for me. It was play number one and it called for me to come off a double screen. Coach said, 'As soon as you catch it let go.'"

Coming off the screen, Bradford rose up and shot a three-pointer that seemed to hit every side of the rim before dropping through.

The Assembly Hall crowd erupted as the streak was now at 73, tying the NCAA mark. It would be a week before the Illini would take the court again when Illinois played Arizona at the United Center in Chicago.

This time, the three-point streak was extended early in the game to set the new mark. Bradford was presented with a ball marking the occasion after the game.

The streak would stretch to 88 straight until a game in February against Wisconsin. During his amazing streak Bradford had 25 games with one three-pointer, 23 with two, 17 with three, 12 with four, five with both five and six three-pointers made, and one with seven three-point baskets.

He would finish his Illini career with 1,735 points, 275 assists, and 360 rebounds, which are all terrific numbers. But the one number that will always be connected with him at Illinois as time goes on will be 88.

89 Record Eight Big Ten Titles and Another Trip to Pasadena—1951–52

Fighting Illini sports absolutely dominated the Big Ten in the 1950s, and perhaps no school in conference history dominated the league like Illinois did in the 1951–52 school year with eight Big Ten championships. From 1950–51 through the 1953–54 season, the Illini claimed titles in 23 of the 48 conference team championships.

On the gridiron, Ray Eliot's 1951 squad is the last Fighting Illini football team to be undefeated for an entire season. After opening the season with seven consecutive wins, Illinois played Ohio State to a scoreless tie in Columbus and needed a win at Northwestern to clinch the title and a second trip to Pasadena.

The team had shown incredible toughness the entire season, including linebacker Chuck Boerio, who would become a subject in Eliot's famous "Proper State of Mind" speech, and two All-American linemen in Charles Ulrich and Chuck Studley. Rex Smith was a pass-catching end and quarterback Tommy O'Connell set Illini passing records that would stand for almost 30 years. The running game was superb with Johnny "the Argo Express" Karras, Don Stevens, and fullback Bill Tate. The defensive backfield featured future College Football Hall of Famer Al Brosky, Herb Neathery, and future Chicago Bear Stan Wallace.

A blizzard hit Champaign for the November 3 game against Michigan when the Illini broke through with a touchdown with less than five minutes remaining for a 7–0 victory. After the tie at Ohio State, it all came down to the game in Evanston. Placekicker Sam Rebecca earned drinks for a lifetime when he kicked a 16-yard second-quarter field goal—his only three-pointer of the season—to give the Illini a 3–0 victory and a championship.

Illinois took the train to California to prepare for Stanford at the Rose Bowl on New Year's Day. After trailing 7–6 at halftime, the Illini broke the game open with a 27-point fourth quarter for a 40–7 victory. The 9–0–1 final record earned Illinois a share of the national title. The game that day was also the first college football game to be televised nationally when it was carried by NBC.

Seven other Fighting Illini teams won Big Ten titles that year including basketball, wrestling, gymnastics, fencing, indoor track and field, baseball, and outdoor track and field. Only one other school ever had eight Big Ten championships in the same season.

The Illini basketball team rode the All-America shoulders of Rod Fletcher and the long legs of center John "Red" Kerr in winning the Big Ten title and advancing to the NCAA Final Four for the third time in four seasons, again finishing third after losing to St. John's by two points in the semifinals and beating Santa Clara in the third-place game. Harry Combes' squad finished the season ranked No. 2 in the Associated Press poll.

The indoor and outdoor track and field teams coached by Leo Johnson swept both conference titles behind sprinters Willie Williams, who one day would be the World's Fastest Human, and Cirilo McSween, while the string of star pole vaulters continued with Dick Coleman winning Big Ten and NCAA titles.

Gymnastics coach Charlie Pond was on his way to winning the Big Ten title every year of the 1950s. Bob Sullivan was the all-around star on that team, winning the NCAA tumbling title and earning three All-America honors, while Frank Bare won Big Ten and NCAA side horse competitions.

On the wrestling mat, coach B.R. Patterson's team featured two-time Big Ten champion Norton Compton and three All-Americans in winning its first title since 1947.

Maxwell Garret's 1952 fencing squad posted an 8–0 conference mark in winning one of his 17 Big Ten titles before finishing fifth at the NCAA championships.

On the diamond, coach Lee Eilbracht was in his first season and led the Illini to a 10–5 record to share the Big Ten title and hosted the NCAA District Playoffs at old Illinois Field, winning the series against Ohio before losing twice to Western Michigan. Gerald Smith led the pitching staff with six wins while Jerry Baranski was the team's leading hitter with an average of .314.

Only Michigan's eight conference titles in the 1943–44 school year during World War II matches the Illini dominance in 1951–52, and no school has won as many in a year since.

90 White Brings West Coast Offense to Midwest

Fighting Illini football had just one winning season, in 1974, from 1966 through 1980. There were some dark days for much of the 1970s under Jim Valek, Bob Blackman, and Gary Moeller.

Valek took over in 1967 following the "Slush Fund" scandal and never gained traction while compiling an 8–32 record in four seasons.

Blackman had won 104 games in 16 seasons at Dartmouth, finishing three seasons with undefeated records. He had the Illini playing competitive football in the Big Ten with only one sub-.500 conference mark, but only one winning season at 6–4–1 in 1974. Unfortunately, this was still in the period when only the Big Ten champion could play in a bowl game, which was the Rose Bowl.

Moeller was hired to bring the success he had experienced at Michigan, but the program fell to a lower depth than Valek experienced with a 6–24–3 record over three seasons, including a 0–0 tie against hapless Northwestern on a steamy day to open the 1978 season, which was as bad as the final score would indicate. The three-yards-and-a-cloud-of-dust style was not working in Champaign-Urbana.

A change in the athletics director when Neale Stoner was hired from Cal State-Fullerton brought a breath of fresh air when he fired Moeller and hired the brash Mike White off Bill Walsh's San Francisco 49er staff after the 1979 season.

An influx of California junior college stars turned fortunes very quickly. Quarterbacks Dave Wilson and Tony Eason, both from the Bay Area, battled through the fall until Wilson earned the starting position in 1980.

White made it clear from the very first play in his opening game against Northwestern that change was happening immediately. Wilson launched a long bomb downfield and even though it fell to the turf incomplete, the Illini faithful at Memorial Stadium rose for a standing ovation.

Passing records quickly started falling as Wilson began throwing to open receivers all over the field. After battling Purdue All-American Mark Herrmann for the single-game league passing record in a mid-October game at Memorial Stadium, ending the game with 425 yards, Wilson rewrote all kinds of records with his 621-yard, six-touchdown performance when he completed 43 passes in 69 attempts against Ohio State on November 8. Wilson became the first Illini quarterback to reach 3,000 yards passing in a season before entering the NFL Supplemental Draft in the summer and becoming the No. 1 overall pick by the New Orleans Saints. Prior to Wilson topping the mark five times, the only Illini quarterback to top 300 passing yards in a game was Tom O'Connell with 305 at Iowa in 1952.

Next up was Tony Eason, who redshirted in 1980 and had two seasons of eligibility remaining. Except for the 621-yard effort at Ohio State the previous year, Eason surpassed Wilson's amazing season with 3,360 yards passing and six games with at least 300 yards passing. In 1981, Eason led the Illini to a 7–4 overall record, including 6–3 in the Big Ten and a tie for third place. There were only 16 bowl games in 1981 and Illinois was passed over for a bowl appearance with many people thinking the court entanglement between the school and the conference over Wilson's eligibility in 1980 played a big part in lack of support.

White and his squad would come back in 1982 seeking their first bowl appearance since 1963. Eason was even better and threw for 3,671 yards and four games over 300 yards. The Illini finished the regular season again with a 7–4 mark and a 6–3 conference record. This time, Illinois was invited to play Alabama in the

Liberty Bowl, where the Illini dropped a 21–15 decision to the Tide in Bear Bryant's final game as head coach.

Eason would be drafted in the first round of the 1983 NFL Draft by New England, where he would lead the Patriots to the Super Bowl after the 1985 season, running into the Chicago Bears and the best defense in NFL history.

Jack Trudeau was waiting on deck and followed as a sophomore in 1983 by leading the Fighting Illini to an historic 9–0 record in the Big Ten as the only team in conference history to defeat every other league team in the same season. In three seasons, Trudeau broke nearly all the records Eason had set in 1981 and 1982 with 8,725 career passing yards, 797 completions, and 55 TD passes. Even with another 7–4 record, the Illini would miss a bowl game in 1984 because of NCAA recruiting violations but returned in 1985 to play in the Peach Bowl with a 6–4–1 regular-season record.

Trudeau would be chosen in the second round of the 1986 NFL Draft by the Indianapolis Colts and would play 10 years in the league.

After two seasons with losing records in 1986 and 1987, Jeff George was the new sheriff in town heading into the 1988 season. However, White was fired in January of 1988 after another rules violation and was replaced by former NFL head coach John Mackovic. White left Mackovic with a loaded roster and the Illini would be invited to the All American Bowl after a 6–4–1 regular season in 1988 and the Florida Citrus Bowl in 1989 with a 10–2 record and No. 10 final national ranking. George would become the No. 1 overall pick in the 1990 NFL Draft by the Colts and would play 12 years in the league.

Illinois had posted winning seasons in eight of 11 years from 1980 through 1990, including two Big Ten titles, as one of the most successful periods in program history. It will always be remembered as the Illini Decade of the Quarterbacks.

91 Doubling Up with Football and Basketball Championships

There are more than 35 different varsity sports offered at colleges across the nation, including 21 at the University of Illinois, but there is little argument that football and men's basketball hold the greatest interest by most collegiate sports fans. The number of television viewers don't lie.

Big Ten championships are hard to win any time, in any sport, and if a school has multiple teams competing for titles, it is a good year. But when the football and basketball teams both sit atop the standings, it allows fans to puff their chests just a little more.

In the 120 seasons that Illinois has offered both football and basketball as varsity sports, both have won championships during the same school year just five times, an average of once about every 25 years.

The first double title came in 1914–15 when Bob Zuppke's undefeated gridders won the league with a 6–0 record and were later recognized as national champions. End Perry Graves and guard Ralph "Slouie" Chapman were the All-Americans on that squad.

The basketball team also earned national championship status in 1915 after going 16–0 during the season, including 12–0 in Big Ten play. Coach Ralph Jones was credited by some with originating the fast break in basketball. Later in his career, Jones was hired by George Halas, one of his former Illini basketball players, as head coach of the Chicago Bears from 1930 to '32, where, among other achievements, he was credited with the revival of the T-formation and the use of a man in motion to throw off the defense.

The Illinois campus was buzzing in 1923 when a young redhead from Wheaton burst on the scene as a football All-American. Red

Grange led the Illini to the 1923 Big Ten title with a 5–0 and Illinois was recognized as national champion after finishing the season undefeated at 8–0.

At New Men's Gym, later known as Huff Gym, Coach J. Craig Ruby led his Illini to a share of the 1924 Big Ten title with an 8–4 record behind center Leland Stilwell, who would later become the longtime team physician for UI athletes.

It was nearly 30 years until the double title happened again in 1951–52, when a total of eight Illinois teams won Big Ten titles. Ray Eliot's football squad was the last undefeated Illini squad with a 9–0–1 record. After defeating Stanford, 40–7, in the Rose Bowl, Illinois earned a share of the national championship to pair with its Big Ten title.

The basketball team under Harry Combes was led by All-American Rod Fletcher and sophomore center John "Red" Kerr, who would end his career as Illinois' all-time leading scorer. The Illini posted an impressive 22–4 record, including 12–2 in the conference, and finished with a final ranking of second in the last Associated Press poll. Illinois advanced to the NCAA Final Four and finished third after losing to St. John's in the semifinal game and defeating Santa Clara in the third-place contest.

It was more than 30 years before another double championship happened with these two sports in 1983–84.

Mike White's football team established a record that will never happen again after going 9–0 in the Big Ten, winning against every other conference school in the same season. Don Thorp was named the Big Ten Silver Football Award winner as the league's Most Valuable Player, while quarterback Jack Trudeau and future College Football Hall of Famer David Williams were leading the offense.

On the basketball court, Lou Henson led the Illini to their only Big Ten title under his watch, ending in a tie with Purdue. The Illini ended the season with a 26–5 record and an impressive 15–3 mark in the Big Ten before earning a No. 2 seed in the NCAA Tournament. In a game that would change rules on who can host NCAA Tournament contests, the Illini season ended in a 54–51 loss to Kentucky on their home court at Rupp Arena. After that result, the NCAA declared a school could not play in an NCAA Tournament game on their home court or when they are hosting.

Point guard Bruce Douglas earned Big Ten Player of the Year honors, and his classmate Efrem Winters was often at the receiving end of alley-oop passes resulting in slam dunks. Both players earned First-Team All-Big Ten honors.

The last time Illinois hoisted both Big Ten championship trophies was in 2001–02.

Quarterback Kurt Kittner and his offensive line led Illinois to the football title after winning seven straight games to end the conference schedule with a 7–1 record. On the final weekend of the regular season, the Illini took care of their business with a home win against Northwestern at Memorial Stadium. To give Illinois sole possession of the title, Ohio State knocked off Michigan, who had defeated the Illini in the conference opener, in their annual matchup. Since the BCS Championship Game was played at the Rose Bowl that season, Illinois accepted an invitation to play LSU at the Sugar Bowl in New Orleans.

Across the street at Assembly Hall (now State Farm Center), Bill Self led his second Illini hoops team to a Big Ten title with a 26–9 overall record and 11–5 in the Big Ten. The Illini piece of the title was won on a near-miracle finish at Minnesota on the final day of the regular season when Frank Williams scored on a floating jumper in the final seconds of the game. Illinois would reach the Sweet Sixteen of the NCAA Tournament before losing by four points to Kansas.

92 Hail to the ... Silver and Cardinal?

The "3-in-1" drill and music was established by the Marching Illini in 1926 and serves as the traditional school song as "March of the Illini," "Hail to the Orange," and "Oskee-Wow-Wow" are played sequentially in one of the most dignified traditions on any college campus.

The middle of the trio almost never came into existence as the original University colors were quite different than orange and navy blue.

On December 8, 1878, the UI Board of Trustees did not select an official set of colors for the University, but by October of 1879, the student newspaper *Illini* reported that silver and cardinal were chosen as the University colors.

By 1888, blue had been used, and on October 1–2, 1891, blue and white together were used. Then, less than a year later, yellow and black were used, and in late November 1893, Dartmouth green was used in an event by the Athletic Association. Over time, the Athletic Association had even used black and yellow, and crimson and olive green, while the Alumni Association had used old gold and black or orange and black.

From all these different color combinations, Illinois could easily have ended up looking like Iowa, Purdue, or even Oklahoma State. Not sure where one would find crimson and olive green used as official colors.

Luckily for those of us today who enjoy the steadfastness and stability of blue and the freedom of orange, University leaders came to their senses and established the best collegiate color combination in the nation.

On October 24, 1894, in a speech at the University convocation, President Andrew Draper established orange and blue as the official colors of the University of Illinois, and campus never looked back.

Excerpts from President Draper's speech that day:

"And now concerning the matter of University colors. It has been said that there never have been any University colors authoratively [sic] adopted. Old gold and black for a long time were recognized as the University colors but were never formally adopted. This question, however, should be definitely settled. The decorating material should soon be ordered for the decoration of the new engineering building. Realizing this, the faculty appointed a committee to look into this matter. This committee, together with representatives of the student assembly, decided to recommend the adoption of orange and white, with green in addition on the athletic field. The Athletic Association, on these colors being recommended, appointed a committee who have done their work wisely and well. After very careful consideration by the committee, it was decided to recommend the adoption of orange and navy blue as the University colors. At a meeting of the Athletic Association this afternoon that body ratified the action of their committee. And now I wish to submit the question to this body. All who are in favor of accepting orange and navy blue as the colors of the University of Illinois please arise? [sic] (All arise.) I am proud to be able to be the first to hold aloft the University colors. [Applause.] I congratulate you upon the selection, for they represent much. Blue is an emblem of steadfastness and stability. Orange has come down to us through 200 years of history. It was the color under which the world's first great battle for liberty was fought. May they long be held aloft and be proudly triumphant, not only on the athletic field, but in the field of literature, of science and of art."

Thankfully, the committees chose the color of the beautiful Illinois sunsets and not the colors of Purdue or Iowa, silver and cardinal, or whatever school uses crimson and olive green. They made the right choice.

93 Illini Golfing G.O.A.T.

The Fighting Illini lineage of great golfers is growing longer each year Mike Small continues to coach. But, when the discussion moves to Illinois' greatest golfer of all time, the list is pretty short ... like one.

While Steve Stricker was being recruited to Illinois from Edgerton, Wisconsin, Coach Ed Beard told Illini freshman golfer Mike Small, "We really need this guy."

Talk about understated. Stricker would become the highest-profile golfer to ever play at Illinois and helped place the Illini program on the map.

After joining the Illini program in 1985–86, Stricker immediately made a major impact, winning Big Ten medalist honors as a freshman, just the first of three individual titles.

Illinois was chasing Ohio State at the top of the Big Ten standings as the Buckeyes won six straight conference championships from 1982 to 1987, and 11 of 12 back to 1976.

In that era, the University of Illinois hosted a fall tournament each fall at Butler National Golf Club in the Chicago suburb of Oak Brook, with many of the nation's top teams competing, including the Buckeyes.

A break in the OSU armor happened in October 1987 when the Fighting Illini won the tournament in a tense battle with the Buckeyes. Beard's lineup of Stricker, Small, Don Edward, Kevin Fairfield, and Heath Crawford proved to themselves they could beat the Buckeyes.

The 1988 Big Ten Championships were scheduled to be played at Savoy's Orange Course, where the Illini often played during practices. The Buckeyes were led by Chris Smith, Anthony Adams, and Gary Nicklaus, the son of arguably the game's greatest player, Jack Nicklaus.

The Orange Course was set up as hard as possible, but the greens had been hit hard that spring with a disease causing large brown splotches. When Jack Nicklaus flew in for the final day of competition, he took one look at the greens and just shook his head. The strong winds that Central Illinois golfers are used to were also in play, but the Illini were used to the conditions.

The Illini used their home course advantage as Stricker's four-round, nine-under-par total of 279 was 14 shots better than Smith and teammate Small to take Big Ten medalist honors for the second time.

Stricker would earn All-America honors as a junior and senior before embarking on a long and successful pro career. Through the 2023 season, Stricker had played in 518 events with 12 PGA Tour victories and 109 top 10 finishes, including 16 in the runner-up spot. He has made the cut in 386 of the 518 events and has nearly $45 million in career earnings.

He has also made an impact on the U.S. National Team, playing on five Presidents Cup teams, three Ryder Cup teams, and serving as captain of the 2017 Presidents Cup and 2021 Ryder Cup teams, leading the U.S. to victory in both events.

Stricker's story isn't complete without mention of a career-threatening slump after losing his Tour Card in 2005. He recommitted himself and in 2006 earned his Tour Card back and wound up 34th on the money list and was named the Tour's Comeback Player of the Year. Winning that award is what makes winning it again in 2007 even more amazing as that was without a doubt Stricker's best year ever up to that season. He posted a PGA Tour victory and had nine top 10 finishes, including a second-place finish in the inaugural FedEx Cup race and finishing fourth on the World Golf Rankings and PGA Tour's money list.

KENT BROWN

He's barely slowed down and has become the most dominant player on the PGA Champions Tour, winning six times in 2023, including a record-tying three majors and finishing in the top 10 in 15-of-16 starts during the season.

Stricker's wife, Nicki, has been a caddie for Steve throughout his professional career. Nicki's father, Dennis Tiziani, is Steve's instructor and the former golf coach at Wisconsin, located around 30 miles from Stricker's hometown of Edgerton.

Stricker has remained very loyal to the University of Illinois and Mike Small's program despite often showing up at Wisconsin Badger events that happen to be just a short drive from his home. Wisconsin natives are just as proud of his background, but he'll always be an Illini.

94 "The Good Kid"— Lou Boudreau

In the first 135 years of varsity athletics, the University of Illinois has retired just two uniform numbers. Hall of Fame coach Robert Zuppke and director of athletics George Huff decided at the end of his collegiate career in the mid-1920s that Harold "Red" Grange's famous No. 77 would never again be used by an Illini football player.

Grange's number would remain the only retired number at Illinois until Dick Butkus' Illini No. 50 was retired in a halftime ceremony of a game against Nebraska on September 20, 1986.

Hard to argue the retirement of either uniform as both are considered two of the top 10 players in the history of college football. Clearly, the bar was set at a very high level.

Baseball was the first varsity sport since the first games in 1879, and out of the thousands of players and more than 140 teams that have worn the Orange and Blue, Lou Boudreau is the only former Illini inducted into the National Baseball Hall of Fame and Museum in Cooperstown, New York.

Boudreau was born in Harvey, Illinois, and graduated from Thornton Township High School, where he led the Flying Clouds to three straight Illinois high school basketball championship games, winning in 1933 and finishing as runner-up in both 1934 and 1935.

Boudreau took his two-sport talents to Illinois, where he helped both the basketball and baseball teams to Big Ten championships in 1937. He teamed with future Illini basketball coach Harry Combes on the 1937 squad and earned All-America honors while playing with Illini stars Lewis "Pick" Dehner and Bill Hapac in 1938.

On the baseball diamond as a sophomore in 1937, Boudreau played third base and batted .347 while helping the Illini to a 14–3 record and the conference title. After the baseball season, the Chicago Cubs and Cleveland Indians both approached Boudreau about playing professionally, but he wanted to stay in college and return to Illinois. Cleveland general manager Cy Slapnicka paid the Boudreau family an undisclosed sum in return for agreeing to play for his team after Lou graduated. The conference became aware of the arrangement and declared Boudreau ineligible for collegiate sports despite Lou insisting he was never aware his mother was getting money.

As a senior at Illinois, he played professional basketball with the Hammond (IN) Ciesar All-Americans in the National Basketball League, a forerunner of the NBA. But his heart was with baseball, and he was loyal to Slapnicka and Cleveland.

In addition to playing professional baseball with Cleveland, Boudreau earned his degree from Illinois in 1940 and worked as the Illini freshman basketball coach in 1939 and 1940. He stayed around as an assistant for the 1942 Whiz Kids and was instrumental in recruiting future Hall of Famer Andy Phillip to Illinois.

After spending most of two seasons in the minors, Boudreau was moved to shortstop as the Indians had an established third baseman in Ken Keltner. In 1940, his first full year as a starter, he batted .295 with 46 doubles and 101 RBI, and was selected for the All-Star Game for the first of six consecutive seasons.

Nicknamed "The Good Kid," Boudreau helped make history in 1941 while helping stop Joe DiMaggio's 56-game hitting streak. DiMaggio had been retired by Keltner at third base on hard ground balls and walked in his other plate appearance. In the eighth inning, DiMaggio hit a bad-hop bouncer that Boudreau was able to corral and start a double play that ended the inning, and the hitting streak.

After the 1941 season, manager Roger Peckinpaugh was promoted to general manager and the 23-year-old Boudreau was named player-manager. His best season came in 1948 when he hit .355 and led Cleveland to the AL pennant and the last franchise World Series title.

Boudreau played with Cleveland and Boston through 1952, then managed the Red Sox from 1952 to '54, Kansas City Athletics from 1955 to '57, and finally the Cubs in 1960. He moved to the Cubs radio booth and called games until 1987. His all-time managerial record was 1,162–1,224 (.487) with one World Series title in 16 seasons. As a player, he hit .295 for his career and was an eight-time all-star and the 1948 AL Most Valuable Player.

He is credited with inventing the infield shift when he moved most of his Cleveland fielders to the right of second base against Red Sox slugger Ted Williams, who was apt to pull the ball much of the time.

"The Good Kid" was elected to the Baseball Hall of Fame in 1970, the same year his uniform number 5 was retired by Cleveland.

In 1992, Boudreau's number 5 jersey was retired at Illinois, joining the legendary football figures as the only Illini retired numbers.

95 Illini in the Super Bowl

Since Super Bowl I in 1967, there have been 37 Fighting Illini players and 18 coaches who have played or coached in 43 of America's biggest sporting events.

UI Athletics Hall of Famers Jim Grabowski and Ray Nitschke won rings with the Green Bay Packers in Super Bowl I in 1967, while offensive lineman Nick Allegretti has won three and played in four for the Kansas City Chiefs in 2020, 2021, 2023, and 2024.

Preston Pearson has perhaps the most unique story of all the Super Bowl participants. He was a basketball player at Illinois, lettering in 1966 and 1967 as a high-flying guard who drew attention by being one of the few players who ever blocked a skyhook shot by Lew Alcindor (later known as Kareem Abdul-Jabbar). The Dallas Cowboys scouting staff saw an outstanding athlete who probably didn't have a future on the basketball court and was drafted in the 12th round of the 1967 NFL Draft as the 298th overall selection despite never playing a down of college football. Pearson would go on to play 14 years in the NFL and make five Super Bowl appearances with three different teams, winning twice.

Special teams snapper Adam Lingner played in four Super Bowls with Buffalo, including three with former Illini defensive back Henry Jones. Tony Eason was the only Super Bowl starting quarterback from Illinois in the 1986 game with the Patriots against the Bears. Former Illini running back Howard Griffith scored two rushing touchdowns in the Broncos victory in Super Bowl XXXIII.

Super Bowl Participants

1967 (I)	Jim Grabowski, Green Bay—RB
	Ray Nitschke, Green Bay—LB
1968 (II)	Jim Grabowski, Green Bay—RB
	Ray Nitschke, Green Bay—LB
1969 (III)	Preston Pearson, Baltimore—RB
1970 (IV)	Bill Brown, Minnesota—FB
1974 (VIII)	Bill Brown, Minnesota—FB
1975 (IX)	Bill Brown, Minnesota—FB
	Preston Pearson, Pittsburgh—RB
1976 (X)	Preston Pearson, Dallas—RB
1978 (XII)	Preston Pearson, Dallas, RB
	Bob Gambold, Denver, Coach
1979 (XIII)	Preston Pearson, Dallas, RB
1982 (XVI)	Chuck Studley, San Francisco, Coach
1984 (XVIII)	Darryl Byrd, L.A. Raiders, LB
	Jack Squirek, L.A. Raiders, LB
1985 (XIX)	Chuck Studley, Miami, Coach
1986 (XX)	Tony Eason, New England, QB
	Calvin Thomas, Chicago, RB
1989 (XXIII)	Ed Brady, Cincinnati, LB
1990 (XXIV)	Jim Juriga, Denver, OL
1991 (XXV)	Adam Lingner, Buffalo, SNAP
1992 (XXVI)	Adam Lingner, Buffalo, SNAP
	Henry Jones, Buffalo, DB
1993 (XXVII)	Adam Lingner, Buffalo, SNAP
	Henry Jones, Buffalo, DB
1994 (XXVIII)	Adam Lingner, Buffalo, SNAP
	Henry Jones, Buffalo, DB
1995 (XXIX)	Greg Engel, San Diego, OL
	Dwain Painter, San Diego, Coach
1998 (XXXII)	Howard Griffith, Denver, FB
	John Teerlinck, Denver, Coach
1999 (XXXIII)	Howard Griffith, Denver, FB
	John Teerlinck, Denver, Coach
2000 (XXXIV)	Robert Holcombe, St. Louis, RB
	Brad Hopkins, Tennessee, OL
	Sherman Smith, Tennessee, Coach
	Mike White, St. Louis, Coach
2001 (XXXV)	Sean Payton, New York Giants, Coach
	Denny Marcin, New York Giants, Coach
2002 (XXXVI)	Robert Holcombe, St. Louis, RB

2003 (XXXVII)	Jameel Cook, Tampa Bay, FB
	Ken Dilger, Tampa Bay, TE
	Simeon Rice, Tampa Bay, DE
	Kirby Wilson, Tampa Bay, Coach
2004 (XXXVIII)	Eugene Wilson, New England, DB
	Walter Young, Carolina, WR
2005 (XXXIX)	Greg Lewis, Philadelphia, WR
	Eugene Wilson, New England, DB
	Brad Childress, Philadelphia, Coach
2006 (XL)	Walter Young, Pittsburgh, WR
2007 (XLI)	Kelvin Hayden, Indianapolis, DB
	Aaron Moorehead, Indianapolis, WR
	Ron Turner, Chicago, Coach
	Harry Hiestand, Chicago, Coach
	John Teerlinck, Indianapolis, Coach
	Leslie Frazier, Indianapolis, Coach
2008 (XLII)	Dave Diehl, New York Giants, OL
	Eugene Wilson, New England, DB
2009 (XLIII)	Carey Davis, Pittsburgh, FB
	Neil Rackers, Arizona, PK
	Nathan Hodel, Arizona, SNAP
	Rashard Mendenhall, Pittsburgh, RB
	Kirby Wilson, Pittsburgh, Coach
2010 (XLIV)	Kelvin Hayden, Indianapolis, DB
	Pierre Thomas, New Orleans, RB
	Mike Mallory, New Orleans, Coach
	Greg McMahon, New Orleans, Coach
	Sean Payton, New Orleans, Head Coach
	John Teerlinck, Indianapolis, Coach
2011 (XLV)	Rashard Mendenhall, Pittsburgh, RB
	Kirby Wilson, Pittsburgh, Coach
2012 (XLVI)	Dave Diehl, New York Giants, OL
	Steve Weatherford, New York Giants, P
2013 (XLVII)	A.J. Jenkins, San Francisco, WR
2015 (XLIX)	Michael Buchanan, New England, DE
	Michael Hoomanawanui, New England, TE
	Tavon Wilson, New England, S
2017 (LI)	Ted Karras, New England, OL
2018 (LII)	Ted Karras, New England, OL
2019 (LIII)	Ted Karras, New England, OL
2020 (LIV)	Nick Allegretti, Kansas City, OL
2021 (LV)	Nick Allegretti, Kansas City, OL
2023 (LVII)	Nick Allegretti, Kansas City, OL
2024 (LVIII)	Nick Allegretti, Kansas City, OL

Kelvin Hayden, who played one year as a wide receiver at Illinois before switching to defense, scored on a 56-yard pick six in Super Bowl XLI against the Bears.

Linebacker Jack Squirek earned some personal fame after he appeared on the cover of the January 30, 1984, *Sports Illustrated* edition that covered Super Bowl XVIII. Squirek's pick-six in the final seconds of the first half gave the Raiders a 21–3 lead over Washington. Squirek is shown on the cover holding the ball over his head as he steps into the end zone.

Former Illini assistant coach Sean Payton coached in two Super Bowls, one as an assistant with the Giants and another as head coach of the Saints. Former Illinois assistant coach John Teerlinck coached in four Super Bowls, two each with Denver and Indianapolis.

96 The Real Linebacker U

No apologies to Penn State, but the University of Illinois can stake claim to the title of "Linebacker U" as much as any school in the nation.

Linebacker is one of the most challenging football positions on the field. It can be both physically and mentally demanding, as the middle linebacker is often responsible for calling plays and requires a good mix of speed, strength, reaction time, and the ability to read the opposing offense.

Starting with All-American Chuck Boerio, one of the 1952 Rose Bowl team stars, to Nitschke, Burrell, Butkus, Hanson, Studwell, Hicks, Brownlow, Howard, Hardy, Holecek, and Rice, among many others, the Fighting Illini have featured some of the best to ever play the position.

Great Illini Linebackers

Chuck Boerio (1950, 1951): Was a favorite of Coach Ray Eliot and is mentioned in his famous "Proper State of Mind" speech telling the Wisconsin offense to "Send Ameche at me" in reference to taking on the other team's biggest challenge.

Ray Nitschke (1955–1957): In a time when players saw action on both sides of the ball, Nitschke was both a fullback and linebacker who would go on to a Hall of Fame NFL career as one of the game's greatest middle linebackers for the Green Bay Packers.

Bill Burrell (1957–1959): Burrell was a tremendous athlete who played guard and linebacker, using his speed and agility to range from sideline to sideline tracking down opponent ball carriers. Burrell was the 1959 Big Ten Silver Football Award winner as the league's Most Valuable Player while also earning consensus All-America honors and finishing fourth in Heisman Trophy voting.

Dick Butkus (1962–1964): Simply the best who ever played the position. He was selected to both the College and Pro Football Halls of Fame. The annual award given to the nation's outstanding linebacker is called the Butkus Award. Butkus also earned the Big Ten Silver Football Award in 1964 while earning consensus All-America honors in 1963 and 1964.

Don Hansen (1963–1965): Two-time All-Big Ten; 11-year NFL career.

Ron Acks (1963–1965): All-Big Ten; nine-year NFL career at linebacker.

Terry Miller (1965–1967): Started his NFL career in 1968, playing five seasons with Detroit and St. Louis.

Tom Hicks (1972–1974): Two-time All-Big Ten; anchored the Chicago Bears defense from 1976 to 1980.

Scott Studwell (1973, 1975–1976): Two-time All-Big Ten; two-time Pro Bowl selection during his 14-year playing career with the Minnesota Vikings, where he retired as the team's all-time leading tackler.

John Sullivan (1974–75, 1977–78): First Illini player to top 500 career tackles and held the UI record until Dana Howard passed him in 1994. Still holds single-season record with 202 tackles and single-game tackles with 34.

John Gillen (1977–1980): Led Illinois in tackles his final three seasons before a three-year NFL career with St. Louis and New England.

Jack Squirek (1978–1981): Led Illinois in tackles as a senior and had a six-year NFL career, helping the Raiders win Super Bowl XVIII with a pick-six.

Darrick Brownlow (1987–1990): Three-time First-Team All-Big Ten and 1990 Big Ten Defensive Player of the Year who followed with a seven-year NFL career.

Dana Howard (1991–1994): 1994 Butkus Award winner; four-time All-Big Ten; Consensus All-American; College Football Hall of Fame; three-year NFL career.

John Holecek (1991–1994): Two-time All-Big Ten; eight-year NFL career.

Kevin Hardy (1992–95): Two-time First-Team All-Big Ten; Consensus All-American in 1995; 1995 Butkus Award winner; No. 2 overall NFL Draft selection; nine-year NFL career.

Simeon Rice (1992–95): Four-time All-Big Ten, including three-time First-Team selection; 1994 and 1995 All-American; No. 3 overall NFL Draft selection; 12-year NFL career; three-time NFL Pro Bowl pick; All-Pro selection and Super Bowl champion.

J. Leman (2004–2007): Two-time First-Team All-Big Ten; 2007 Consensus All-American; three-year NFL career.

Brit Miller (2005–2008): All-Big Ten selection; four-year NFL career.

Martez Wilson (2007–2008, 2010): All-Big Ten; three-year NFL career.

Jonathan Brown (2010–2013): Two-time All-Big Ten.

Matt Sinclair (2001–2004): Three-year NFL career.

Nate Bussey (2007–2010) Two-year NFL career.

Dele Harding (2016–2019): First-Team All-Big Ten.

Jake Hansen (2016, 2018, 2019–2021): All-Big Ten; two-year NFL career.

97 Josh Whitman and Illinois AD History

The athletic directors of major college athletic programs play an instrumental role in making major decisions that directly affect hundreds of student-athletes, coaches, and staff members each year. Their decisions on hirings and firings, budget decisions, policies, and everything inside these multi-million-dollar departments are critiqued by fans, donors, media, campus colleagues, and anyone who follows the program. The pressure can be overwhelming.

Illinois' first athletic director was named in 1892 when Edward K. Hall came to the UI from Dartmouth to serve as both AD and football coach at a salary of $1,200. Three years later, Henry Everett became the third Illinois AD and served as the UI's representative at the January 11, 1895, meeting at Chicago's Palmer House Hotel that formed the Big Ten Conference.

When George Huff was named AD in 1901, little did anyone know or expect the impact he would have on the University until his death in 1936. He started his association with the UI as a student and was a member of the first Illini football team in 1890, lettering the first two seasons. Huff also lettered three times as a baseball player.

As was the custom in the day, one person in athletics would have many different responsibilities, and Huff was no different. "G" coached football from 1895–99 while also serving as head

Illini Athletic Directors

1892–1894	Edward K. Hall
1894–1895	Fred Dodge
1895–1898	Henry Everett
1898–1901	Jacob Shell
1901–1936	George Huff
1936–1941	Wendell Wilson
1941–1966	Douglas Mills
1967–1972	Gene Vance
1972–1979	Cecil Coleman
1979	Ray Eliot (interim)
1980–1988	Neale Stoner
1988	Ron Guenther (interim)
	Karol Kahrs (interim)
1988–1991	John Mackovic
1991–1992	Bob Todd (interim)
1992–2011	Ron Guenther
2011–2015	Mike Thomas
2015–2016	Paul Kowalczyk (interim)
2016–Present	Josh Whitman

baseball coach from 1895 through 1919. Huff won more than 70 percent of the baseball games he coached and directed his teams to 11 Big Ten titles. He also had a knack for hiring great coaches and spearheaded the movement to build Memorial Stadium and New Gym, renamed Huff Gym following his death in 1936. He was considered the "Father of Fighting Illini Athletics" as a man who dedicated his life to University of Illinois athletics.

Doug Mills, who served in the role from 1942 through 1966, was also known as the coach of the famed Whiz Kids on the basketball court. As AD, his leadership led to Illinois dominating several sports at the Big Ten and national levels in the late 1940s and through the 1950s.

Neale Stoner stated that the "'80s Belong to the Illini" and lit a fresh fuse of excitement in the athletics department after a stagnant period in the late 1960s and '70s. His hiring of Mike White had the Illini back in the Rose Bowl for the first time in 20 years and his support of Lou Henson helped that program sit among the best in the nation.

John Mackovic was the last athletics director who also coached before taking the head football coaching position at Texas following the 1991 regular season. He was instrumental in leading the transition from the Athletics Association to the Division of Intercollegiate Athletics and a home within the University structure.

Ron Guenther was a master fundraiser who led efforts to construct several new athletics facilities while renovating and updating Memorial Stadium during his years at the helm. He led the Illini program to some incredible high points, including two Final Fours along with Rose Bowl and Sugar Bowl appearances. The Illini just couldn't find football consistency under his tenure, but the record shows that inconsistency stretches back to the 1920s.

Josh Whitman took on the role as athletic director in 2016 as the youngest AD at an Autonomy Five institution at the age of 37 and has established himself as one of the fastest-rising leaders in collegiate athletics. Under his watch, every sport and facility has seen upgrades and increased resources to help compete at the highest level.

Whitman started at Illinois as a tight end on the football team in 1997, helping the Illini to the 1999 Micronpc.com victory over Virginia and earning Academic All-America status. After a four-year NFL career, he returned to Illinois and completed his law degree. A short stint practicing law led into a return to collegiate athletics as AD at Wisconsin-La Crosse and Washington University before being named at Illinois. During his time at Illinois, Whitman earned national recognition when *Sports Business Journal* named him to its prestigious Forty Under 40 list in 2018.

The University of Illinois can have no better leader to guide the athletics program through all the swift-moving changes that are happening in the collegiate space.

98 Orange Krush

When Lou Henson started his Fighting Illini coaching career, he noticed early in his tenure the need for more involvement from the Illinois student body in creating a hostile environment for opposing teams.

During the summer of 1975 Henson did something about it by asking then-athletic director Cecil Coleman for permission to add 164 seats on the large Assembly Hall concrete floor, with a plan to sell them to students. The student seats cost $40 for the season.

The first two seasons, it was known as the Orange Crunch before turning into the present-day Orange Krush. The initial leaders of the group were Alan Solow and Peter Korst, who would work at selling the ticket package to friends, neighbors, fraternities, sororities, and dormitories in an attempt to fill the new space with high-energy students.

Henson' first team went 14–13 but the seeds for success could be seen and the program was headed in the right direction. After scrambling to fill the seats the first year, student organizers had too many requests in the second season. They held a lottery to see who would get choice spots and those who didn't get picked had to move to other areas of the arena.

In those early years, the Orange Krush would wear anything with their favorite color, including orange bowling shirts that a local sporting goods store had and were wanting to move off their shelves.

The early Krush members also started the tradition of standing until the opposing team scored, which still happens today but includes the entire State Farm Center crowd.

The Orange Krush and Fighting Illini fans have a well-earned reputation as some of the most rabid in the nation and a major reason why the University of Illinois is considered one of the country's most prestigious athletics departments.

The Orange Krush remained the official student support group through the Henson era that ended in 1996. When new coach Lon Kruger took the head coaching position, he had some new ideas for the Krush, using their membership as a fundraising group to help support local charities.

The Orange Krush Foundation was established in 1998 with half of the money raised from the pledge program supporting ticket expenses for the members, covering costs associated with a road trip to another Big Ten school, and in support of various scholarships including the Lou Henson Coaching Endowment Fund. Over the years, the Orange Krush Foundation has donated more than $3 million to a variety of community charities.

Orange Krush has also established a reputation for secretly invading opponent arenas around the Big Ten, traditionally using a bit of a "tale" to gain access to the number of tickets needed for the trip. The Krush will wait until the opening tip of the game before taking off shirts covering their Orange Krush gear and chanting "You've been Krushed!"

Despite opponent ticket offices being aware of the Orange Krush tactics, the group has invaded just about each Big Ten arena within reach of a bus trip. Some of their creativity has earned visits and photos with opposing coaches (Michigan's Tommy Amaker), tours of campus, and seats close to the floor that would normally be available to local fans only. The opposing schools have imposed restricted ticket sales for games against the Illini because of the access the Krush has gained over the years.

Seating for Orange Krush includes approximately 700 seats in the lower bowl of State Farm Center and is distributed on a first-come, first-served basis.

The Orange Krush is properly recognized by many national media as the best student support group in college basketball. Their support at State Farm Center, as well as in the community, only confirm it.

99 The Eternal Debate— Flyin' Illini vs. 2005 Illini

For Fighting Illini basketball fans of a certain age, the debate that can't be settled is which was the better team, the Flyin' Illini of 1989 or the national runner-up squad of 2005?

The only consensus is when you ask the players of each team, who are fiercely loyal, as one would expect.

Preseason expectations for both teams were very high, with the Flyin' Illini ranked No. 9 in the nation in the preseason while the 2005 squad started fifth in the nation as Big Ten favorites. The Big Ten was loaded in 1989 with Iowa and Michigan both ranked ahead of the Illini at seventh and third, respectively, and Ohio State starting at 17. Indiana moved into the Top 20 for the final nine weeks of the regular season, climbing to No. 3.

Heading into the NCAA Tournament, Illinois was No. 3, Indiana No. 8, Michigan No. 10, and Iowa No. 14, even as the Hawkeyes were 10–8 in Big Ten play.

The Fighting Illini players felt underrated in the preseason being ranked behind both Iowa and Michigan. The early schedule wasn't especially difficult outside of 19th-ranked Florida in the fourth game until meeting up with No. 10 Missouri in the Braggin' Rights game and 17th-ranked Georgia Tech in Honolulu.

Lou Henson's best team relied on incredible athleticism from his top eight players, all of whom were between 6'4" and 6'8", allowing for a smothering, switching defense and a reason they earned the nickname of "Flyin' Illini." They were arguably the highest-flying team in Big Ten history.

Kendall Gill, Nick Anderson, Kenny Battle, Stephen Bardo, Lowell Hamilton, Larry Smith, and Marcus Liberty were the core group of players, with Hamilton serving as the primary post player. Playing against size wasn't really an issue as the quickness advantages more than made up for a few inches of height. Gill, Smith, and Bardo's defensive ability and length on the perimeter made it extremely hard for opposing guards to start offense or to shoot over the top. Anderson and Battle were 6'5" and 6'6", respectively, and were rim rattlers.

A key point in the season, at both ends of the spectrum, came on January 22, 1989, when Georgia Tech came to Champaign for a rematch of the earlier game in Honolulu. The Illini were ranked second the nation and Duke had lost the day before, so an Illinois victory would likely move them into the top spot for the first time since 1952.

In one of the most memorable basketball games in State Farm Center history, the Illini took down Tech, 103–92, in double overtime to leave the court with fans chanting, "We're No. 1, We're No. 1!" after starting the season with 17 straight wins. On the other end of the scale was a broken foot suffered by Gill, who was playing at an All-America level. The Fighting Illini would go 8–4 in the 12 games missed by Gill and fell two games behind the Hoosiers in the Big Ten rankings before Anderson's "Shot in the Nick of Time" in the 70–67 win at Bloomington.

Illinois finished incredibly strong with a 118–84 win over No. 15 Iowa on Senior Day at Champaign and an impressive 89–73 victory over No. 8 Michigan on the final day of the regular season. Despite finishing in second place in the league, they earned a No. 1 seed in the NCAA Tournament.

The 2005 squad started out at No. 5 in the preseason rankings and posted impressive wins over No. 24 Gonzaga and No. 1 Wake Forest within four days, leading both teams by more than 30 points during the games.

After moving into the nation's top spot in the rankings, the Illini swept through the remaining non-conference games and first 15 Big Ten games to start the season with 29 straight wins. Only a three-pointer with just seconds remaining in a one-point loss at Ohio State kept the Illini from a perfect regular season.

This Illini team had a three-headed guard group of Deron Williams, Dee Brown, and Luther Head; a versatile center in James Augustine; and a matchup problem at forward in Roger Powell. Bruce Weber's squad also had quality depth with Jack Ingram, Nick Smith, and Warren Carter on the front line and Rich McBride in the backcourt.

The guard play that season was superb, as all three earned consensus All-America honors. Brown, nicknamed "The One-Man

Fast Break," was named the Big Ten MVP and Defensive Player of the Year, while Williams led the team in assists as arguably the nation's top point guard, and Head led the team in scoring at 15.9 points per game.

No team in Illinois history shared the ball like the 2005 squad, with all five starters averaging at least 10 points per game. And no game will be held in higher regard than the 15-point comeback victory over Arizona in the NCAA Regional Final.

In comparing the two teams, the Flyin' Illini likely had better size, athleticism, and depth, while the 2005 team was extremely balanced and connected. They could both shoot the ball extremely well, while defending and rebounding. The Flyin' Illini created more havoc by forcing opponents into 17 turnovers per game, while the 2005 opponents averaged 15.

Neither team had the word "quit" in its vocabulary and both teams are among the best teams to not win the national championship in their best seasons. Both teams were loaded with players who rank among the best 10 in school history.

The 2005 team was the better passing team with the three guards all topping 150 assists, but the style of play of each team was quite different. The Flyin' Illini averaged 86 points per game and had a scoring margin of nearly +13. The 2005 team averaged 77 points per game with a scoring margin of nearly 16 points per game. As the game evolved over the 15 or so years, defenses became much more physical and scouting greatly improved. If one were to watch video of both years, teams just didn't allow the easy movement that players made in 1989.

Final breakdown is that the 2005 guards hold a slight advantage in shooting, athleticism, and playmaking, even though the Flyin' Illini had a size advantage. The 2005 squad had better size in Augustine, Jack Ingram, and Nick Smith, but that was offset by the Flyin' Illini's ability to switch and athleticism on the front line. The Flyin' Illini had more firepower coming off the bench with

Larry Smith and Marcus Liberty. The real advantage of the Flyin' Illini came to who would guard Anderson and Battle. They caused massive matchup issues for everyone in 1989 and would have done the same in 2005.

By a Nick Anderson bucket at the buzzer, it's the Flyin' Illini in a nail biter. That is, unless Williams knocks down his own three-game winner. This is fact, though. Both teams were winners despite coming up just short in the national tournament.

100 Celebrating Fantastic Finishes

Sports has a way of bringing out the emotions of the fans, both positively and negatively. Watching special players, incredible plays, and exciting endings is why millions of fans purchase tickets and attend live sporting events each year.

An unexpected victory or play that can pull a victory out of the hands of a defeat creates a memory of a lifetime. Often, these finishes create an emotional moment when fans want to join in the celebration and storm the field or the court. Over the last 40 or so years, there have been some amazing finishes that led to wonderful court or field rushes.

Following are the Top 10 such rushes since 1983. A 1998 victory over Middle Tennessee State to break an 18-game losing streak won't be on this list, even though hundreds of students rushed the field after the 48–20 Illini victory. Nor will the iconic dogpile after Nick Anderson's game-winning three-pointer at Indiana. Everyone on the pile was connected to the team as the few dozen Illinois fans in attendance couldn't join in on the floor.

Top 10 Field and Court Stormings Since 1983

10. February 5, 2019—Basketball—Illinois 79, No. 9 Michigan State 74

Fighting Illini head coach Brad Underwood was in his second year at Illinois and in the middle of building the program. The Illini were on their way to a school-record 21 losses on the season, but freshman Ayo Dosunmu was Underwood's most important recruit at the time, and the young talent promised better times ahead. Illinois' swarming defense helped force 24 Spartan turnovers while Dosunmu scored 24 points, including a key three-pointer right after ESPN announcer Dan Dakich said on air, "This won't end well for Illinois."

9. October 15, 1983—Football—No. 19 Illinois 17, No. 6 Ohio State 13

The Fighting Illini mounted a game-winning drive in the final moments keyed by two pass completions from Jack Trudeau to Scott Golden and scoring on a 21-yard sweep around the right end by Thomas Rooks. After beating No. 4 Iowa two weeks earlier, Illinois fans were starting to dream of roses. The Memorial Stadium goal posts came down quickly after fans swarmed the field.

8. November 19, 1983—Football—No. 4 Illinois 56, at Northwestern 24

This is the only road game on the list because who storms the field or court at a road game? Well, the crowd that day at Dyche Stadium in Evanston was predominately wearing orange and blue and the victory clinched Illinois' first Big Ten football title and Rose Bowl in 20 years. Hundreds of Illini students and fans rushed the field and tore down the north goal post, carrying it out of the stadium and a few blocks east, where it was dumped into Lake Michigan.

7. February 7, 2013—Basketball—Illinois 74, No. 1 Indiana 72
The top-ranked Hoosiers controlled the game until about four minutes remaining before a late run led by D.J. Richardson and Brandon Paul gave the Illini a shot at the end. And what a shot it was. With 0.9 seconds remaining, the Illini had the ball on the baseline near the corner on the right side. During a time out, Coach John Groce drew a play with Paul assigned to throw the pass that would end up in the hands of Tyler Griffey for a wide-open layup for the game winner.

"I just made a simple curl cut and left two guys behind me, and Brandon got off a heck of a pass," Griffey said. "Zeller and Watford were both right in front of me and just kind of stayed there."

Griffey was swarmed by fans as officials reviewed the play to make sure it was released in time. Video showed it was clearly off in time and the celebration was on in Champaign!

6. February 6, 2010—Basketball—Illinois 78, No. 5 Michigan State 73
Even though the game wasn't scheduled to start until that evening, thousands of Illinois basketball fans and Orange Krush members braved icy and snowy conditions to attend ESPN's *College GameDay* show from Assembly Hall early that morning. The Illini basketball team followed up later that night with a 78–73 victory over the fifth-ranked Spartans behind Demetri McCamey's 22-point, 11-assist performance. A Mike Davis slam just before the buzzer set off a wild court storm and celebration that would envelop the Illini team.

5. February 6, 2001—Basketball—No. 7 Illinois 77, No. 4 Michigan State 66
This was one of several Top 10 matchups for Bill Self's first Illini squad and this one had Big Ten title implications. In possibly the most anticipated home game in more than a decade, a local radio

station declared it the first-ever "Paint the Hall Orange" game where all fans were requested to wear orange, which is exactly what happened. The Spartans were three-year defending Big Ten champs since the two teams shared the title in 1998. Cory Bradford used six three-pointers to help score a game-high 22 points. The court-storming will be remembered by many as the game when fan-favorite Lucas Johnson was carried off the floor after scoring three points in just nine minutes of action. The teams ended up sharing the Big Ten title with identical 13–3 records and both squads earned No. 1 NCAA Tournament seeds.

4. February 4, 1993—Basketball—Illinois 78, No. 9 Iowa 77

There was no way to ignore the emotion in this game, from both teams. The Iowa program was still mourning the stunning death of star Chris Street in a car wreck just a few weeks earlier. Illinois and its fans were steaming over alleged recruiting violations claimed by Iowa assistant coach Bruce Pearl that had placed restrictions on Illini recruiting efforts and kept the team out of the NCAA Tournament in 1991. The game was tied at 76 on a Richard Keene three-pointer when one of the most incredible finishes in program history occurred. First, on the Iowa end, a Hawkeye shot bounced hard off the side of the rim. As Deon Thomas reached to rebound, the ball hit off his arm and banked in to give Iowa a two-point lead. After conferring at the table, officials placed 1.5 seconds back on the clock. Former high school quarterback T.J. Wheeler was tapped to throw the pass from the end line. Andy Kaufmann cut around a double screen. Wheeler's pass was on target as Kaufmann caught the ball in front of the Illini bench, took a dribble, and fired a three-pointer that hit nothing but net before being buried by his teammates and hundreds of fans storming the court.

3. October 19, 2019—Football—Illinois 24, No. 6 Wisconsin 23

Illinois was celebrating its 109th Homecoming this weekend as the sixth-ranked Badgers entered the game dominating opponents during a 6–0 start to the season.

A stingy Badger defense had posted four shutouts already and Wisconsin had an impressive 35–14 win over 11th-ranked Michigan on its résumé. The Fighting Illini were 2–4 under Lovie Smith and coming off a four-game losing streak. The Badgers were posted as 30.5 point favorites by sports books.

The Illini took advantage of some defensive takeaways to put themselves in position for the win. Brandon Peters hit Josh Imatorbhebhe in the end zone for a 29-yard touchdown to bring the Illini within two points with more than five minutes remaining. In the next Wisconsin possession, Tony Adams made an interception with 2:32 remaining. The Illini moved into field goal territory and drained the clock to set up a game-winning 39-yard field goal by James McCourt as time expired for a 24–23 victory that emptied the stands onto Zuppke Field and buried McCourt in the best football field storming since 1983.

2. October 29, 1983—Football—No. 9 Illinois 16, No. 8 Michigan 6

It was Halloween weekend on the Illinois campus, so there was sure to be a big party that night no matter the outcome, but the Fighting Illini victory over the Wolverines raised the celebration level several notches and put the Illini squarely in the driver's seat for the Big Ten title and Rose Bowl.

It was easily the most anticipated Illinois home football game in decades and the Fighting Illini defense and offensive stars didn't disappoint. Played in front of a Memorial Stadium record crowd of 76,127 and national TV audience, quarterback Jack Trudeau tossed two touchdown passes, including the iconic 46-yard strike

Fighting Illini football fans rushed the field and tore down the Memorial Stadium goalposts following a monumental 16–6 victory over Michigan during Halloween weekend to take a stranglehold on the 1983 Big Ten championship and trip to the Rose Bowl.

to David Williams. A special teams safety when Joe Miles tackled the Wolverine punt returner in the end zone with 1:22 sealed the victory.

The goal posts at both ends didn't stand a chance as the emotion of 20 years without a Big Ten title erupted into a celebration that lasted until sometime the next day. For those on campus, it was a weekend never forgotten.

And the best court storm in Fighting Illini basketball history is …

March 6, 2022—Basketball—No. 20 Illinois 74, No. 24 Iowa 72

The Fighting Illini basketball team and their fans woke up on the final day of the regular season one game behind Wisconsin for the top spot in the Big Ten after 10th-ranked Purdue surprisingly dropped two games at Michigan State and Wisconsin the previous week, moving the Badgers into the driver's seat for the title. All Wisconsin needed was a home victory against last-place Nebraska on that final Sunday. Most Illini fans held little hope for a miracle in Madison, but as the game played out early in the afternoon, the Huskers were hanging around. Nebraska guard Alonzo Verge Jr. scored a game-high 26 points, including the last nine as part of a 12–0 Husker rally in the final minutes of a 74–73 win.

Suddenly, Fighting Illini fans everywhere knew what was on the line that night when Illinois hosted Iowa in the final game of the day and Big Ten regular season. A victory would earn the team a share of the Big Ten title after appearing all hope was lost. A Big

The floor rush and scene on the State Farm Center court following a dramatic Fighting Illini victory to clinch a share of the Big Ten title in the final regular-season game of the 2022 season produced an unforgettable experience for everyone involved.

Ten official who was in Indianapolis drove a championship trophy to Champaign just in case it was needed.

The buzz and energy that night nearly blew the roof off State Farm Center. Kofi Cockburn had 21 points and 14 rebounds, and Alfonso Plummer scored 15 as the Illini had to overcome a 15-point first-half deficit.

The Illini were leading by just three points with a minute remaining as students and fans started moving to the lower levels of State Farm Center. A free throw by Iowa's Keegan Murray with 15 seconds remaining made it 73–72 before the Illini countered with a free throw by Da'Monte Williams that made the score 74–72. Hawkeye Kris Murray had a three-point attempt from the right corner that seemed to take eternity from his hand to the rim as the missed shot bounced into the hands of Illini guard Trent Frazier and time expired.

The rush to the floor by the Krush and any fans who could get there was fast, furious, and like nothing anyone had seen in the nearly 60-year history of the building. The celebration lasted through a championship trophy presentation and cutting of the nets by the Illini players and coaches. There were still people hanging around the floor nearly an hour after the completion of the game and winning of an unexpected Big Ten title.

Acknowledgments

The number of people I need to thank for helping with *100 Things Every Illini Fan Should Know and Do Before They Die* could easily fill an entire additional book.

First and foremost, thanks to my wife, Amy, for the encouragement to take on and complete this project. I'm not sure she had a real understanding how crazy a sports information director's life could be when we married in 2015. I tried to explain and give her warning, but she married me anyway. Thank you! I love you and appreciate your love for me more than you'll ever know.

Thank you to my entire family for allowing me to follow a career path that I probably started when I was about eight years old, and apologies for making life so complicated by missing events and family time because of the crazy life of working in collegiate athletics. My immediate family has had to put up with a complicated schedule and lifestyle for nearly four decades.

My parents and siblings probably realized something was weird with me when I started my baseball card collection in 1971 at eight years old. I studied those cards so closely I could recite just about every word printed on the back. I became a circus sideshow at family events when family members would cover the entire card leaving just a sliver of the photo open and I was just about perfect at identifying any of the hundreds of cards in my box.

I was hooked on sports and sports trivia at an early age.

I read every sports history book I could get my hands on. I started devouring the sports sections of two daily newspapers.

I will always remember the day Tom Kacich, a journalism instructor at the University of Illinois in addition to his job at the Champaign *News-Gazette*, suggested I speak with UI Sports Information Director Tab Bennett about working in his office as a student assistant.

It was a meeting that changed the trajectory of my career. Assistant SID Dick Barnes said I could join the staff as a student assistant the next fall and off I went. The next step was two years as a graduate assistant in the office and then I was fortunate enough that new Illinois SID Mike Pearson agreed to add me to the staff on a full-time basis. My foot was in the door, and I never left the room. Thank you, Mike, for the lessons you taught me as a mentor and for your friendship. Your series of *Illini Legends, Lists & Lore* books were critical in researching ideas and background for this book.

The book certainly wouldn't be possible if it weren't for the incredible performances by Fighting Illini athletes, coaches, and administrators. Thanks to the athletics directors and coaches I've worked with over the years. ADs John Mackovic, Bob Todd, Ron Guenther, Max Urick, Mike Thomas, and Josh Whitman had the trust in me to be their SID, and I will forever have respect for them and the immense amount of stress they worked under.

Thanks to all the incredibly talented and loyal individuals who worked as colleagues with me in the sports information offices at Illinois and Kansas State. There are no harder-working people in the athletics world. I learned so much from working with you and having you as part of my life and career. If I start listing everyone, we'll have to add several more pages. I wish Derrick Burson all the best after he took my chair in a cleaned-out office that I used for 23 years. Derrick's dedication and loyalty will always be appreciated. Additional sports information colleagues who have earned my eternal thanks and respect include Brett Moore, Derek Neal, Danny Mattie, Cassie Arner, Matt Wille, Mike Koon, Ed McGregor, and Julie Herman. Many of my colleagues have turned into lifelong friends. Marty Kaufmann, Warren Hood, Dave Johnson, photographer Mark Jones, Dan Wallenberg, and Jason Heggemeyer are just a few of the folks who hold a special spot in my life.

Thanks to the Tuesday lunch group of Loren, Steve, Kevin, Don, Bill, Mike, and Ron for offering chapter ideas and asking questions that prompted new thoughts on possible chapters of this book. The Illini knowledge and history around the table each week is amazing.

Last but not least, thank you to all the Fighting Illini fans who show up for games, are engaged with Illinois Athletics and make what we do in collegiate athletics possible. There are no better fans in the nation. Go Illini!